Nothing Bet
Than Deal

Insights from Sixty-Two
Near-Death Experiences

KEVIN R. WILLIAMS

CONTENTS

DEDICATION

To my beloved Mother, Phyllis Scofield, whose tragic death during the writing of this book, taught me a lesson about life and death that I had never known before. Although death may bring overwhelming tears of joy to those who cross over, it may also bring overwhelming tears of sorrow to surviving family and friends who, at the same time, may also have overwhelming tears of joy knowing that there is nothing better on earth than being dead and crossing over to heaven.

FOREWORD

It all begins for us at birth. We are thrust from the womb onto the carousel of life, carried away in a blur of activities from childhood to adulthood and then to old age. Each of us have our dreams, our relationships and we go to school; we work and play, day after day, week after week, year after year. Life is certainly busy.

And yet we tend not to think about the fact of our inevitable death. It's kind of scary. It doesn't seem to make any sense that we will no longer exist as we know it. The fact is we will die and there is no way to avoid it. Like the child being born, we have no choice but to yield ourselves to the unknown.

Like the seventy billion who have already passed this way through life, we will join their ranks at the rate of 130,000 a day. And in that same day, 400,000 new lives will be born. The cycle of life and death continues at an ever-increasing pace.

The fear of death has given rise to a host of speculations about an afterlife. Religions, philosophies and cults have multiplied over the millennia, all trying to answer our need for comfort about this seemingly absurd fate that awaits each of us. And now science has turned its gaze toward the matter of death.

Beginning in the mid-1970s, noted researchers such as Raymond Moody, Elizabeth Kubler-Ross, Kenneth Ring, P.M.H. Atwater, Michael Sabom, and Melvin Morse, have brought the subject of NDEs to the popular front.

In 1981 and again in 1991, George Gallup Jr. conducted a poll on close brushes with death. He was astonished to find out that some 8 to 12 million people in the United States have had an NDE. This is a population about the size of New York City. NDE researchers speculate that the figures may even be higher since the experiencer is often reluctant to talk about it.

-- NORMAN VAN ROOY
from his documentary, Shadows: Perceptions of Near-Death Experiences, Part 1 (1994)

PREFACE

Socrates had this to say about death: "To fear death is nothing other than to think oneself wise when one is not. For it is to think one knows what one does not know. No one knows whether death may not even turn out to be the greatest blessings of human beings. And yet people fear it as if they knew for certain it is the greatest evil."

Thousands of years later, NDEs are showing us that death is indeed the greatest blessing of human beings. According to a great number of people who have had an NDE, there is nothing better than death. One experiencer, Dianne Morrissey said, "If I lived a billion years more, in my body or yours, there's not a single experience on earth that could ever be as good as being dead. Nothing." [1]

Such insights into life after death are intriguing to say the least. After years of researching the NDE and gathering various accounts from books and visitors to my website (www.near-death.com), I have collected a few of the most profound of these insights to profile in this book.

I first learned of the NDE in the early 1970's after reading the groundbreaking book by Raymond Moody, Life After Life. His findings were a major factor in inspiring my own research into the NDE. Since then, I have read every major work concerning the phenomenon and many of the not so well known ones as well. As a result, I have developed a deep love for things concerning the NDE and the afterlife in general. Because of this deep love for these things, I am committed to bringing to the world the truths I have discovered about life after death.

Many of these truths are universal. You will find these truths even speak to your heart and tell your mind of their truthfulness. Because many of these truths are universal, practical and of "common sense", I am confident they are in fact true.

Before learning of the NDE, I became a fundamentalist Christian. This brand of Christianity is known for believing the NDE to be "of the devil." As my knowledge of the NDE grew, I came to realize from what I researched the fact that God is not limited only to just those who profess the Christian faith. The NDE expanded my mind into understanding the vastness of God's love for all people, no matter what their religious or cultural persuasion. Since then, my heart has been burdened to reach Christians all over the world, to show them the truth of the NDE in order to increase their faith as well. The purpose of this book is not to promote religion, but to promote the great truths and spirituality found in the NDE. One of these truths is that God is not limited to any one religion or even religion at all. God cares only about a person's heart, not a person's religious affiliation or church membership. The NDE reveals that the way to heaven is through love because love is God. Love is not limited to only one religion or culture because love is universal. This truth is too immense and profound to be fully understood or embodied in any one religion.

I am not the source of these truths. I consider myself a person who has picked the most beautiful flowers from other people's gardens to create one of my own. Neither the gardeners nor I matter much, but it is the flowers themselves that matter most and the life force making them so lovely.

ACKNOWLEDGMENTS

I first learned of spiritual concepts at a very early age from my grandparents Walter and Marie Williams, who taught us Sunday school lessons in the Nazarene Church. They planted the seed of love for the spiritual that has, over the decades, grown into a tree of life. I am deeply indebted to them and their love. They taught me at an early age the love of Jesus, which has never left me. Now, in their advanced age, it is I who am caring for them out of love. Without their early guidance, I am not sure where I would be today.

I want to acknowledge my father, who taught me the true meaning of being a Dad; my mother, who is now in heaven with her father and Jesus; my brothers and sisters, who taught me companionship from a very early age. I especially want to acknowledge my brother Glenn, who led me to spirituality at a time I really needed it. An excellent writer and editor, he has supported my research by editing this book, for which I am truly grateful. Without his help, this book would have been extremely more difficult to produce. Although my siblings and I ultimately have embraced different religious philosophies, it is the love binding us together I cherish most. I thank them for the love and support they have given me.

I would also like to acknowledge Dr. Stephen Hoyer, who provided me the near-death experience of the late May Eulitt and also recommended to me Xlibris as a publisher. I must also acknowledge those NDE researchers who have had a tremendous influence on my life. As mentioned earlier, Dr. Raymond Moody's groundbreaking work, Life after Life, was responsible for me becoming interested in NDEs. Dr. Kenneth Ring has been a big help with his research and has graciously allowed me to use a large amount of his material for my website. I thank P.M.H. Atwater, whose work I greatly admire, for listing my website in her Complete Idiot's Guide to Near-Death Experiences -- a book I have deemed "Book of the Year" on my website.

I would also like to thank all the experiencers who selflessly allowed me to profile their profound experiences. These include Linda Stewart, May Eulitt, David Oakford, Rene Turner, Karen Schaeffer, Ricky Randolph, Kerry Kirk, Brian Krebs and Joni Maggi. I am forever indebted to these individuals.

INTRODUCTION

Over the last several decades, I have read literally thousands of published NDEs. Of these, I have found sixty-two which I believe to be the most profound. What classifies these experiences as profound are the tremendous insights they give into the nature of life and death.

The NDE reveals the true meaning of life and it is this: we are here to learn to love. This world is part of a divine university of higher learning where learning to love is what life is all about. The NDE suggests that life and love itself is what many people identify as God. Love is the power holding all things in the universe together. Love is where we came from and love is where we will return. Love is the law of the universe.

The NDE reveals the importance of learning the many lessons of love. One of the most important lessons learned by experiencers is that practicing unconditional love is the method by which we can return to our divine origins -- that is, heaven. It does not matter what religious affiliation you belong to. Merely to love someone is to receive a glimpse of heaven. Through love, heaven begins inside you here on earth. The best way to get to heaven is to take it with you through the love you have given and received in life. Hell is the spiritual condition of being separated from love. It begins here on earth and can be carried over after death.

CHAPTER 1: NDE TESTIMONIALS

"Life is eternal; and love is immortal; and death is only a horizon; and a horizon is nothing save the limit of our sight." -- R. W. Raymond

MAY EULITT

The following is one of those very rare NDEs shared by several people at the same time. An excerpt is described in the words of May Eulitt to Stephen Hoyer, Ph.D. from their book entitled "Fireweaver." [2]

During the fall of 1970, when I was 21 years old, I shared a near-death experience with my cousin James and his best friend, Rashad, who was from India. Both young men were on a break from school and were staying with my family on our farm. One afternoon the three of us went to the cornfield to cut fodder. To get to the field we had to go through a metal gate, and we took turns climbing down to open and shut it. By late afternoon a storm started brewing in the west, and we decided to quit for the day. It was James' turn to open the gate, and as he did so, he reached up for my arm to climb back up onto the wagon. I was leaning the wrong way, and his weight pulled me toward him. Rashad grabbed my other arm to steady me, and we were in just this position when the lightening hit us. I saw the lightning sparkle along the top of the gate. The next thing we knew, we were in a large room or hall made of dark stone. The ceiling was so high and the gloom was so thick we couldn't see the top. There were no furnishings or wall hangings, just cold, black stone all around. I knew I should be afraid, but I just felt peaceful, floating along there in the gloom with my two friends in the great, dark hall. The stately walls of this place loomed above us and seemed to radiate both great power and also great masculinity. I remember thinking it would have suited King Arthur. It was at that point, I realized the three of us were united in thought and body. Images of Arthur came to me from James and Rashad. James saw only a comic version of the once and future king. Rashad seemed to be envisioning himself in the time of Arthur. As we all became conscious of each other's thoughts, I suddenly knew James and Rashad better than I have ever known anyone else.

We realized there was light coming into the chamber from an archway at one end. It was more than just light. It was a golden, embracing warmth. It gave off a feeling of peace and contentment more intense than anything we had ever felt. We were drawn toward it. We weren't talking, but we were communicating with each other on some other level, seeing through each other's eyes. As we came to the archway and passed through, we entered a beautiful valley.

There were meadows and tree-lined hills leading to tall mountains in the distance. Everything glistened with golden sparks of light.

We saw the sparkling lights were tiny, transparent bubbles drifting in the air and sparkled on the grass. We realized each tiny sparkle was a soul. To me, the valley appeared to be Heaven, but at the same time I knew James and Rashad were seeing it differently. James saw it as the Gulf of Souls. Rashad saw it as Nirvana, and somehow we knew all this without speaking. The light began gathering at the far end of the valley, and slowly, out of the mist, a pure white being began to materialize. I saw an angel with a strong, bright face, but not like you'd usually imagine. She was closer to a strong, Viking Valkyrie. I knew she was the special angel watching over the women of my family, and I perceived her name to be Hellena. James saw this same being as his late father a career naval officer, in a white dress uniform. Rashad perceived the being to be the Enlightened One, or Buddha.

The being spoke first to Rashad and welcomed him. He said Rashad's time on earth was done. He was worthy now of Nirvana. Rashad asked why James and I were there and was told that we were part of the reason why he was worthy of Nirvana. His two great friends loved him so much they had willingly accompanied him on his last journey. At the same time, however, James received a different message. He had been worried about what his father would think about his anti-war protest activities, and his father told him he was proud of him for standing up for what he believed. He knew he was not a coward because a coward would not have made this journey with Rashad. I received yet another message in which Hellena told me she was glad I had remembered the example of strength, honesty, wisdom, and loyalty taught to me by my family.

We spent what seemed like an eternity in this place as we talked to our separate yet joined entities. They said they appeared to us in this way because back in the real world we were physically joined when the lightning struck us. They said it also symbolized the joining of all religions and doctrines. They said I would live to see a new age of tolerance, where the souls and hearts of humanity would be joined as the three of us were.

The guides taught us that doctrine and creed and race meant nothing. No matter what we believed, we were all children joined under one God, and the only rule was God's true law - do unto others as you would have them do unto you. We should treat all people as if they were a part of our soul because they were. All living things in the universe were connected to one another. They said soon humanity would mature enough to assume a higher place in the universal scheme of things, but until then we must learn acceptance and tolerance and love for each other. They said there would come a new age when people would not be able to endure seeing others homeless and hungry. We would realize that only by helping each other could we truly help ourselves.

Eventually we were told it was time to go. We would not be allowed to stay longer because it was not yet time for me or for James, only for Rashad. The enlightened one told Rashad he would have a little time before he returned to take care of his worldly affairs. James' father told him he would return to this place soon after Rashad, but the two of them had to go back for now so that I could. I said I would willing to stay here in this valley with them, but Hellena told me I had not fulfilled my destiny; I had children yet unborn.

We drifted slowly toward the archway. The pull became stronger and we were literally thrown back into the world. We floated for a while there, hovering above our bodies. Some of my cousins had been in the next field and had seen what happened. We saw them all come running to where we lay. James and Rashad's hands were still stuck to my arms. We saw my cousins pry their fingers loose so they could turn Rashad over to help him.

When our hands were pried loose, James and I reentered our bodies. We felt as if we were on fire, but it turned out we had only minor injuries. Rashad, it seemed, being on the end, had taken most of the charge. The doctors said the lightning had caused damage to his heart, lungs, and liver. He remained in the hospital for several weeks. During that time, tests revealed James had a brain tumor that would eventually claim his life.

As soon as Rashad could travel, James took him home to India. He offered to stay, but Rashad told him he wished solitude for his final time. Rashad took on the life of the Ascetic, in the Vedic tradition. He asked his wife to stay with her family because he wanted his last days to be spent in spiritual awakenings. About a year and a half later, on a cold day in January, Rashad returned to Nirvana. James and I knew when his soul left the world without being told.

James lived about three years after he found out he had the brain tumor. He gave most of his considerable inheritance to a charity that educated young people in India. I, on the other hand, have survived for another thirty years (so far) with the knowledge this experience I shared with my closest friends has been a guiding force in my life. I strive every day to meet my destiny, whatever it may be, with the same quiet dignity and resolution they showed when they met theirs. They have truly been my pathfinders, and I know the connection I shared with them so long ago is the same connection we all share. We just sometimes fail to realize it. [3]

DAVID OAKFORD

In the early summer of 1979, David Oakford was 20 years old and having problems dealing with his life situation. His childhood was not designed to enable him to properly deal with life in general. He had no self-esteem and everything he did to find peace within just did not work. He was pretty miserable and he felt lost and unloved. He turned to drugs and alcohol. He needed to find the peace within himself and he felt it calling him. It was at a party that David took an overdose of drugs and had an NDE. His NDE is one of the most profound you will ever read. The following is an excerpt from David Oakford's NDE. You can read his entire account in his book entitled "Soul Bared." The following is David Oakford's NDE in his own words.

I laid down to use the stability of the earth in an effort to maintain a hold on reality. I knew I had to do that in order to be able to come back down.

The next thing I knew I was riding in my friend's car. I thought we went up north, crossed the Mackinaw Bridge and came back again. We rode past my childhood home and I saw my parents sitting on the porch.

I felt drawn to the trees. I could see and feel their strength. I saw their roots going deep into the ground. I mean I actually saw the tree roots physically reaching below the ground. I told my friends about the car ride after the experience and they told me the only place I went was to the chair they carried me to after I passed out on the porch.

I did wake up in the chair my friends say they put me in a bit later. When I woke up I could feel the organs in my body working, each one separately as well as all together. I could not see my friends anywhere. I could see in all the rooms of the house at the same time. The stereo was playing the Doors Absolutely Live album, except the volume was way too loud for me. Since I did not see any of my friends around I got up and tried to turn the music down, but could not. No matter what I did the music kept playing. I knew the stereo too. I had a real problem with the noise. It was tearing at me and I could not figure out why nor could I adjust the volume.

I called out to my friends and nobody came. I tried to unplug the stereo but that did not work either. Every time I tried to touch the cord to unplug it I could not grasp it. It just kept on playing "LA Woman" and the sound rattled my very being.

I ran all over the house calling for my friends, yelling repeatedly that the music was too loud but I was not heard. I pleaded for the music to be turned down. I tried to go outside but I could not feel the doorknob. I could see the daylight outside but could not go outside. I ended up hiding in the bathroom in an unsuccessful attempt to escape the noise. I looked in the mirror and could not see myself. That frightened me greatly.

I went back into the family room and saw my body sitting in the chair. It looked like I was sleeping. I wondered how I could be looking at myself. I got a bit scared then because I could see me from outside of me, from all different angles except from the inside angle I was used to seeing myself.

I was alone. I was confused and very scared. I tried to get back into my body but could not. I could not touch the ground either. I was floating. I rose up into a spot above my body and kind of just hung there. I could no longer move. I called out for help and nobody came. I tried to go out the door but like the stereo I could not touch the doorknob. I was scared and alone and did not know what to do. I did not understand what was happening to me.

I asked God to help me. I did believe in God then, but I was kind of angry at him because of the crappy life I was experiencing. I reasoned if God were really the omnipotent and omniscient being I was taught he was he would not have let me experience the pain I had experienced throughout my life. I thought if there was a time I needed God, it was now! I was not disappointed with the result of my plea for help.

I looked over by the door to the outside and saw a beautiful being standing there. His feet did not touch the floor. His feet just blended into thin air. He looked both female and male and was young. I could not tell his/her sex. His hair was curly and he was about my height. He had this glow about him too. The glow was green close to him, then blue, then pure white in the upper areas. He said, "I am here to help you" but when he spoke his mouth did not move. I did not actually hear him speak with my ears. I felt what he was saying.

When I saw this being and he spoke to me, I was no longer afraid. I actually felt peace and comfort like I had never felt before. I felt the peace I was searching for throughout my entire life. The feeling was very familiar to me, like I had felt it before but not in this life.

This wonderful being called me by a name I do not remember. I told him he must have the wrong guy and the name he used for me was not my name. He laughed and said I was a great "master" and I had just forgotten who I was. I did not believe him, because I did not really know for sure what a "master" was then and if I were this great master I would not have had all the problems I had. I felt I was an evil being because that is what I was told in my life several times by many.

He told me his name, but I do not remember it. He told me he had been with me always and told me he knew I had a very hard life and he would help me understand why if I really wanted to. He told me he would help me remember who I am. He said he would understand if I did not believe him and offered to prove to me he knew everything about me.

He told me things I did when I as a child proving to me he was always with me. He told me about things I had only thought about. He told me I could go anywhere I wanted to go and he would show me how to do it if I wanted him to. He said that if I needed to come back and see my body I could. My body would be fine because I was still connected to it somehow.

When we spoke to each other we did so telepathically. The expression on his face was a happy one all the time.

I told him I would like to see the pyramids in Egypt as well as the southwest United States. He told me all I had to do was trust him, think about where I wanted to go, and we would go. I thought about the pyramids and we were there in an instant. I do not know why I chose the pyramids, the thought just popped into me so I went with that. While we were there he told me some things about the pyramids and Egypt I do not remember now. I really wish I could remember what he explained while we were there because I do know it was highly significant and had to do with humanity's future. The energy was the lowest in areas where there were man-made structures, the cities of the world. The energy I saw came from the human beings living in the cities. It was explained to me that humans are the basic producers of energy in cities because of their relatively low vibration level the energy is lower in general. I could see the higher sources of energy in the cities though. I was shown people who had higher energy levels and some of them actually talked to the being I was with. I saw dark souls during the time the being and I spent on Gaia. The dark souls were earthbound spirits who refuse to go to the light. They prey on the energies of humans still in human form and try to use those souls to prevent the evolution of spirit. I was told I was protected from these dark ones as long as I chose to focus on the love in me. The dark ones did not even try to affect us, in fact they gave us nasty looks and went away. I was told I would know these dark ones when I see them and I was told to tell them to go to the light. The light is a porthole to the place all souls go if they choose.

I could see energy around the humans too, all different levels and colors. The being explained the human energy to me. He said the energy coming from humans is what spirits use to evaluate the spiritual condition of particular humans. He said the lighter and more brilliant the color the more advanced the spirit is. He said seeing the "aura" around a spirit is useful in determining how much a particular spirit needs to work on his development. He said the higher beings know where to go and what to do to help an earthbound soul so they may advance themselves if they so choose. He told me all souls have this energy, this is why I could see it on every human I saw. He said I was of the same energy type as he but my vibration is lower when I am in human form and in time my energy would raise to match his intensity provided I chose to take the initiative to consciously evolve my soul.

He told me there is much to this planet that spirits can see which humans do not see with their eyes because their vibrations are so low. He showed me life in the trees that I could see as a spirit but could not see in my human form.

He explained that beings of higher vibration do live on earth but they are not human, they are part of earth itself. He explained these beings were the caretakers of physical life on the planet. He said these beings take care of what we call nature. There are beings taking care of the plant life, the mineral life and the waterborne life. These lower echelon beings work together to ensure that all aspects of nature is protected and remains healthy. When the planet was evolving, these ethereal beings were the ones keeping the balance of nature.

He explained to me that the planet we call earth really has a proper name. He told me the earth is really called "Gaia". He said Gaia has its own energy and that Gaia is really a true living being. I asked if this energy could be seen and he said that we have to be away from Gaia to appreciate and see it. He said humans are the ones who can manipulate Gaia's energy through their choices. He said if humans choose to live in harmony with the energy on Gaia, it is good for Gaia. He said if humans abuse Gaia, they hurt Gaia by altering its energy structure. I was given an example of how humans have deforested the planet and reduced the energy available faster than it could be replenished. He said Gaia was very strong but has been weakened considerably since humans have chosen to use the resources in a manner inconsistent with the laws of the universe.

I asked him if we could go into space and see Gaia's energy and he said yes. He said there were no limits on where we could go. I concentrated my thought, trusted, and we then went into what is known as space.

Away from this planet I could see Gaia all at once. It was so beautiful. I could see the aura around Gaia. The aura affected me greatly. I felt a deep love for this beautiful place. I could hear Gaia move and was told the sound was the energy flowing in and out of Gaia. My special being told me that Gaia is the most unique planet because it is designed for humans to live on forever. It was created for spirit to play, learn, and grow. He said the balance of nature on Gaia allows spirit to be in human form when a spirit lives in harmony with nature.

Nature exists to compensate for the decreased vibration and was created for spirits to adapt enough to adjust and be in the physical human body while still having access to energy that will help them advance. He explained that humans were designed by God to live eternally on Gaia and are not supposed to "die". He said "dying" is a human created earth term meaning little in the world of spirit. The reason humans supposedly die is that they have fallen away from the balance of nature and allow themselves to be affected by what they create that violates the natural laws of the universe. He said humans have fallen away from living in balance with nature. He said they must relearn about the harmonic balance if they want to survive as a race and live on Gaia forever. He said it was still possible for humans to learn about this harmony and it is the next overall goal of humans on Gaia. I was told humans would eventually realize they must restore the harmony but great damage will be inflicted before humans will fully realize what they have been doing to Gaia and work to reverse what they have done.

We traveled past all of the planets in our solar system. Near each planet I could hear the energy just like on Gaia. I saw the auras around each one of them too. I saw spirits on all of them as well. My friend told me all planets are places for spirits to live, learn and thus evolve. I saw great cities on each and every one of those planets. It was explained that other life in the universe is not readily seen because the beings were all of higher vibration and most spirits in human form have yet to attain the higher vibration required to see them.

16

The being told me each planet has a theme for learning and any of them can be chosen by a soul when we are between physical lives. He said we practice on the other planets to be ready to live on Gaia. He said Gaia is the ultimate experience for a soul. It is ultimate because our souls evolve faster here than anywhere else. It was said the lessons we need to learn are difficult to learn without having a physical form.

He explained how we pick a physical life on Gaia. He explained to me I picked the parents I was born to so I could learn what I needed to learn to grow enough to come back and do spirit work on Gaia after I attain a certain level of growth. He said I was being told all of these things so I could help souls come together and return Gaia to harmony.

He explained some things to me about God that I do not remember. They had to do with the universe and the size and structure of it. I do remember he said God is not to be seen for he is everywhere. He told me God loves Gaia deeply, much as a man loves his wife.

He talked about Jesus too. He told me Jesus was a master God sent to earth to teach humans how to act toward each other and find their way back to the path of harmony with each other as well as with Gaia.

I was told Jesus is the being entrusted by God to ensure souls evolve. He said Jesus is of the highest in vibration than any other soul. He said God holds Jesus in the highest of favor because he was the best example of what humans need to do. I then got to see Jesus. I saw his light. Jesus' light was the purest I have ever seen. There was no need for words. There were only love feelings I cannot even begin to describe.

I was told that loving one another is what souls need to do in order for peace and harmony to be the standard on Gaia.

I was told there is a hierarchy in the universe dedicated to preserving the harmony of the universe. I was told humans are an integral part of this harmony and the free will we have is a part of souls allowing humans to provide service to the universe.

After he explained those things to me I was able to see our whole solar system all at once in full color. The planets were all in a line and I could see all of them from Pluto to the sun. I felt very blessed and very important. I was given this great gift and I did not really understand why. There I floated, a person who went out his way to inflict pain on other souls, yet I was never asked about what I had done. In fact I was given the honor of being given answers to questions most people wonder about all of their lives.

I thanked this loving being for explaining and showing me what he did. He told me there was more for him to show me if I was ready to experience it. I told him I was ready. I did not know why I was chosen but I was not about to question why. It just seemed small to me then.

We started to head back toward Gaia. We went to a place in the shadow of Gaia. It was a great city in the clouds. The city had these beautiful white buildings as far as I could see. I saw spirits living there all of which had vibration but no real physical body. These inhabitants went to and from the buildings - going to work and play too. I saw a place where spirits went to get what I thought was water. There were no vehicles there. Spirits seemed to get around the same way my being and I got around, by flying.

The city had no boundaries I could see. This was a place full of life of all kinds. There was nature there, many pure plants, trees, and water just like on Gaia but more pure. Nature there was absolutely perfect. It was untainted by human manipulation. This place was just like Gaia only without the problems and negativity. I felt this was what is called heaven in earth terms.

I saw spirits going to and from the Gaia and the city. I could tell the development of the spirits going to and from by the energy they emanated. I could see that animals came to and from earth just like humans do. I could see many spirits leave Gaia with guides and could see spirits returning to Gaia without guides. The being told me that some of the spirits passing by were the ones doing the work with humans on Gaia. I could make out the type of spirits doing the work and the spirits coming to the great city to become replenished to eventually go back to Gaia to experience and further evolve. I could feel the emotions of the ones coming back for replenishment. I could feel some of them were sad, beaten and scared, much like I felt before my being came to me.

My being took me into one of the larger buildings. Inside I saw many spirits working. They were doing things similar to jobs on earth. When we walked by the spirits, they looked at me. I think they were checking me out because of the being I was with.

We went upstairs and I saw spirits that knew me. They greeted me and asked me how I was doing. They gave me advice that I do not remember. I thought I was going to be given a job there, but the being knew I thought that and told me there was something I needed to do first.

I was ecstatic. I was in heaven despite everything I had done during my life on Gaia. I was experiencing what most people only dream about. The love I felt there was the same love I felt when I saw Jesus. I had been searching on Gaia for what was really the same place I was in then. I was searching on Gaia for the feeling I had that very moment. I had found what I spent my whole life searching for. I was truly happy. I was home and I knew it. I was ready to stay and do whatever work I was given to do.

My being took me to another building that was special. It was bigger than the rest and had the greenest foliage I had ever seen growing on it, decorating it like a shrine. We went inside a set of double doors glowing with life. The inside was decorated with a wood paneling the being told me was "living" wood from the trees growing at this wonderful place. He led me to some big double doors and told me to wait on this bench while he went inside.

A bit later he came out of the room. He told me to go into the room and said he would wait for me and to not worry. He cautioned me to ensure I was truthful with the beings in the room. He said they were no judges, rather they were the ones who evaluated a soul's development based on a soul's history. He told me to remember who I was and to refrain from fear. I knew I had to leave this being sooner or later but I was glad he would wait for me. I was a little scared to leave him, but I felt I was protected and knew I would be protected here.

I went in and saw a group of several spirits seated at a table. The table was made of the glowing wood and was perfect in every way. The spirits around this table had the highest vibration I had seen so far with the exception of Jesus.

I looked at these beings and recognized them. I do not know where I recognized them from, but they all had a familiarity about them. They just looked at me.

All of a sudden, I saw my parents on earth before I was born. I saw how they came to be together and watched them have my brother and sister before me. I saw their positive and negative sides and evaluated them according to what I knew I needed to do on Gaia. The beings asked me how and why I picked these particular parents and asked me to tell them. They said I knew how and why I picked them and asked me to tell them why. I do not know where it came from but I did tell them how and why and they agreed with me. I picked them to help them on their path as well as to achieve my learning.

I saw my soul go to my mother and go inside of her. I saw myself being born from an observer standpoint as well as having the actual experience. I proceeded to see my entire life from the observer point of view and from the points of view of those my actions affected. I felt the feelings they felt directly resulting from things I had done to them. I saw both the positive and the negative things I had done as they had truly happened; nothing was left out or presented inaccurately.

I experienced the harshness of being born again. I experienced leaving heaven and the transit to Gaia. I saw myself as a helpless infant who needed his mother for everything. I experienced my father's love as well as his anger. I experienced my mother's love, her fear and her anger as well. I saw all of the good and bad from my childhood years and re-experienced what I had done then. I felt all of my emotions and the emotions of the souls I had hurt as well as loved. From all of this I learned it matters deeply what choices I make on Gaia.

I learned just how powerful we humans are and how we can affect each other in positive and negative ways. It was amazing to see how my innocent actions had such a powerful effect on souls I had no idea I was affecting. The experience was one I will never forget. I experienced the whole spectrum of feelings of my life in a relatively short period of time as we humans see it. Where I was, time did not really exist.

I could see how I became what I had become on Gaia and why I became that way. Everything I did in my life affected the evolution of the souls around me. I saw the reasons for all of my actions and understood why I did what I had done. There was a place for all of my positive and negative actions. There was no action necessarily wrong, but there were actions I took that did not enhance positive growth. I was both a victim and a beneficiary of my actions. This was not a fun experience to go through. I could see how wonderful it could be if one chose to act to affect other souls positively most of the time.

Afterward, the beings in the room asked me questions about what I saw and how I felt about my life up to then. I knew I had to provide an honest assessment - I could not lie. I hesitated when they asked me whether I affected others more positively than negatively. I thought about lying.

These beings knew what I was thinking and I had to tell them I felt I could have done a better job on Gaia. I knew what I had come to Gaia to accomplish and was well on my way to doing that but I knew I was not finished yet. They agreed and told me that I still had many things to do and that I may want to go back and do them. I was told it was understood how difficult it would be for me but it was necessary for the universe for me to finish. They said it may be wise to go back and live my life how I had originally planned it. They said I had set lofty goals for my life on Gaia and the events in my life were achieving the goals I had set. They said I originally came to Gaia to learn and share with others using the gifts I have accumulated over several lifetimes. They said I am needed on Gaia to help souls bring themselves and Gaia back to harmony. They said I have great potential to affect other souls, to help them grow and Gaia is the best place to do that. I was told the events I had experienced thus far were preparing me to make a large contribution to the universe and my experiences were not to be considered personal attacks in any way. I did not want to accept it. I wanted to stay. I told them that. I told them I was tired and wanted to stay because life on Gaia is hard and unforgiving. I felt going back would be dangerous for the universe because I was not advanced enough in my spiritual evolution. They said that was precisely why it would be in my best interest to go back to Gaia. They said I was more advanced than I give myself credit for. They said it was possible for me to stay but I would need to finish my work on Gaia sooner or later. The type of work I was destined for can only be done on Gaia. I could stay if chose to but I would only be prolonging the completion of what I needed to do for this universe. They explained the fastest way to finish my work would be to go back to Gaia as soon as possible.

I was stunned to say the least. I resorted to bargaining but it was no use. I still did not like living on Gaia and did not really want to go back. These beings understood me but remained firm. I had a decision to make that was really the hardest decision I would ever make.

I did come back to Gaia and am now living the life I was (later in the experience) told I would live. Believe it or not, I ended up shelving this experience away, classifying it as a really vivid "trip". It was not until I evolved more that I realized the gift I was given.

I share this experience now because I feel it can, if so chosen, spur thought and foster choices affecting the planet in a positive way.

If I learned anything from this experience it was that every choice I make is duly recorded, noted and will return later, when I leave here again. My goal is to save people the pain I felt in my review and hasten the evolution of humans on Gaia, helping Gaia as well as the universe.

I am one who had a near-death experience and was given a choice to return to this planet in a physical sense again. I chose to return out of love for this planet - a love so great I would give up the slot I have "back home." I did this also in order to help to heal the place through the sharing of what I was shown of the in between and through the choices I make, (hopefully loving and kind ones).

Without the free will to return I would not be here in the physical doing what I am doing. The physical pain, war, poverty, pestilence, horror, rape, murder, abandonment etc., etc., etc. which is here on this planet is the result of humans coming here and making their free choices in order to learn and evolve. Unfortunately learning does tend to create a mess at times and the physical pain etc. is a part of that mess. It makes sense to me that the same free choice concept is instrumental in cleaning up the mess.

I liken it to camping and choosing to clean up or not clean up the mess one makes. If you choose to clean up your mess, this helps the planet to stay as is because one does not contribute to the mess. If one does not clean it up, it adds to the mess. If one cleans up his or her own mess and then some, it contributes to healing the planet.

In my near-death experience I was also shown there are many souls in "heaven" who are more than willing to come to this place regardless of the state it is in. I was shown if I did not choose to return I would be in the schools existing in heaven, working toward the growth I need to accomplish regardless of the form I am in. That was an attractive choice to be sure except I had a problem with how long it would take me to grow enough to do what my soul wishes to do. (I have a burning desire to experience other places in other universes and to do that I need to grow more.) The prerequisite for that is ensuring my soul has the IQ for it.

It is my understanding that a soul can choose to remain in heaven and operate on the level he/she (whatever) is on to infinity, but I seek more because I know without doubt there is more.

At any rate, the idea remains that for this place to start feeling and looking like heaven is to create the love felt there here. I would like to see that on this planet and I know it can be done. If I need to, I will come back here all over again to make it happen.[4]

RENE TURNER

On February 1982 in Newcastle, Australia, Dr. Rene Turner left her optical instrument repair firm after a day's work. She got in her car and drove down the highway on her way home. As she came to a stoplight where a road crossed the highway, she slowed down to a stop. Here, her memory ends.

Her partner, who was riding with her, reports, "As we approached the lights, they changed to green. As we went into the crossing, the car aquaplaned and hit a large power pole just after the intersection. Stuart, who was lying on the mattress in the back of the panel van, was thrown forward into the back of Rene's head, driving her into the steering wheel."

At the hospital, the professor of neurosurgery reported Rene's death to her parents and said they should be grateful because she would have been a vegetable had she survived. During this conversation, a young frightened nurse rushed into the office and blurted out, "She is alive! She sat up and spoke!" The professor chastised her for interrupting them and lectured her about how "dead bodies" can move and make noises.

But the nurse was emphatic; "She sat up and said, 'Don't give me any more drugs!'"

At this point, Rene's mother took the professor by his and Rene's father's elbow and marched them down the corridor. They found Rene in a back corridor where she had apparently been placed so the nurse could remove equipment prior to her transfer to the morgue. She was found in a deep coma and breathing. She remained that way for ten days.

The following is Rene Turner's NDE in her own words.

I don't know when the above events in my experience took place. I have no memory of the process of dying or leaving my body. I was moving headfirst through a dark maelstrom of what looked like black boiling clouds, feeling I was being beckoned to the sides, which frightened me. Ahead was a tiny dot of bright light steadily growing and brightened as I drew nearer. I became aware that I must be dead and was concerned for Mum and Dad and my sister, and somewhat upset with myself as I thought, "They will soon get over it," like it was, in passing, just a fleeting thought as I rushed greedily forward towards this light.

I arrived in an explosion of glorious light into a room with insubstantial walls, standing before a man about in his thirties, about six feet tall, reddish brown shoulder length hair and an incredibly neat, short beard and mustache. He wore a simple white robe. Light seemed to emanate from him and I felt he had great age and wisdom. He welcomed me with great love, tranquility, and peace (indescribable) - no words. I felt, "I can sit at your feet forever and be content," which struck me as a strange thing to think/say/feel. I became fascinated by the fabric of his robe and tried to figure out how light could be woven!

He stood beside me and directed me to look to my left, where I was replaying my life's less complementary moments. I relived those moments and felt not only what I had done but also the hurt I had caused. Some of the things I would have never imagined could have caused pain. I was surprised that some things I may have worried about, like shoplifting a chocolate as a child, were not there, whilst casual remarks which caused hurt unknown to me at the time were counted. When I became burdened with guilt, I was directed to other events that gave joy to others, although I felt unworthy. It seemed the balance was in my favor. I received great love.

I was led further into the room, which became a hall. There coming towards me was my grandfather. He looked younger than I remembered and was without his hare lip or cleft pallet, but undoubtedly my grandfather. We hugged. He spoke to me and welcomed me. I was moved to forgive him for dying when I was 14 and making me break my promise to become a doctor and find a cure for his heart condition. Until that moment, I had not realized I had been angry with him!

Granddad told me that grandma was coming soon and he was looking forward to her arrival. I inquired why she was coming soon as she had been traveling from her home in Manchester to New Zealand to Miami for continual summer for a number of years! Granddad told me she had cancer of the bowel and was coming soon. Granddad seemed to have no grasp of time when I pressed for how soon. (Grandma was diagnosed three months later and died in August. I had upset my mother by telling her about it when I regained consciousness). After Granddad and I had talked a while, he took me further into the room that became a hall again. We approached a group of people whom I started to recognize.

The person who first welcomed me came and placed his hand on my shoulder and turned me towards him. He said, "You must return. You have a task to perform." I wanted to argue. I wanted to stay. I glanced back at Granddad and was propelled quickly towards the entrance. At the threshold, all became blackness, nothing, no awareness.

I awoke from my coma slowly, over several days, half-dreamed memories of familiar voices and glimpses of faces. The clearest moments were several occasions where I would awake from deep sleep to find a nurse with a syringe and refuse any drugs. I had no idea why! I had three lots of surgery to repair my face, skull, and eye socket. I left the hospital with pain, double vision, Anosmia, and damage to eighth cranial nerve. It left me with nausea and a disturbed balance. I was for two years angry at G-d for sending me back in such torment with a task to do and with no clues or instructions, except for one thing. I was given a clear message I have no idea how to pass on. It is this: "It is time to live according to your beliefs, whatever they may be - to put your house in order because the end times are upon us!" This can't be my task. There was no booming voice or any way I knew the message got there. I am also unsure of the identity of the gatekeeper - no nametag and no introduction!

It took me five years as a zombie before I was able to rehabilitate myself. I have gainful employment, formed the Head Injury Society of New Zealand in 1987, and am paraded as the example of how well it is possible to recover from acquired brain damage. I still don't know my task - still have pain, Anosmia, Diplopia, etc.

The memory of the near-death experience is more real than what I did yesterday. [5]

KAREN SCHAEFFER

Karen Schaeffer experienced one of the most unique NDEs I have ever read. In it, she is shown the future, but is given the option of changing it.

The following is her experience in her own words:

As a teenager, I had several psychic experiences often occurring in dreams. As I grew older and life more hectic, these experiences diminished - almost disappeared until the pregnancy of my first child.

Shortly after his birth I had the most horrific dream that I would be in a terrible car crash that would take my life. For months I was terrified and was extremely cautious and on the lookout for that monster vehicle. By the time my son was 7 months old, I convinced myself it was only a dream... nothing of what was to come. I had a brand new teaching position, a baby, a home and my husband to take care of ... I had put too much energy into this thing. Then it happened.

I had left school right away that day. I wanted to pick up my son from his grandmother and hurry back to school to watch a baseball game. It was a picture perfect way to spend the afternoon with my son. As I was exiting the freeway with usual caution, I made a left hand turn on a light that had been green for some time. This was my lucky day I thought. Then in an instant I was gone.

Immediately I was in the most beautiful serene place I had ever been. My grandfather, another person whom I had known in a previous lifetime, and a guardian were ready to help me with the transition. They told me of the accident, showed me the site. It was my time to come home they said.

The overwhelming love and happiness of that place was so inviting.

I could feel myself becoming lighter each moment. In a fit of fear and panic I began crying. No, I couldn't be dead. What would happen to my son? He was seven months old! He would never remember me. His father didn't even know how to take care of him. I didn't want him raised by his father's parents. No, no, no ... this was not the time to go. They were wrong.

In an embrace of love they calmed me by showing me that my son, my entire family would be okay after my death. My mother could lean on my grandmother. It would take time, but she would heal. My husband, hurt, sad, and lonely would also heal and eventually find love once again.

Death is part of the lessons we are to learn on earth, and my death was an important lesson for those involved in my life. I was shown my funeral, taught how to be near those I loved and told I could eventually communicate with those whose spirits were open. I could accept this. They would be fine.

I was feeling lighter all the time. But wait... my son. I couldn't leave my son! Babies need their mommies. I needed to be his mommy. I couldn't let go. So much patience was shown to me - so much love.

My guides explained that the feelings I was having were still a connection to my human side. Once my Humanness wore off, I would feel light as air, utter happiness, and extreme love.

Words do not do the feelings justice. They worked to help me throw off my human weight. The feelings were so great and seemed to pull me in stronger and stronger; yet my connection to my son was so strong.

We wandered in this beautiful place for what seemed an eternity. We discussed my life. We discussed religion. We discussed secrets of the soul that as humans we must forget, lest we'd never be able to thrive on earth. All the while I was in awe. Some things were just as I always dreamed an afterlife would be. Some things I was just plain wrong and I remember thinking, "Wow!" Where were my other loved ones? When could I see my other grandparents who had passed? In time - they were on a different plane. When my transition was complete I could choose to go to other levels when I was ready.

Every now and then thoughts of my son would make me heavy once again. I couldn't bear the thought of him growing up without a mother. I was told others would be a mother for me. First grandparents, and then they showed me Jake's life. He was the most beautiful boy, so happy, but with a touch of sadness that seemed to pierce his soul. This was his lesson to tackle. He knew coming into this life the main lessons he was to learn. It was meant to be. I saw a new mom for Jake when he was about 7 or 8. A beautiful woman, kind hearted who definitely cared for Jake, and treated him well, but she was to have her own child with my widowed husband and the love she showed for her own child was different and unequal to the love she showed for my child - her stepchild. This isn't what I dreamed for Jake. This couldn't be. I was happy for my husband. He was okay. He was happy. My son was a different story. Other lessons were learned in the constant-patient job of transitioning me to the other side. I had to let go. At times I became hysterical and then moments later I was calm and serene.

I saw a female child, who had been meant in Jake's place, but before conception, plans changed and there was a need for Jake's spirit to take her place. There was much upheaval that Jake could help mend (and he did).

At a time when I felt the closest to accepting my death, I experienced a resurgence of sorrow and pain, longing for my son, for my life. I couldn't let go of my human life. My guides tried their hardest. They never gave up. They never became discouraged. It is unbelievable the amount of patience and love they exuded. Finally, my hysteria was calmed by a higher spirit who seemed to envelop me in love. My guides were instructed to allow me to return. Despite their pleas to allow them more time, they were told that at this point, my spirit would not rest. It was best to let me return, to settle my spirit, learn further lessons. My pleading won my return for the time being. I understood that before my descent, my friends and family had lessons being postponed, but they would have to learn the lessons resulting from my death at some time later.

Arrangements were made for when, where, how my spirit would return and which lessons I was to have enriched or acquire new. Some lessons learned in my arrival on the other side would have to be forgotten, and it was not good for my soul to know when I was dying again or else as a human I would focus on only that, especially as the time neared.

The last things I remember were being taken back to the accident site, and just before my descent, I was told when my children were older it would be time to come home for good. I accepted it immediately, but then, wait! What qualifies as older? Does it mean only a few years older? Teenagers? Will I live to see them marry and have their own children? This was a difficult aspect to deal with immediately after the accident.

I had a life with my son again. I had to spend it right for I had no idea how much longer I had left.

I was told I was lucky to survive. A large utility truck ran a red light and hit the driver's side of my tiny compact car. Despite wearing a seatbelt the doctors say I would not have survived if it were not for the airbags to open, something that is not supposed to happen in a side impact.

The first year after the accident was an attempt to live the best I could, the happiest I could. I was suffering however from severe pain from a fractured shoulder bone, broken ribs, and two hip fractures. I was told the pain should disappear in six months to a year at the worst. Three years later, the pain has not gone away. The second year however seemed to be the worst. I became so suicidal. All I wanted to do was to return to this place, this life so awesome, so love-filled, and so joyous. My son, and later my daughter were the only things that made me go on. I was here for them. Today, only three years later I have accepted my return to earth, long to return to my after-life home, and struggle to find peace and happiness until my time here comes to its final end. [6]

LINDA STEWART

Linda's journey to understand God began in the rugged environment of a Texas childhood filled with "rattlesnakes, tornadoes, and hellfire-and-damnation." Her early concept of God was molded by the pervasive, extremist religious community of the Bible Belt, exemplified by the Southern Baptist religion practiced by her parents. The wrathful, vengeful God as taught by her religion instilled in Linda a deep fear of God, death and the afterlife.

Her lifelong search for a loving God and release from the paralyzing fear of death culminated in a brief journey to Heaven after a debilitating illness. The NDE transformed Linda, showing her that God is only a loving God, who does not judge and punish. She came to understand the Oneness of all existence; this understanding has permeated her life with peace and the unfaltering knowledge of God's goodness. Linda now spends her time counseling, lecturing and making television appearances. She has written a book entitled, Entertaining Angels Unawares, which is in the hands of an agent who is seeking a publisher. The following is her NDE in her own words.

When I finally gave up my will to live, relinquishing my life unto death was sublimely easy after my long illness and loss of everything that had made life worthwhile for me. The decision to leave this world hung suspended in an extended moment of absolute quiet. Passionless, I watched my spirit leave my body as a feeling of "otherness" engulfed me. I felt a strange detachment from my physical body and the life I had created. I was no longer connected to a pitiful, suffering mass of flesh. I was not that body and yet, I still existed but in a new state of being. Gone was the wrenching pain that accompanied my every waking moment. The strain of expanding my lungs to gasp for air had disappeared. Fatigue, which had weighted my life for years, had lifted. Depression no longer drained my mind of hope. Sight and sounds did not sear my head with pain, leaving me emotionally bereft. And yet, I still existed. I felt weightless and calm.

Although I knew I was not in the lifeless body lying on my bed, and that the eyes and brain I had previously identified as mine were in that inanimate object with which I no longer identified, I was still aware of sight and thoughts and sensations. I observed my new reality with tranquility. Slowly I looked around and below me I saw a vast, endless blackness. Like a void or black hole, I was irresistibly drawn toward the darkness. Gradually, I felt myself sinking toward it. I thought, without fear or any emotional reaction, "Isn't that strange?" I had been so afraid I was going to be judged and sent to either heaven or hell. But it appeared I would simply disappear into the dark nothingness. As even my new awareness waned, I yielded to the heaviness overtaking me as darkness filled my mind. My vision became obscured as I began to merge into the blackness.

Offering no resistance, I released my hold on any remaining shred of consciousness and personal identity. At the very moment I felt the last of me disappearing into nothingness. A powerful, energetic force swooping beneath me, lifting me, and carrying me upward suddenly buffeted me.

Barely conscious, my only awareness was a sensation of rising. I seemed to be traveling upward at an unimaginable speed. A clean sensation of wind rushed over my face and body with tremendous force and yet there was no discomfort. Vast distances seemed to fly by me. The higher I rose, the more my head cleared. I became aware of a deep sense of peace and warmth permeating my senses. Confused, because the energy enveloping me had a definite presence, I tried to see what was happening and who was carrying me. Who or what cared so deeply for me? I felt peaceful and loved immeasurably. I knew I was in the arms of a being who cherished me with perfect love and carried me from the dark void into a new reality.

As my mind cleared, scoured of the remnants of mortal, past associations, I was finally able to open my being fully to spirit and my vision cleared.

With the eyes of my soul body, I looked to see what held me in such love and I beheld a radiant, spirit being, so magnificent and full of love, I knew I would never again feel the sense of loss. I have no way of explaining how, but I knew the Spirit was Christ. It was not a belief, perception or understanding, but my recognition of Christ came from my new perspective of spirit.

I did not see the Spirit as I had seen Jesus of Nazareth depicted in paintings, but the innate knowing of my heart remembered and acknowledged Christ. The radiant Spirit was Christ, the manifestation and expression of pure love. Because of my Christian education, I knew no other name to call what I felt as I looked at him. Others might have called him Buddha, or Yahweh, or Great Spirit in the Sky, but the naming did not matter, only the recognition of absolute love and truth was important. Safe in the gentle yet powerful embrace of his love, I rested, secure that everything was okay, exactly as it was supposed to be.

Ascending ever farther, I lifted my eyes to see a great light in the vast distance. With Christ as my guide, I rapidly approached the light. Ecstasy filled my soul as I looked at the radiance, many-fold brighter than a sun.

The light was everywhere and everything, the brightest I had ever seen and dazzling beyond description. Brilliant enough to blind or burn; yet I was not harmed.

The light moved over and through me, washing every hidden place of my heart, removing all hurt and fear, transforming my very being into a song of joy. I had thought the love I felt from Christ was complete; yet, the light toward which we were soaring was the fulfillment of my search, the loving Source of all that exists, the God of truth and unconditional love, the origin of creation.

My understanding of love was forever changed. The majesty and glory of that vision was an ineffable moment defining forever more, the direction of my new truth. I was home and I wanted nothing more than to remain in the light of God. Christ had delivered me into the light and I stood in the presence of God. I was filled with complete knowing: The light was love and love was God. Waves of consummate love emanating from the light obliterated every burden I carried and every thought keeping me from knowing God. I was made aware of my purity. With new clarity, I realized I had been walking through life ghostlike, wrapped in a shroud of fear, huddled against illusions. I stood like a lover, open to the liquid flow of golden light filling my empty shell to overflowing.

There was no limit to the outpouring as I came to the rapturous awareness of the infinite nature of God's love. There was no place that God did not exist and I was within God. I am an inseparable part of the light. The truth, of who I am, indeed, who we all are, is perfect love as a creation of God. All of God's creation is one creation and I am one with creation. God and I are one, Creator and created.

I had spent a lifetime of fear of judgment and now, standing with God, I had been known completely and found faultless. I knew God regarded me as perfect. God loved me because love is the totality of God. God loves without limit. Finally it all made sense. God could only love me because God is only love, nothing other than love. The only reality is God; there cannot be another and GOD IS LOVE.

I had reached my true home. I turned to Christ and said, "This is beautiful. I am home. This is where I want to be. I want to stay." And Christ answered, "You can stay for a little while and then you must return."[7]

RICKY RANDOLPH

In December 1982, Ricky Randolph, a Georgia Department of Corrections Correctional Officer, was involved in a hunting accident and had an NDE. Since then, he has had many psychic experiences that were verified by family and friends. Ordained as a Baptist minister at age 17, his life in childhood was filled with psychic events. The following is his unique NDE in his own words. It can be described as unique for a very good reason and that reason is miraculous. As the saying goes: "miracles happen."

I was looking forward to this morning, as I had planned a hunting trip on the ninety-eight acre farm, bordering the Chattahoochee River, my family and I lived on. I arrived home and gathered my gear trying to get as early a start as I could. My wife had already left for work as most people do who have normal working hours. I usually called her when I was going hunting but being in a hurry on this particular morning I didn't. I had about a two mile hike to my tree stand and arrived there around 10:15 am. My stand was about 20 feet high on the front side facing a thick patch of pines. The backside faced the river below and dropped off to huge boulders in the river below. I tied off my rifle to be pulled up after my climb to the top and began my upward ascent. I reached the top and positioned myself to pull my rifle up. Then without warning I heard a snap! I would later return to this site many times to reflect on my life. On one visit with a friend I measured the distance from the top of the stand down to the boulder I landed on - eighty feet!

As I began my fall to the river below I could see the river coming up fast I knew this was the end for me and though it was just seconds before impact, it was as though I was in slow motion.

So many thoughts raced through my mind. My wife, my daughter, my family, and no one knows where I am. Would I ever be found?

Then, darkness! How long this darkness lasted I don't know. Then something wonderful happened. I felt myself leaving my body. I was floating a few feet in the air above the river. I looked on my body with mixed feelings. I was bleeding from my mouth, nose, ears, and saw a trickle of blood underneath me on the boulder. As I was reflecting on the state of my body, I felt a pulling and began to rise very fast! I was traveling at a high rate of speed upward through the atmosphere.

As I left the atmosphere, I looked back and could see the earth. Such a beautiful sight. It was so brilliantly lit. As I looked ahead I could see the planets. I thought to myself this cannot be. Where is Jesus? I was never told anything like this could or would happen when I died. Faster, and faster the speed was increasing. I saw other star systems and galaxies as I raced onward. I entered what seemed to be a hole of some sort. It was long and dark. However around me I saw streaks of light made up of every color in the spectrum. I saw a faint light growing brighter and brighter in the distance up ahead. As I entered the light I felt it all through my being. I was not afraid anymore.

Then all of a sudden I was standing before a massive set of steps. They led up to what seemed to be a bridge or walk of some kind. In the distance I saw a sight so magnificent and astounding - city made up of what seemed to be glass or crystal.

The lights were of many colors radiating from it. Never have I ever seen such a sight. I began walking toward the city in a daze of unbelief.

So many questions raced through my mind. I had to know where I was. What was happening to me?

I reached the front of the city and saw a double door looking to be about thirty feet or so in height and width. It shined as if it was polished. As I stood there wandering, the doors began to open. I took a step back and looked inside. I could see what appeared to be people walking about on the inside, much like they do in a mall here on earth. These people though were dressed very different. For one thing, they all seemed to be dressed in some sort of robes with hoods. I entered through the doors in amazement at what I was seeing! The inside was massive. It seemed to be square in shape, with a balcony all around leading down to different levels. I walked up and looked downward over the balcony. It seemed to go on forever.

As I looked up I saw many passing by me, yet no one seemed to notice me. Then as one was approaching me he suddenly stopped. He slowly raised his head and I could see his face. He appeared to be human in every respect but one - his eyes. No pupils! Yet they seemed to change colors in colors of blue! His hair was snow white. I wanted to speak but before I could he turned and pointed to a long hallway. Though we never spoke I knew I was to go down this hallway. Then as if nothing had ever happened, he continued on. I knew I had to as well.

Something was beckoning me forward. I walked a long walk down to the end of this hallway. I did not turn to the right or the left. I knew, somehow, my questions were about to be answered. Again I saw before me a massive double door. It seemed to be of some type of metal - whether gold or not I could not tell.

Suddenly the doors opened. I heard a voice, though not as we speak, but from inside of me it seemed, to say, "Enter." I did as I was told and the doors shut suddenly behind me. I was afraid for the first time. Total darkness. Total silence!

Then after a space of time the length of which I could not determine, a bright light began to glow in the room. Brighter and brighter it became. It was somewhat above me and in front of me. I tried to look but was almost blinded from it. I held my hands up in front of me and could make out the appearance of a figure setting on some type of seat.

Then without warning it happened.

"What have you done with your life?" The voice penetrated my very being. I had no answer.

Then to my right I saw what seemed to be like a movie, and I was in it. I saw my mother giving me birth, my childhood and friends. I saw everything from my youth up. I saw everything I had ever done before my eyes.

As my life played out before my very eyes I tried to think of good things I had done. I was raised in church and had been very active in church functions, yet as I pondered on this, I saw a man in his car that had run out of gas.

I had stopped and given him a lift to a local store about a year ago. I had bought him some gas as he had no money and helped him get on his way. I thought to myself, why am I seeing this? The voice was loud and clear.

"You took no thought to help this soul and asked nothing in return. These actions are the essence of good."

I saw all the people I had hurt as well and was shown how my actions had set in motion the actions of others. I was stunned! I had never thought of my life having an effect on the actions that friends, family, and others I had met would take. I saw the results of all I had done. I was not pleased at all.

I looked on until the events came to an end. Indeed I had done so little with my life. I had been selfish and cruel in so many ways. I was truly sorry I had done so little. Then again loud and clear I heard the voice speak again, "You must return."

I did not want to return though. I was content to stay and longed to stay even after the things I had seen and heard. "I have so many questions," I replied, "things I need to know and don't understand."

"You must return and help others to change by changing your life. Physicians will want to perform surgery on you. Do not let this happen. If you do you will never walk again. One who brings answers to the questions you have will visit you. When I call you will come again. You will recover from all that has happened if you do these things. Look and see what lies ahead."

I turned and saw the earth in turmoil. Wars and death, terrible sights! Cities fell and new ones were built. I saw the United States and a volcano exploding covering many cities in darkness. I looked on and saw the collapse of our government, as we know it. People killing for food and water. Horrible sights. I saw what seemed to be a giant explosion in the earth's atmosphere and much land was destroyed. I looked on and saw a new type of people, younger and of a peaceful nature. The cities were few that were left, but these people seemed to be content.

"It is time for you to go," I heard again. But I wanted to see more.

Then the doors opened and I felt myself almost be carried down the hallway. I passed through the doors of the city and felt myself shooting through this hole I had come through. Faster I went, unable to stop.

I entered the atmosphere of earth and saw the river below. I saw my body still lying there motionless.

Then it was like an electric shock so tremendous I felt my body jump. I opened my eyes and saw the trees above and the skyline. Then, Oh God, the pain. I was struggling for every breath, choking on my own blood.

I managed to roll onto my stomach. The pain was all I could bear. I looked at the sky and saw the sun was lower than I remembered. I looked at my watch. It was 5:30. My only thoughts were how I could get help. I noticed my rifle was not far from me, still attached to the rope I had tied around my waist. I began pulling it toward me. I managed to grab hold of the barrel and pulled it up to me. I fired a shot about every ten minutes hoping someone would come.

It was getting late and I knew I would not make it much longer, so I began crawling on my stomach, pulling myself with the stock of my rifle. I managed to crawl up a trail running down to the river. As I crawled and crawled, the pain was so great I passed out many times. Through thick brush and briar patches I crawled. I wanted to give up I was so tired and in so much pain. I knew though I had to make it at least to where I could be found - I hoped.

I looked out in front of me and saw the road I lived on through the trees. I could hear sounds in the distance.

"Yes, thank you, God," I thought to myself.

I finally found myself at the road and began a feeble cry for help. I was too exhausted though and just lay there in the road.

My father-in-law was returning from work and found me lying in the road.

"It's all right," I heard him say, "help is on the way."

That was the last I remembered until I saw the lights inside the ER. A doctor stood at my feet.

"Can you feel this?" he said.

"Feel what?" I asked. He had been sticking my feet and legs. I was paralyzed.

"We cannot help you here, son," he said. "We are sending you by ambulance to a hospital that can handle your injuries."

Whether from the pain or medication, I was out like a light.

The next afternoon, I awoke to find two doctors standing at the foot of my hospital bed. They introduced themselves as my attending physicians and proceeded to explain to me that I must undergo surgery at once. The bones in my back that were broken were putting pressure on my spinal nerve causing paralysis. Then I heard the warning I had heard before.

"Do not let them perform surgery, or you will never walk again."

I understood completely, but knew they would not. I told them I must see my wife and daughter first.

My wife arrived with my daughter shortly after the doctor's visit. I told her what they had said. She advised me that I must realize they were doing what was necessary to help me. I did not know how to tell her what I had experienced. I tried to tell her it was my belief I should not be operated on. Although she disagreed, she honored my wishes.

When the doctors returned and I told them of my decision, they were very upset! I listened to lecture after lecture.

"OK," one of them said, "if you never want to walk again, that's up to you." Then they left.

That night I lay upon my bed and wept sorely. Was I insane? What was I doing?

A light began to fill my room. "You will be well," I heard a voice say. Then it was gone. I composed myself and dosed off to sleep.

Days turned into weeks, weeks into months.

Then one morning I felt a tingling in my feet! I was overcome with joy. I told the nurse I wanted to get up and walk. She stared at me and said, "We'll see, we'll see." I knew I was healed without a doubt. The nurse put a call into my doctor and the next morning he stopped by.

"So you think you can walk?" he said.

"Yes," I replied.

"Well, we will see."

A few hours later, I was taken down to the Physical Therapy room. They carried me down and raised me up to a vertical position. The nurse helped me in front of a set of parallel bars. I gripped the bars and placed my feet firmly on the floor. One step. Two steps.

"My God, he's walking!" the nurse said to the nurse who had brought me down. The next few days were hard. I took many trips to Physical Therapy and had numerous x-rays done per my doctor's orders. My wife and family were all amazed, yet I knew. I had been told. The rest had to be true as well.

My doctor was more amazed when he found no bones pressing on my spinal nerve! I use his quote: "This is not normal! It seems a higher power has done for you what we were going to try and correct with surgery. I have never seen anything like this before."

Since that day, my life has changed and I have been able to help others in ways I never dreamed. I wanted to share this with all, as it is what has led me onward in my quest for Truth. [8]

KERRY KIRK

The NDE reveals that God is not concerned with a person's sexual orientation, but is concerned about a person's heart. The next NDE involves a lesbian who learns this very fact while having an NDE. The following is her NDE in her own words.

The following happened to me during the summer of 1981. I was nineteen at the time. It was a time my life when I had pretty much decided there could be no God, no great being in control of the world around me. If there were he wasn't doing a very good job. I didn't realize it at the time, but once I had made this "decision," I started going downhill. I became selfish. That is, self-centered, but not very self-concerned.

I should mention that I had been having episodes of tachycardia for several years. I was never diagnosed (up to that point) with any kind of heart defect. Had I been asked I would have denied any problems with my heart. I thought it was very normal to get light headed and almost pass out during periods when my heart would race. Duh!

One evening I was in the back seat of a car traveling to San Francisco from Los Angeles. All of a sudden my heart began to race and the nausea hit. Next everything started spinning and I could see lots of colors. Then I had a sense of blackness come over me. Like a dark damp cloud. I was terrified. I have never been so scared. In my fear I said, "Jesus."

Immediately I witnessed a fight. It seemed there was a battle between a being in white/light and this blackness. Immediately following, the light overtook the darkness.

I found myself on my face in worship in front of this being of light. I felt a warm feeling. The most intense love filled me. It was an energy that penetrated every fiber of my being. I had never felt such a complete and total love. It was that unconditional love I hear many people talk about.

I know there was conversation between us but I cannot remember what was said. I feel like it was a time of healing for me – a kind of regeneration if you will.

In the next instant, I was floating above the car moving down the highway looking at myself in the back seat. I knew it was I sitting there, and yet I was up here. I wasn't afraid or confused. Everything was as it should be.

There was someone there to my left. I don't think it was the same being I had just been with. He (I had a sense it was a he) seemed to be in a white robe or something. Funny, I never really looked at him. His identity didn't seem to be important. I think he was there to guide me. I didn't make myself go, it was more like he took me or led me.

We began moving through space. I was aware of this because the stars and planets were passing very quickly. It was very exciting, I felt so free.

The order of the next [series of episodes] I am unsure of. I know each was a distinct episode, but it is hard for me to put them in an order or time frame.

The next thing I knew there was a white "room." I can't say it had walls but it seemed to be somewhat enclosed. Maybe its boundaries extended to the edge of the light that filled it and that is why I call it a room. There was a man in a white robe behind a podium with a book on it. I knew it was the book of life from the Bible. I remember thinking, "Uh oh, that stuff was for real." I suddenly realized that the "God" I had been presented wasn't anything like the reality. I saw it doesn't matter if you call him God, Allah, Great Spirit or whatever, He is the same thing.

The different religions just have different ways of explaining the same Creator. I also realized that little voice inside us prompting us to do good things comes from this Creator. It is that light of love inside each of us. I don't remember specifically being told this; more like I just knew it.

I came to a place, maybe a room, maybe a space. I was shown my life. If it was my entire life, I do not remember all of it. The only part I remember now was just the last week or so. Because I had given up on God. I saw how selfish I had been. I felt the pain I had caused one person in particular and it bothered me very much. The things I had the most guilt for was hurting other people, lying, not being sensitive to their feelings, just being selfish. The fact I was a lesbian didn't even seem to matter then. That was surprising to me, given what I had been brought up to believe.

There was another room or area. It seems like there were others there, I sensed some were female, some male, but I can't say I recognized anyone.

I was shown a diagram. I could see it represented choices – choices leading to other choices which then lead to other choices. Basically, actions have consequences.

I began receiving "all knowledge," or at least that is what it felt like. They were there teaching me. This didn't come to me as words like you and I speak. It was more as complete thoughts. When I think, it is generally in words and pictures, this is how I received the information - as complete words and pictures in my mind. As I could form a question in my mind I had the answer. Not just the answer to that question, but the why and how and the answer to every other question the answer would bring up. EVERYTHING in the entire universe fit together like a jigsaw puzzle. EVERYTHING MADE SENSE. I remember thinking, "I have to remember this."

I looked over to the right and in the distance I could see a beautiful valley with lots of people. There was someone looking out over all of it I felt it was Jesus. I then looked down and saw a line. My foot (Yes, I did have a spiritual "body" as did the others I encountered) was stepping over the line to go to be with the others. Then I was told, "If you cross that line you can't go back; it would mean you would have to die." Funny as it may sound, up to that point I didn't realize I would have to die or was about to die. It never occurred to me. I didn't realize I was separate from my body even though I had seen it in the car. I felt complete. I remember laughing and thinking this isn't how I pictured death.

I said I wanted to stay. I was then told the people I was with (in the car) as well as my mother would not understand and it would hurt them deeply. I understood.

At some point I was shown a map and was told to leave and go to Virginia.

The angels were singing and it seems like I could see the clouds all lit up (it was nighttime).

The next thing I knew I as sitting in the back of the car. I could hear the most beautiful music.

I didn't tell anyone what had happened to me for a long time. I felt out of place the next several days. I wanted to go back. I knew instinctively that I could not do anything to bring it about though. I tried and tried to remember everything I learned when I was filled with knowledge but it isn't there. [9]

BRIAN KREBS

Some people have reported having an NDE while experiencing an alien abduction. The most famous case of this kind comes from Betty Andreasson and is documented in Raymond Fowler's book, The Andreasson Affair. [10] Other experiencers have seen alien-type beings during their NDE. There appears to be a connection between these aliens and the beings of light reported in so many NDEs. The following NDE is from Brian Krebs and describes just such an encounter.

I had my first near-death experience when I was a child, perhaps two or three. This would be about 1953. It involved me drowning. My memories of it were of seeing my body below me. I remember seeing a bright, warm, loving orb above me. I panicked Dad and Mom below. I didn't know it was anything to talk about and no one would have believed me. It never was a thing I felt I had to relate.

Then in 1971 ... I had been knifed with a stiletto that severed an artery above my liver. I remember looking up and seeing a light. I then looked down at my body and then I was confronted by at least two beings. They were human in appearance and they seemed to float in midair. I realized I was far above my body and not in any earthly space. The beings tried to keep me from going to the light. I don't know why, they just seemed terrified and didn't want me to go. But I did. I shot up like an arrow through what can only be described as a tunnel.

I saw the tunnel as a peripheral blur of stars and I saw a loving light before me. Then I stopped. I was there with this orb of glowing love and understanding. It didn't seem foreign to me. It was not frightening. It was totally assuring and there was no feeling of anything but my awe and the love and knowledge and wisdom this orb projected. In size, it would be not like looking at the sun, but looking at the earth when you are on it. It was immense and total, and its power was love.

I felt a presence next to me, a man, and he asked if I was ready for my life review. I said yes - all of this not a verbal thing, but just in the form of knowledge. Then I saw something like an HO scale train set below, a city. I went to this city and I went through my life. I went through every moment and every feeling. I was not afraid as I was still in the light. I talked with the man about my life. But I do not remember any specifics.

I then remember standing, as it where, in the light of the Orb of love. I felt the goodness and love and knowledge of it. My mind was in a state of deep, deep, concentration of thought.

I then went to twelve beings of greater knowledge. They were in front of me and stood in a row. They were not human. They had no feelings of anything like judgment or authority, but seemed strong in themselves. They seemed taller than I did and they wore silver white robes. They had white skin, large heads and large eyes. I do not remember them having a mouth. Above them was a spirit. It was like a star as we see one from earth, but in size it appeared the same size as the heads of the beings. The spirit went to my left and hovered above the first being. I remember it was like a video of knowledge springing from the being's hands, which were held in front of them.

Each being had something to relate. They opened the knowledge they had when the spirit moved above them. The last told me what I could do if I came back and the significance of it. I only remember seeing young man with his head back in pain as if his neck was injured. I said, "Oh! Aaron! My son!" They said, "No, not that son." And I realized whom they meant. (In 1978, my only other child was born a son).

Then I made the decision to come back to earth. And I remember it was such a hard decision. It was so difficult because everything there was so beautiful and there was so, so, much love. I had the feeling of freewill, yet a feeling of duty was present - of obligation. And the second I realized that I shot back into my body.

After two near-death experiences and having studied many NDEs, I am convinced there is order to the experience.

I do get angry when people come to conclusions about the near-death experience because they think it is not orderly and therefore find it to be a part of our imaginative minds. For the ones that have not heard this, here goes:

Rule 1: At any given microsecond, you may return to your body. You have a trauma of some kind making you leave your body. You might feel a vibration. You might feel nothing, except that you are suddenly out of your body.

Rule 2: Nobody remembers every single detail and the meaning to it while having an NDE.

So, now you are out of your body you may look down and see your body. You may take off for another room or zip back into your body. You may go into the void. This is the home of many a grim story. See, after death you may end up quite stuck in this void. It lacks one thing: love. It is the hell the Pope just figured out. It is not being of love, not recognizing it. Those who are stuck there may frighten you by just being or by intentional gestures to frighten you. They are stuck and they are confused and they will put the "HELL" in hell.

Rule 3: Beyond this point your soul must be convinced your body is dead.

See, sometimes things happen which doesn't cause death. I mean we all ultimately live to tell of NDEs, but we must be convinced the body business is behind us to go further.

So, there you are outside the body. Now those who love you might show up. They do so for a couple reasons. One, they may want you to stay, that is, go back to your body. Or they may want you to think of love. I just love the way George Rodonaia said it. While describing the void, he said that he thought, "I am, and if I am, why for not can I be happy?" And he was. Then he thought, "If I am, and I can be happy, why for not then can I feel love?" And he did. You see, the way out of the void is simple. You must think of love.

Now if you are a Christian and you think of Jesus and you see Jesus as love, then you will be thinking of love and to think of love. To recognize it as a reality, that is the key to getting out of the void. Now, you are in the void and you think of love and you are love and you will see love, just a speck, but you will concentrate on it and then you will connect with it. This connection is called the tunnel. It is a pathway to the Creator.

I recently heard someone talking about taking some sugar and some water and mixing them together. The sugar would disappear and the water would become sugar water. But in time the water would evaporate and the sugar would remain as sugar and the water would turn to vapor. The point was that the sugar had the memory of the water and the water the memory of the sugar. As I thought this out, I tried to think how to explain it better. Being of a scientific background, I thought, "Okay, let's put the sugar and water together in a test tube. Let's mix them. Then to speed things up, let's add heat, which makes vibrations and causes the water to turn to vapor. But wait. Let's put a rubber stopper in the test tube and a glass tube leading to another test tube. That would allow the water to reestablish itself as water in the other tube." You see? Then you have water with a memory of the sugar and the sugar with the memory of the water. You also have a very good model to explain how to get out of the void. As the tube concentrates the water, so the tunnel concentrates the spirit.

Now, many things can happen in the tunnel. Say for instance you get depressed and you gobble down too many pills. You would choke if not for the washing of booze you gave them. You might end up in the tunnel off to the side where you are requested to think. So you sit there thinking. Some other soul would pass right on by that, not notice, or may notice. Things, earthy problems can be worked out there, out of the void and in the tunnel. Ultimately though, if you don't return to your body, you zip right past all this and end up at a point that you may refer later to the end of the tunnel. It may be though that you are in one of the rooms of the tunnel or zones. There you see a garden, a river, a gate, and someone will appear to help you decide whether you should go on or think a while or talk or be reassured enough to return to your body. But, go through the gate or over the river past the decision to go back or stay and think, and you end up at the end of the tunnel. There at the end of the tunnel is the Creator.

Rule 4: If you make it to the end of the tunnel you will feel more love and acceptance and wisdom and knowledge and understanding than you ever have. And you will remember it. And you will not leave it out of your description of your experience. There you are and there is love - overwhelming, pure, beautiful love. Now let's not forget Rule 1, that you may at any time zip right back into your body! You should begin now to see why there are so many "different" descriptions of the NDE: because a person may go only to a given point and the description of what they saw will be limited to that level.

So, now you are there in front of the Creator, and you might well see your Higher Self. You will then go through a life review. You do this in the light of the love of the Creator. In this love, you see all you have done wrong and right and the effects of it and you are unafraid because the Creator's love is there. There is nothing but the truth. That accomplished, you may (Rule 1) zip back into your body. You may then do whatever you think you need to and those descriptions vary. One consistent theme is that you have spirits to help you. As Dannion Brinkley did, I had twelve "spirits" giving forth information about the past, the present and the future. They may help you decide to stay or go back to earth. Once the decision is made, zipppppp, you're back. [11]

JONI MAGGI

One does not have to be near death to experience an NDE. NDEs are induced through such methods as extreme stress, deep meditation, drug hallucinations and right temporal lobe brain stimulation. The next NDE comes from Joni Maggi. It occurred while she was in an altered state of consciousness. The following is her NDE in her own words.

Close your eyes for a moment and try to imagine you are face to face with the sun! What an extraordinary feeling! I thought to myself, "How can I be face to face with the sun and not feel the burning heat?" This first thought shocked and puzzled me - to be thinking in the way I would normally think.

It was literally so bright I could not sustain the gaze, so I turned away. At that moment I noticed a silver cord, attached around the navel area going down, down, down to a person I saw lying on my bed. It was I! I had a curious non-interest in it.

Suddenly, I was in dark outer space, floating as it were on my back, in what I can only describe as total "bliss" (one of a few words, which I'll explain later, I had never understood before that point!) I'm not sure how long this ecstatic feeling lasted but it was what I suppose is called Cosmic Consciousness or cosmic bliss. I knew the Universe is upheld by love (though if you ask me now I would not be able to explain that!) I knew the planets are alive and conscious. I knew they would never bump into each other on purpose or cause any damage - there was no violence but rather a total harmony in their existence.

I then looked down and could see the earth – far, far away and down in this dark sky. I knew it was a place of violence, a realm shrouded in darkness and difficulties so to speak.

At one point I saw what I could only describe as a group of beings - perhaps beings of light would describe them best. I then zoomed over to them - literally willed myself over to them (Swoosh!) and was there instantaneously.

They were seated (?) in an oval circle and there seemed to be a leader of some sort at the head of the group. First of all, I felt the most overwhelming love coming from them! It cannot be compared to anything here on earth. For one, I felt it was an inclusive group -

rather than an exclusive one. (Here on earth we seem to have trouble letting new people into groups but there it was as if all of them at the same time were welcoming me!) I heard them - in my mind - say, "Welcome Home! You have been on such a long journey!" I had the feeling they were sharing life experiences and learning from each other, as if in a sort of classroom.

I didn't have time to find out, because at this point I said to the leader, again telepathically, "I cannot stay! I have to bring up my son!" with real sense of urgency. (At the time my son was 4 years old and I knew somehow I had the absolute obligation to bring him up and take care of him. Years later, when I thought of this, I understood we live in a "moral" Universe.)

I immediately started coming down again. And as I was coming down, I saw - as if written on the entire dark sky this message:

"There is nothing worth worrying about! Not even death!" And again I knew - or understood in an instant - that death is exactly like falling asleep.

What happens is you let go of daily consciousness and slip into another. Or for that matter, like waking up - you let go of sleeping consciousness and find yourself in our recognized reality. It was an incredible feeling of peace to know there is no death!

All of a sudden, I was awake and I literally ran to my table to write everything down because I knew the "veils" (another new word for me) were going to fall and I would forget or lose the feeling of the experience. I had the feeling a shaft of light had come down through the top of my head. The top of my head was literally tender!

The third word I came to know was ""grace" (which up to that point I thought meant the prayer Christians say at the dinner table). I had been an atheist - or agnostic - up until my experience but after that, though the veils did fall down again, I have spent the last 20 years, trying to recapture that feeling, that absolute knowing. I feel closer and closer to it all the time now.

I felt I had been "given a gift"" of tremendous value! I could not, and can not to this day understand how that works or what that means. I only know I had been in a state of emotional crisis - I was living at the time in South America and undergoing a painful separation from my husband so I found myself alone, depressed and with a very young child. I had also been asking myself the question, "What one thought gives peace?" for a very long time. Somehow, I feel that my earnest and extremely deep need to find an answer to the ups and downs of life was answered in that unspeakably profound experience.

This is the first time I am sharing my experience so openly with others because my family and friends of course at the time did not believe me or understand me. Plus the fact I myself had lost contact with the light and only years later did I start to remember it and piece it together again coherently. Now, it is probably the most important thing I can do - to remember it and to share it with others. If it hadn't been for the experience I probably would not have pursued the spiritual path with such relentless passion as I understand there is a spiritual need which cannot be filled by any other thing than... how shall I call it? The spirit.

I also know it was real! Actually, I could say it was the only real thing that has ever happened to me. At this point I cherish sharing my experience with others and hope to learn afresh from their experiences to continue to get a wider and wider appreciation and understanding of this phenomenon.

I still have many unanswered questions: Why was I "blessed" with this experience? (I think it was because without it I never would have been able to go on, but even so, who "gave" it to me or how did I receive it?) Why are other people not given the same experience, though some search for it so longingly? And it has only whetted my appetite to know more - everything! Everything about our life purposes, life after death, etc.! Unfortunately I cannot, as I mentioned, retrieve the feeling of it and sometimes I still forget and find myself in darkness and pain. But just remembering it and sharing it helps me - and who knows, maybe others - to know more and more about it, especially now that these phenomena are coming more and more to light! [12]

CHAPTER 2: NDE SUMMARIES

"Normally we do not like to think about death. We would rather think about life. Why reflect on death? When you start preparing for death you soon realize that you must look into your life... now... and come to face the truth of yourself. Death is like a mirror in which the true meaning of life is reflected." - Sogyal Rinpoche

NDEs vary from person to person based on many factors: religious bias, cultural background, historical time period, etc. They also vary as to depth of experience. Some people only experience the out-of-body phase of the experience, while others go well beyond. What follows are brief summaries of the rest of the NDEs that are a part of my research. Such a format helps when doing comparisons between experiences. Each summary is given in the present tense to give the feeling of the NDE as it is happening.

JOSIANE ANTONETTE

Born in France and trained as a nurse, Josiane had an NDE in 1966. Afterwards, she became aware of her ability to "communicate with the other side." For over 30 years, she worked with the dying and the living, in hospitals as a chaplain, universities as a teacher, as a spiritual counselor, healer and ceremonial leader. Her understanding of living, dying and the spiritual realms has touched many people. In her book, Whispers of the Soul, she describes her NDE. She is also the author of another book entitled Matters of Spirit and she is the founder of The Bernadette Foundation.

Josiane leaves her body and sees her life pass before her eyes as in a movie. She momentarily reenters her body and sees restless spirits around her who seem lost. Suddenly, light beings appear and she is surrounded with love. She receives a vision of the earth appearing lifeless and gloomy on one side. On the other side, the earth appears sunny and full of life. She watches as the darkness takes over the whole earth. A voice tells her this is the world in the absence of light, love and free will. The darkness of the world is then replaced with light and beauty. She sees the solar system united by a transparent web of unparalleled brilliance. The voice tells her to never forget what she has seen. She becomes filled with an overwhelming love as she merges with the light.

She returns to her hospital room where her lifeless body is. There she meets her deceased cousin along with other beings of light. As they leave, Josiane begs to go with them. Her cousin tells her she has work left to do here on earth. With this, she enters her physical body. [13]

MELLEN-THOMAS BENEDICT

Mellen-Thomas was an artist dying of cancer. In 1982, he succumbed and had an NDE. He was dead for over an hour and a half. During that time, he rose up out of his body and went into the light. Concerning his NDE, Dr. Kenneth Ring noted, "His story is one of the most remarkable I have encountered in my extensive research on near-death experiences."

Mellen-Thomas leaves his body and discovers he has 360-degree vision and consciousness. He travels toward a brilliant light, but halts his experience to ask questions. He sees the brilliant light transform into several avatars such as Jesus, Buddha and Krishna.

The light also transforms into a mandala of every soul from earth. Mellen-Thomas refers to this as our "Higher Self matrix." He sees the earth surrounded by a grid-like structure connecting every human being to this "Higher Self matrix." His consciousness expands to fill the universe all the way to the Big Bang and beyond.

In the void between an infinite number of Big Bangs and universes, he becomes aware of the fact he perceives all things through God's perspective. He experiences the full consciousness of God in infinite knowledge. Here, all his questions are answered. He experiences all the levels of heaven and hell. The process of consciousness expansion reverses and his consciousness deflates to its original condition. He expects to be reincarnated as a baby, but is surprised to find himself back in his own physical body. [14]

DANNION BRINKLEY

In 1975, Dannion was talking on the phone during a thunderstorm. A bolt of lightning hit the phone line, sending thousands of volts of electricity into his head and down his body. His heart stopped, and he died, but in the process, he had an NDE. When he revived in the morgue after twenty-eight minutes of death, he had an incredible story to tell. He was told of events that would shake the world before the year 2000 - including the Chernobyl nuclear disaster and the Persian Gulf War. Of the 117 revelations that he recalls, 95 have already come to pass. His book, Saved by the Light, describes his NDE and his revelations of the future.

Dannion leaves his physical body and watches as a friend tries to revive it. He is sucked through a tunnel and into a paradise of brilliant light. A being of incredible love and light appears and Dannion experiences a life review. He is taken to a "city of cathedrals" where twelve beings of light appear. Each of the twelve beings represents a human personality type similar to the zodiac. One at a time, they each present to Dannion a kind of video screen foretelling some future event. He is drawn into each of these screens to actually experience the future event. Afterward, he returns to his physical body. [16]

BEVERLY BRODSKY

Raised in a conservative Jewish family in Philadelphia, Beverly went through her teens as an atheist. Since learning of the Holocaust at age eight, she had turned angrily against any early belief in God. How could God exist and permit such a thing to occur? In 1970, her questions were answered when a motorcycle accident led to an NDE. Her NDE is found in a book by Dr. Kenneth Ring entitled Lessons from the Light. Dr. Ring describes her NDE as "possibly the most moving in my entire collection."

Beverly leaves her body and floats over her bed. She is met by a radiant being of light she believes to be the Messiah or an angel. Holding hands, they fly through the window and out over the Pacific Ocean.

They travel through a tunnel forming in the sky toward an incredibly bright light she identifies as God. She has a very intense discussion with God and learns some important answers to questions plaguing her mind. She also begins to remember knowledge she once had before being born into the world.

As soon as all her questions were answered, she becomes one with all knowledge and God. She tours the universe and all its wonders. She is filled, not just with all knowledge, but with all the love of God. She experiences ecstasy beyond her wildest dreams. She then returns to her physical body. [17]

DON BRUBAKER

Happily married with three children and a busy broadcasting career, Don rarely thought about life after death. After his heart attack and NDE, all of that changed. Don was clinically dead for 45 minutes during which he experienced the glory of heaven and the fire of hell. His book, Absent from the Body, describes his afterlife journey. His NDE is unique because he actually travels back in time to experience one of history's greatest moments.

He leaves his body and travels through a tunnel. A large, eerie red eye peers at him and he realizes it to be his own. While in the tunnel, he is stricken with panic and believes he is in hell. A voice, he identifies to be God's, tells him not to fear. He has been chosen to write about what he is experiencing. He is told he must testify about the reality of hell.

Afterward, he is drawn into a vast, flaming "oven" filled with other people. They laugh as they realize the flames are not painful. Suddenly, he is alone in the dark with God communicating to him. In an instant, he is aware of everyone in his life whom he was ever angry with.

Afterward, he floats in a glorious deep blue sky. Christ appears shining a tremendous amount of light. Christ gives him a choice of staying or returning to the physical world. Thoughts of his family cause him to choose to return. Before he returns, he is taken back in time to witness the crucifixion of Christ. [18]

GRACE BUBULKA

Over twelve years ago, Grace was a nurse experiencing an NDE that changed her life. It wasn't until ten years after her NDE that she felt comfortable telling others about it. Now

Grace shares her NDE with others through seminars and lectures. Her book, Beyond This Reality, describes her profound experience with the afterlife.

She hovers above her body and watches as doctors try to save her life. She travels through a tunnel toward a bright light and notices she is a speck of light traveling with an infinite number of other specks toward the light. She enters into the light and merges with it. In the light, she becomes ecstatic. An infinite sense of all knowing comes to her while in the light. The light reminds her of her obligation to her children and she knows she will have to go back. She has a life review witnessed by everyone in the light. Afterwards, she returns to her physical body. [19]

EDGAR CAYCE

The book entitled There Is A River, describes the true story of a devout Christian and Sunday school teacher, Cayce (1877-1945) was a man who had out-of-body experiences amazingly resembling NDEs. In 1910, the New York Times carried two pages of headlines and pictures in which he was declared the "World's Most Mysterious Man." In 1954, the University of Chicago accepted a Ph.D. thesis based on a study of his life and work. He is also considered to be the father of holistic medicine by JAMA, the prestigious medical journal. He was a wonder to the medical community because of his ability to diagnose and specify a treatment for gravely ill people often hundreds of miles away through his out-of-body experiences. He gave roughly 14,000 hypnotic readings in his lifetime which are kept at the Association for Research and Enlightenment. Each reading involved going into a trance resulting in an out-of-body experience.

Once the hypnotic suggestion is made, he leaves his physical body and travels through a tunnel with a brilliant light at the end. The sides of the tunnel reveal to him the various afterlife levels appearing to wind around in a wheel formation. The first level of the tunnel is inhabited by horrible looking beings similar to what one would see in a nightmare. Higher up on the next level, misshapen forms of human beings appear with some part of their body magnified.

As he travels through the tunnel, beings on either side of the tunnel call out to him for help, trying to get his attention. He knows that any deviation from traveling through the tunnel toward the light would mean he would not be able to return to his body and he would die.

Farther up the tunnel, he sees gray-hooded beings moving downward. Up higher on the next level, more gray-hooded beings appear except they are moving upward. The color of their robes get lighter and lighter as he moves up. The next higher level resembles the physical world with houses, trees, etc., except everything is motionless. As he rises higher through the tunnel, there appears more light and more motion in what appears to be normal cities. Rising higher, he sees more light, more beautiful colors, more laughter, and beautiful music. In the higher levels, there are no houses and such, only a blending of sound and color.

Suddenly, he comes upon the "Hall of Records," an enormous building without walls or a ceiling. Here an old man hands him a large book containing the records of the individual he is giving a reading for. According to Cayce, this record is the person's so-called "Book of

Life" which every person is constantly filling by thinking, speaking and doing. When he completes a reading, he would then return to his physical body. [20]

CECIL

P.M.H. Atwater is one of the most respected researchers of the NDE phenomenon. In her latest book, Children of the New Millennium, she presents the first serious look at the NDEs of children. One of these children was an eleven-year old named Cecil. He and his brother were swimming when they had a problem. He tried to get his brother out of the water, but in a panic was pulled under several times and they drowned. His brother died; but Cecil had an NDE.

He leaves his body and travels toward a brilliant light. He travels into cities made entirely of light. Each city represents a kind of cosmic grade in school where people progress. Three men appear as a welcoming committee to escort him to the first city. He hesitates to go because he knows there is no turning back. The brilliant light of God appears and a voice asks Cecil why he hesitated. Cecil answers he is too young to die and has a lot of questions. He asks what death is. The light shows him a car accident where some people are killed. Some do not leave their bodies because they do not believe in life after death. Cecil asks what hell is. The light shows him an old woman worrying about her children and everything. Cecil asks if there is a Satan and the light tells him no. Cecil asks how he can know right from wrong. The light replied, "Right is helping and being kind. Wrong is not only hurting someone, but not helping when you can." The light asks Cecil why he wants to return. Ultimately, Cecil discovers the real reason he wants to return is to "leave the earth a little better than he found it." [21]

LINGA CHOKYI

A curious phenomenon, little known in the West, but familiar to Tibetans, is the "delok". In Tibet, "delok" means "returned from death," and traditionally deloks are people who seemingly "die" as a result of an illness, and travel in the "bardo" (one of many Tibetan Buddhist afterlife states). They visit the hell realms, where they witness the judgment of the dead and the suffering of hell, and sometimes they go to paradises and Buddha realms. The delok is sent back to their bodies with a message from the Lord of Death for the living, urging them to spiritual practice and a beneficial way of life. They spend the rest of their lives recounting their experiences to others in order to draw them toward the path of wisdom. During the sixteenth century, one of the most famous delok was named Lingza Chokyi. Dawa Drolma is the author of the book entitled Delog: Journey to Realms Beyond Death which is the source for the information about Linga Chokyi.

She finds herself outside of her body but fails to realize she has died. She sees her corpse but thinks it is a dead pig lying on her bed and wearing her clothes. She frantically tries to talk to her family, but no one hears or sees her. Her weeping children cause her tremendous pain, but she feels joy when the death rituals are being performed on her behalf.

After a while, she hears her deceased father calling her and begins to follow him. She arrives in the first afterlife level (bardo) and sees a bridge leading to the hell realms. Here, the Lord of Death counts the good and evil actions of the dead. She sees a great man (a yogin) enter the hell realms in order to liberate people. She is told there is an error concerning her name and family and it is not yet her time to die. She returns to her body. [22]

CLARA

Another child of P.M.H. Atwater's study of childhood NDEs is a fifth grader named Clara. She became sick with extreme pain in her lower right side and was rushed to the hospital. It was there that she had her NDE. Dr. Atwater has also released a new book on childhood NDEs entitled The New Children and Near Death Experiences.

Clara leaves her physical body and watches doctors working on it. Someone leads her through a tunnel where she hears a playground full of laughing children playing. Another person approaches telling them they are not yet ready for her.

She is taken to a large building where others are working. She is led to meet Christ who tells her telepathically what she must do. Jesus has her look into a television-like device to see her future. What she sees makes her very happy. Jesus tells her she will forget what she witnessed in the device when she returns. It happens exactly as she was told. [23]

LYNNCLAIRE DENNIS

In 1987, while hot-air ballooning in the Swiss Alps, Lynnclaire died from a lack of oxygen when her balloon reached too high of an altitude. During her NDE, she came into contact with what she calls "the Pattern", a mandala she describes as "primarily a matrix of personal and global healing." Seeing the Pattern, she knew she was looking at life itself. It was light; it was time and space. It was the energy of all matter, the heart of all that mattered. Her book, The Pattern, documents her experience.

Lynnclaire finds herself in a beautiful valley. She wonders if she is in heaven. She sees her lifetime as it existed without the bounds of time. She hears beautiful music and begins to dance joyously. Her deceased grandmother appears and she realizes they are in a place of infinite love.

They enter a meadow that becomes an amphitheater. On stage, every person greets her who played a part in her life and who has already died, including her miscarried baby. They all share a message of love. The last person who appears on the stage is unknown to her, yet this person is someone who speaks directly to her soul. This special person, whom she identifies as "the Presence," tells her she will be a catalyst for change and love. Everyone leaves the stage and she enters a sacred place before the light. She is embraced by "the Presence."

She then finds herself climbing a mountain toward the light and realizes she is in the space between two worlds and is going home. A tunnel appears that takes her to the top of the mountain. At the end of the tunnel, she sees what she calls "the Pattern," which is God. As she prepares to take the next step to merge into the light, she is pulled back by her husband who is frantically giving her physical body CPR. [24]

JEANIE DICUS

In 1974, Jeanie's heart went into fibrillation and she died. Her resulting NDE is documented in one of P.M.H. Atwater's books, Beyond the Light. It affirms many concepts behind the NDE such as reincarnation, the mechanics of the life review and the why people cannot remember their life experiences before birth.

Jeanie leaves her physical body and floats above it. She sees doctors operating frantically on her physical body. Jesus appears and asks if she wants to be reincarnated. She asks for some time to rest and think about it. She holds a conversation with Jesus telepathically.

God appears as a tremendous light and gives her the choice to stay in the light or be revived and remain in a coma. She chooses to stay in the light. She feels ecstatic in the love and light of God.

She is taken into a domed room where the walls are covered with television-like screens. On each screen, an event in her life is being played out. God asks her what she has done with her gift of life. She mentions the time and energy she spent on her daughter. Jeanie realizes she is judging herself, rather than God judging her, and that God is satisfied with her answer. She asks many questions of God and receives many answers. Afterward, she returns to her body. [25]

NED DOUGHERTY

As a most successful nightclub owner, Ned lived life in the fast lane. Despite his religious upbringing as a Roman Catholic, he had no interest in a spiritual life because he didn't believe in an afterlife. He was too busy searching for a good time to be bothered with such things. This all changed when he had an NDE resulting from a heart attack during a heated fistfight with a business associate. His NDE changed his life and gave him a conscious awareness of his mission in life. Later he served on the Board of Directors for the International Association for Near-Death Studies. His experience is documented in his book entitled Fast Lane to Heaven.

Ned leaves his physical body and falls as if into a dark pit. He reaches the bottom and sees in the distance the light of God. He can see and hear the ambulance workers trying to revive his physical body. As the ambulance takes his body away, he finds himself hovering in midair.

Suddenly, all of his worldly possessions flash before his eyes. A tunnel forms and an old deceased friend appears. Together, they travel through the tunnel and come out into a universe of bright stars. The brilliant light of God appears and embraces them. Tremendous knowledge and revelations enter into him. He and his friend descend into an amphitheater filled with thousands of spirit beings who emanate all their love and attention to them. He is reunited in a kind of homecoming with deceased family and friends.

The amphitheater grows quiet as a luminescent sphere envelops him and he experiences his life in review. Afterwards, he finds himself in a beautiful garden. A beautiful "lady of light" appears and takes him to the Hall of Records where he is shown images of the future.

Afterward, he finds he is back in the garden again. A person resembling Jesus is seated next to him with children all around him. The lady of light shows him more scenes of the future. As the scenes end, the luminescent sphere dissolves and he is once again in the amphitheater standing next to his friend. The cheers of thousands of spirit beings communicate a tremendous amount of support for him. Then, he returns to life, escorted by his friend. [26]

BETTY EADIE

Her book, Embraced by the Light, became a New York Times bestseller. Her NDE is considered to be one of the most detailed and most profound NDEs ever documented. The argument can be made that her NDE and book was responsible for causing other experiencers to come forward with their own NDEs, thereby proliferating the knowledge of the NDE to millions of readers.

Betty leaves her body through her chest and floats above her bed. Three hooded monk-like beings she identifies as her guardian angels appear and tell her they have been with her for "eternities" and that she has died prematurely. Concerned about her family she left behind, she leaves and visits them at her home but discovers they cannot see her.

She returns to her body and her guardian angels at the hospital. She is then sucked through a tunnel toward a very bright light. At the end of the tunnel, Jesus embraces her. Jesus tells her it is not yet time for her death. She begins to remember forgotten pre-birth memories while receiving an unlimited amount of knowledge. Two close friends appear whom she knew before she was born. They embrace and go on a tour of the spirit world.

They enter a large room and see people creating heavenly garments using heavenly looms of some kind. In another room, she sees people working with a large computer-like machine. They enter another room similar to a library. It is a library of the mind. They go outdoors to a garden where beautiful mountains and rivers can be seen in the distance. It is a realm more beautiful than words can describe.

Beside a waterfall, she observes a magnificent rose and becomes one with it briefly. A group of people gathers around her for a graduation party. Her guardian angels are there and they tell her she has died prematurely and must go back.

Wanting to explore the universe, she is escorted by two light beings into the vastness of space. She travels to other worlds similar to earth having intelligent beings on them. She returns to the garden and is taken to a place where many spirits are preparing for life on Earth.

Her guides show her a drunken man lying on the sidewalk. They ask her what she sees. She sees only a drunk wallowing in his own filth. Her guides show her who the man really is. They reveal to her the man is filled with light and love and who is greatly admired in the spirit world for being a reminder to people of the need to help others.

She is shown the earth as it appears in space. She is shown how prayers shoot like beacon lights from the earth. She sees angels rushing around answering these prayers. She is observing all of this while in the garden.

She is led from the garden and into a large building before a "Council of Elders," consisting of twelve men and Jesus. Here, she is again told her death was premature and she must return to earth. Jesus shows her life in review in the form of well-defined holograms. Jesus comforts her when she sees the negative aspects of her life and begins to judge herself too harshly.

After her life review, she is told her mission in life is not complete and she must return. She steadfastly refuses. Jesus decides to reveal her mission in life with one condition. If she decides to return to earth, the memory of her mission will be removed. She agrees to this and is shown her mission. Immediately, she agrees to go back. Suddenly, thousands of angels appear to sing her farewell.

She finds herself back in the hospital where it all began. Her mission in life was completely removed from her memory. [27]

DR. RICHARD EBY

As a professor and obstetrician with a successful practice, Richard fell off a balcony in 1972 and hit his head causing an NDE. When her revived, he closed his medical practice in order to follow his calling into a full-time ministry. He is now proclaiming the gospel wherever TV, radio, or audiences request his unusual testimony. His NDE helped to shape his ministry and message. His NDE is published in his book entitled Caught up into Paradise.

Richard finds himself out of his body and hears Jesus tell him, "Dick, you're dead!" He asks Jesus many questions to which he replies, "Didn't you read my book?" The answers are given to him corresponding to what is written in the Bible. He explores the paradise Jesus prepared for him. He begins to get lonesome for his wife and tries to find her. He returns to earth after his grieving wife prays for his return. [28]

BLACK ELK

The Native American medicine man Black Elk, of the Lakota Sioux nation, lived between 1863 and 1950, surviving the collision of two eras, when the ancient primal world of his people was shattered by the violent invasion of the new industrial culture. This remarkable medicine man did not even speak English when he told his visionary experience to the author John Neihardt, who wrote about it in his book entitled Black Elk Speaks. In this classic of Native American literature, Black Elk's NDE glows through his perceptions of a sacred natural world.

Black Elk is a dying boy when two men appear in the clouds to tell him his grandfather is calling him. He is raised up into the clouds and feels sorry to leave his parents. He sees a vision of a classic Native American mandala consisting of a circular hoop and the center of the world on an axis stretching from the sky to the earth. Numerous horses prance around surrounded by lightning and thunder. He is told to follow the bay horse.

The horse leads him to a rainbow door. Inside sit six grandfathers who are as old as the stars. The oldest grandfather welcomes him and says, "Your grandfathers all over the world are having a council, and they have called you here to teach you." He becomes frightened because he knows these are not old men, but the Powers of the world.

Each grandfather gives him a special power. The first grandfather gives him the power to heal. The second grandfather gives him the power of cleansing. The third grandfather gives him the power of awakening and peace. The fourth grandfather gives him the power of growth. The fifth grandfather, the Spirit of the Sky, gives him the power of transcendent vision. The sixth grandfather transforms into a young Black Elk and back to an old man. The grandfather tells him his people will have great troubles.

The boy hears a voice telling him, "Behold the circle of the nation's hoop, for it is holy, being endless, and thus all powers shall be one power in the people without end." He stands on the highest mountain and watches this hoop of the world. He says, "I saw more than I can tell and I understood more than I saw; for I was seeing in a sacred manner the shapes of all things in the spirit, and the shape of all shapes as they must live together like one being." He receives his powers from the grandfathers and is sent back to his body.

Many years after his NDE, he tells his story to a medicine man. He helps him reenact the vision as a ritual. Black Elk becomes a powerful medicine man and heals many people. [29]

ANGIE FENIMORE

A wife and mother haunted by abuse in childhood and overwhelmed by despair, Angie was in a desperate state of mind. In 1991, she committed suicide in the hope to escape her sense of emptiness and suffering. But the resulting NDE led into a realm of darkness instead of light. Her book, Beyond the Darkness, describes the hell she experienced which is far more horrific and personal than the old fire-and-brimstone metaphors. It is a world of terrifying visions and profound psychic disconnection.

Angie commits suicide and passes into a warm tunnel and re-experiences her own birth. She notices a large screen in front of her and is drawn into a three dimensional slide show of her entire life. She instantaneously relives her entire life from everyone's point of view, including that of herself. She sees her childhood from an adult point of view.

After her life review, she finds herself in vast darkness. Looking to her right, she sees she is shoulder to shoulder with some teenagers who have also committed suicide. She is sucked further into the darkness to a plane she is told is purgatory. There are thousands of people there. Everyone there was too self-absorbed in their misery to communicate with others. She hears their thoughts and gets terrified at the solitude there. She realizes this is a place where there is no hope.

Suddenly, a great voice emanates from a pinpoint of light she identifies as God the Father. Filled with power, anger and love, God asks her, "Is this what you really want? Don't you know that this is the worst thing you could have done?" She replies, "But my life is so hard." God replies to her, "You think that was hard. It is nothing compared to what awaits you if you take your life. Life's supposed to be hard. You can't skip over parts. We have all done it. You must earn what you receive."

Jesus appears and says, "Don't you understand? I have done this for you?" Angie becomes one with Christ and understands perfectly about the sacrifice of Christ. Jesus pleads her case to God. God tells her, "I told you how to get through this," referring to the scriptures.

She is shown the future, as it would be if her suicide succeeded. She realizes nobody else in purgatory can see God talking to her. This is because they lack the will to seek God as she does. She realizes beings of light have been all around her all along. As she gains more light, she is lifted from the plane of darkness and finds herself back in her physical body. [30]

DAVID GOINES

When David was thirteen years old, he was riding his bike to school and was hit by a concrete mixing truck. The resulting NDE revealed to him many of the secrets of the afterlife. Many questions concerning "Why are we here?" or "What is the meaning of life?" were answered. At the end of his experience, he was given a choice - a choice that is offered to us all. It is a choice we all must make when we die.

David leaves his physical body and observes people working on it in the emergency room of a hospital. One nurse tells another, "Well, it certainly makes you wonder if it's worth saving this mess."

Frightened by these words, he steps through the wall of the hospital and finds himself in a dark void. Taking another step, he finds himself in a beautiful garden. He sits on a bench and a kind and old gentleman appears sitting with him. David asks if he has died. The old man replies that he is not dead, but his body is in a lot of trouble.

The old man explains why David can be two places at the same time, in the hospital and in the garden. The old man tells him he is there with David to remind him his true home is with God. David begins to remember forgotten knowledge concerning life before his birth. The old man disappears.

David sees a path and begins to walk down it. Jesus appears and asks, "Will you come unto me?" David steps forward and pauses, remembering he has a whole life to learn and experience. He tells Jesus, "No, I still have many things which I must do." He then finds himself back in his body, wondering why he said "no" to Jesus. [31]

REV. KENNETH HAGIN

Being raised a Southern Baptist, Kenneth thought he had done all that was necessary to get a place in heaven. He made a commitment to Christ, was baptized with water, and was a lifelong member of the church. He was a believer and follower of Jesus Christ and he knew this assured him a place in heaven. It came as a real shock to him when he found out it didn't. At the age of 15, Kenneth had an NDE resulting from a malformed heart – a condition he was born with. His NDE is described in his book entitled I Believe In Visions.

Kenneth leaps out of his body and descends into a pit. The pit gets hotter the further down he descends. He discovers the very gates of hell and is drawn like a magnet to it.

An unknown creature appears at his side and takes his arm to escort him through the gates. He realizes once he goes through the gates, he cannot return. As he is escorted toward the gates of hell, an unknown voice speaks causing everything to shake. The creature unhands him.

He is then pulled away and returns to his physical body. This whole experience happens again two more times in succession exactly in the way it did the first time. [32]

HELEN

In Jean Ritchie's book, Death's Door, she documented the suicide attempts and subsequent NDEs of a woman named Helen. Her NDEs demolished the myth held by many religious people that suicide and homosexuality are one-way tickets to hell. Although Helen is now very comfortable with her homosexuality, coping with it has not always been easy.

When she was seventeen, she drank heavily and experimented with drugs. Her problems greatly escalated and led her to decide to take her own life. After taking an overdose of pills and drink, Helen's heart stopped four times according to medical staff. This led her to have an NDE.

Helen commits suicide and floats out of her physical body. She feels a tremendous sense of peace. She floats into a supermarket-like place where she sees her deceased relatives beckoning to her. Outside, through the windows, she sees the family and friends she left behind beckoning to her. She decides to return to her physical body in the hospital.

In a later NDE resulting from another suicide attempt, she travels to a beautiful realm through a tunnel toward a bright light. She feels tremendous peace and warmth there. She has a sense it is her decision to either stay or return. She awakens in the hospital.[33]

JOHN HERNANDEZ

In 1996, Arvin Gibson, a retired nuclear engineer and a prominent NDE researcher, interviewed a firefighter named John Hernandez who had a most unusual NDE while working with other firefighters in a forest. What makes his NDE unusual is that it happened at the same time as several of his co-workers were also having an NDE. John's experience was sufficiently interesting that Gibson's local chapter of IANDS invited Jake to tell his story at one of their meetings. Arvin Gibson's book, Fingerprints of God, documents the NDE.

John and a crew of firefighters succumb to a fire they were battling. He leaves his physical body and sees the rest of his crew outside of their bodies as well. In the glorious peace that ensues, a brilliant light appears in which he sees his deceased great-grandfather. He tells John it is his choice to stay or return to life. John was told neither he, nor any of his crew who chose to return, would suffer ill effects from the fire. John and his crew return to their bodies and all are well as promised. [34]

VALVITA JONES

At the time of her NDE, Valvita was a woman of Christian faith, a wife, and a proud mother. She entered the hospital due to a serious infection after having a cesarean section. Her NDE is documented in Rita Bennett's book, To Heaven and Back.

Valvita leaves her physical body and observes doctors trying to revive it. She then passes through "three heavens." In the first heaven, she meets Christ and his great love. They travel through two more "sky-like heavens" until she comes into the presence of the light of God on an invisible throne extending all the way to earth.

Falling prostrate, she hears God speak to her about her and her life, while she has a life review. After her life is reviewed, Jesus touches her hand and she is given the strength to stand up. Jesus leads her to some kind of arena, steps away from her and walks toward the light of God. Jesus then stops, turns sideways and stretches out his arms as a bridge between her and God.

Everything she knew from scripture flashes into her mind. God and Jesus begin discussing her case. Jesus says, "My blood is sufficient. She's mine." This removed all her doubts and feelings of unworthiness. She becomes ecstatic and starts rejoicing. Jesus returns to her and rejoices with her.

A look in Jesus' eyes tells her she had to return. Jesus tells her she has work for her to do. She then returns to life. [35]

CARL JUNG, M.D.

Carl Jung was the world-renowned psychiatrist who founded analytical psychology. He had an NDE after having a heart attack. As he reflected on life after death, Jung recalled the meditating Hindu from his NDE and read it as a parable of the archetypal Higher Self, the God-image within. Jung centered on the archetypes of the collective unconscious in his autobiography entitled Memories, Dreams, Reflections, which describes his NDE.

Carl finds himself in outer space viewing the earth from about a thousand miles above. He sees the beautiful blue aura surrounding the earth and it is the most beautiful sight he has ever seen. He turns around to see a temple floating in space with him. At the temple's entrance, a Hindu sits waiting for him. As Carl approaches, his earthly consciousness is stripped away. He begins to carry with him everything he had ever experienced. He knows inside the temple would be all the people to whom he really belongs. He knows inside he will find the answers to everything.

This scene is suddenly interrupted by an image of his doctor protesting Carl's death. Carl becomes disappointed because he knows he will not be allowed to enter the temple. Instead, he returns to his physical body. For three weeks after his NDE, he is depressed for having to return to this "box system" on earth. He now sees this physical world as a place where people must live and work in box-like rooms. He becomes very angry with his doctor for bringing him back. Because of his experience, he realizes his doctor will soon die. This later turns out to be true. [36]

DR. GERARD LANDRY

As an anesthesiologist who worked twenty-seven years in medicine, Gerard had a very good life as a Christian, husband and father. Then in 1979, he had a heart attack that resulted in an NDE. It is documented in Rita Bennett's book, To Heaven and Back.

Gerard finds himself in heaven with a great number of other people all dressed in white robes and each person holding a crown in their hand. Someone tells him, "We were waiting for you."

Suddenly, Jesus appears on the cross and glances at him with a look of great love and compassion. Everything Gerard read in the Bible becomes more real to him there. Jesus says to him, "Gerry, my peace be with you. You are healed. You will feel no pain. You will have no anxiety. You will have no fears or guilt from the past. In one week you will be home from the hospital."

Jesus then tells him to tell his family that all their prayers are answered and are being answered. Jesus also tells him to read the Gospel and other books of John. When he asks why he must do this, Jesus replies, "John is my friend. He knows all about my love." His experience ends here. [37]

LAURA

Another child of P.M.H. Atwater's study of childhood NDEs, is a three-year old named Laura, whose father, in a blind drunken rage, raped, sodomized, and beat her to death. At the most extreme outpost of pain, she cried out to God and in that moment was torn from life.

Laura is carried into the sky by brightly colored angels. She is taken before the feet of a beautiful female angel who asks to hear about her life. The infinite light of God is there which heals her. Then a struggle between the angels in heaven and the doctors on earth occur in a literal tug-of-war to bring her back from death. The doctors win the struggle and she returns to physical life. [38]

LYNN

Another child of P.M.H. Atwater's study of childhood NDEs, is a thirteen-year old named Lynn who underwent open-heart surgery to correct a condition she had since birth. She had her NDE after a complication occurred during surgery.

Lynn floats out of her physical body and around the ceiling. She observes doctors working on her body. She observes her grieving parents in the waiting room. She travels through a tunnel toward a brilliant light. From the light, two of her deceased dogs run to greet her. The light tells her it is not yet her time to die. She reaches up and touches the face of God. Her deceased relatives greet her and one of them shares with her an important piece of information to give to someone when she returns to physical life.

Jesus appears and tells her the reason for her heart condition she was born with. Jesus tells her it was given to her as a challenge to help her grow and stay compassionate. Jesus tells her about her future.

As she enters the tunnel to return, she notices some disoriented people hiding in the tunnel afraid to come into the light. She is told not to worry about them because a guide is coming along to help them. After her NDE, the important piece of information she was given to share with someone was verified to be true. [39]

LAURELYNN MARTIN

At the height of her promising tennis career, Laurelynn had a routine surgical procedure that caused her to have an NDE. In her book, Searching for Home, she describes her NDE. It is an NDE that Dr. Kenneth Ring said, "can change your life" and is "surpassingly rich in the spiritual insights it offers."

Laurelynn leaves her physical body and watches doctors try to revive it. She floats through a dark void that is warm and loving. In the distance, she sees a brilliant light and she travels toward it. Once in the light, she has a feeling of being home. She greets others including her deceased brother-in-law. She is then led through her life review. When it is over, her brother-in-law tells her she is not ready must return to her body which she does. [40]

MEBRUKE

According to the tenets of the Muslim faith, death is the complete end of physical life and the beginning of a period of rest until the day of resurrection when Allah judges the living and the dead. Many Muslims believe that the righteous can see visions of God after death and the wicked see visions of hell. Except for these possible visions of heaven or hell, Muslims believe the soul remains in a kind of "soul sleep" until the Day of Judgment. In his book entitled Parting Visions, Dr. Melvin Morse described a Muslim NDE by a thirty-year old Saudi Arabian named Mebruke. She was swimming in the Mediterranean Sea off the coast of Italy when she drowned and had an NDE.

Mebruke sees a very beautiful white light that has a peaceful effect on her. While underwater, she hears a voice tell her, "You are not to die like this." Suddenly, a powerful force of energy shoots through her physical body sending her to the surface. Shortly after this, she is rescued and taken aboard a boat. [41]

DR. DIANNE MORRISSEY

When she was twenty-eight years old, Dianne was electrocuted while working on her fish tank resulting in a very profound NDE. Her experience transformed her entire life in a very big way. Today, she is a certified hypnotherapist and has taught 25,000 people to see and feel God's presence during the dream state. Her book, You Can See the Light, trains people to do this very thing for themselves.

Dianne leaves her body and observes her dog pawing at it. She discovers her spirit body is transparent and has the ability to walk through walls. She tries to communicate with a living person outside her house, but she walks through the person and is unnoticed by him. She sees a silver cord connecting her spirit body to her physical body.

A tunnel appears and she travels through it. She emerges from the tunnel and a radiant angelic being appears. This being shows her an instantaneous three-dimensional display of her entire life. Afterward, she returns through the tunnel and emerges into another dimension. She sees a duplicate of herself lying on a bed. She then realizes the absurdity of being at three places at the same time. As she moves closer to the bed and reclines on it, her duplicate disappears. As she lies in the bed, she raptures with great feelings of love and peace.

A pinpoint of light appears which gets closer and closer until she finds herself in the very presence of God. She is given the choice to either stay with God or return to her physical body. The light of God touches her and she is transformed, becoming one with God.

Suddenly, she is sucked through the tunnel again and emerges before her angelic being. The angelic being begins asking her questions such as, "What do you want to do?" Diane replies, "I want to go into the light, and I want to touch things." She is sucked through the tunnel once again and emerges before her lifeless physical body. Realizing she wants the light, she is sucked back into the tunnel and back to the angelic being. Dianne is torn between staying in the light or returning to the physical world where she can actually "touch things." She goes back and forth through the tunnel several times more.

She realizes she has done little while in the physical world - how few lives she touched. She is pulled through the tunnel and reenters her physical body. Afterwards, she wonders how she could have possibly decided to come back. [42]

DR. DON MORSE

As a scientist who believed in the absolute finality of death, Don went through life with an increasing anxiety about his eventual fate. Then an NDE led him on a quest to uncover what science knows about the nature of death. His subsequent spiritual journey led him through the entire realm of science and religious beliefs until he came to an inescapable conclusion: Some form of an afterlife must exist. In his book, Searching for Eternity, he summarizes the vast research and data leading to this conclusion.

Don feels himself spinning around and around in ever widening circles. Out of the pitch darkness comes an incredibly bright, white light. He is shown his life in review. He flies above the clouds and travels to the cemetery where his body is going to be buried. He sees a newspaper with his own obituary in it. He returns to his body and is back in the hospital.[43]

VASUDEV PANDEY

Dr. Satwant Pasricha and Dr. Ian Stevenson documented sixteen cases of NDEs in India. Indian experiencers frequently report being taken to the after-death realm by functionaries who then discover that a mistake has been made and send the person back, whereupon he or she revives. One of their subjects was Vasudev Pandey who nearly died of "paratyphoid disease" when he was about ten years old. He had been considered dead and his body had actually been taken to the cremation ground. However, some indications of life aroused attention and he was revived.

Two beings take hold of Vasudev and take him away. After some distance, he feels tired and the two beings drag him.

He is taken before a black Hindu with no clothes who says to the two beings in a rage, "I had asked you to bring Vasudev the gardener. Our garden is drying up. You have brought Vasudev the student."

He regains consciousness with the gardener standing in front of him. The next day, the gardener is dead.[44]

APOSTLE PAUL

Many of books of the Bible were written by Paul, a Hebrew Pharisee who converted to Christianity after receiving a vision of Christ. In 1945, an ancient Gnostic book entitled the Apocalypse of Paul [45] was discovered in Egypt. Together with a number of other manuscripts, this book outlines the early Gnostic Christian idea of what happens after death when the soul is judged. According to Paul's Apocalypse, each soul has to rise as best it can through a hierarchy of heavens and face the increasingly difficult challenges posed by the guardian angels of each heaven.

In the Apocalypse of Paul, Paul first meets the Holy Spirit in the form of a child. The child leads him to the third heaven. The child warns him they are about to enter a realm of archangels and demons. They pass by the place where souls go to be reincarnated.

The child leads him to the fourth heaven where they see a soul having his life reviewed. The soul is subsequently reincarnated because of misdeeds. The child leads him to the fifth heaven were he meets his fellow apostles. Here they see angels scourging souls in order to drive them on to judgment.

In the sixth heaven, he sees a strong light shine down on him. In the seventh heaven, he sees an old man bearing a striking resemblance to Jehovah as described by the prophet Ezekiel. The old man asks Paul where he is going. Paul gives him a password which is the Gnostic sign necessary for one to know to move into higher realms.[46]

In the eighth heaven, Paul embraces the twelve disciples and they all rise to the ninth heaven. When he reaches the tenth heaven, he is transformed. [47]

REV. HOWARD PITTMAN

In 1979, Howard was a Baptist minister of 35 years when he died while on the operating table during surgery. During his NDE, he traveled through a number of afterlife realms until he was taken before the throne of God. In his booklet entitled Placebo, he describes his NDE and the message he was told to share with the world.

Howard leaves his physical body and angels lift him to the second heaven where he sees demonic spirits among the living on earth. He becomes nauseous at this sight. An angel tells him he is feeling this way because there is no love in this world.

He is escorted to the third heaven through a tunnel he describes as the passageway from earth to the third heaven. He is taken to the very gates of heaven, but instead of entering, he is instructed to watch others enter one at a time. An angel forbids him to enter because he would not be able to return. Howard realizes if he could not return to his physical body, his physical body would die. This troubles him because he is very concerned about the physical body he left behind.

He is told to stand by one side of the gate and present his case to God. He is assured God would hear and answer him. Howard begins talking of his good works. He asks God for an extension of his physical life. In anger, God rebukes him by telling him he lived a life only for himself. Dejected by this show of God's anger, he is escorted back to his body. Then he realizes God did not actually answer his question. Howard pleads with the angels to take him back so God can answer his question.

He is escorted back to the gate before God and he pleads his case again. He promises God he will do better next time. God reminds him he has promised this before. He is shown all the promises he made to God that he didn't keep.

Suddenly, he becomes filled with light causing him to see God in a whole new way. Instead of a God of wrath, which he saw previously, he sees God as a God of love. He becomes sorrowful for the promises he broke to God.

God expresses sympathy for him. Howard realizes his physical body is not important after all. God tells him why he was taken to heaven in the first place. The reason is because God has an important message for him to tell others. The message has to do with the Second Coming of Christ, which he is told is soon to happen, and the fact the Christian church has fallen away from the faith. [48]

PLATO'S ER

The oldest surviving report of an NDE in Western literature is Plato's story of Er, a soldier who awoke on his funeral pyre after sojourning in the afterlife. Plato integrated at least three elements of Er's NDE into his philosophy. These included the departure of the soul from the cave of shadows to see the light of truth, the flight of the soul to a vision of pure celestial being and its subsequent recollection of the vision of light, the very purpose of philosophy. In his book, Republic, he concludes his discussion of the immortal soul and ultimate justice with the story of Er. Traditional Greek culture had no strong faith in ultimate justice. The dead lingered in a dark, miserable underworld Hades, regardless of their behavior in this life, with no reward or punishment. But Plato drew on the idea of an otherworldly reward or punishment to motivate virtuous behavior in this life. The first point of Er's story is to report on this cosmic justice.

Twelve days after Er is slain in battle, his body does not decay and is laid on a funeral pyre for burial. He revives from death and tells others his experience:

He leaves his body and journeys with other souls to a mysterious region where there are two tunnels side by side in the earth and two tunnels side by side in the heavens. Judges sit between heaven and earth to judge the souls. Souls judged as righteous enter to the right, upward tunnel leading to the heavens. The souls judged as unjust enter the left, downward tunnel leading to the earth.

As he draws near to be judged, he is told he must be a messenger to inform humanity of this other world. From the upper left tunnel from heaven, he sees souls arrive in preparation to be reincarnated to earth. These souls are happy and talk of how beautiful the world is from which they came. From the lower left tunnel from the earth come souls who are lamenting over how great the suffering was they endured in the world from which they just came.

Journeying on, he sees a bright pure rainbow light resembling a "cosmic axis" holding together eight spheres revolving around the earth (the solar system?). Each sphere (planet?) is guided by its Fate. Before the groups of reincarnating souls, one of the Fates displays a number of earthly destinies from which the souls may choose. For example, the destiny of a tyrant or an animal or an artist can be selected. Before returning to earth, each soul drinks from the "River of Forgetfulness" to forget all pre-birth memories. Er, however, is not required to drink and forget. [49]

JAN PRICE

A nearly fatal heart attack caused Jan to undergo an NDE. While many experiencers are greeted by a being of light during their NDEs, Jan was greeted by her deceased dog. Their new relationship while in heaven is quite interesting and amazing. Her NDE reveals what happens to beloved pets when they cross over to the other side. In her book, The Other Side of Death, Jan describes her NDE and her adventures with her dog in the afterlife.

Jan leaves her physical body and sees angels helping her rise higher. A beautiful light pours through her. Her beloved deceased dog appears and she communicates with it telepathically. Her dog gives her a guided tour of the afterlife.

First, they go to the home her dog created with its mind and where her dog currently dwells. Next, they go to a cliff where they can observe what is happening in the physical world. Next, they enter a "Temple of Knowledge" resembling a Greek temple. Here, people are engaged in various artistic endeavors.

Moving further inward, they see wise ones who are stationed at intervals waiting to assist people who choose to approach them. She approaches one of them and is given much knowledge. Her wise one shows her a city of light consisting of three simultaneous dimensions. In the first dimension, everyone and everything is dingy, with much darkness and evil. The second dimension is brighter and much more colorful and appears very much like the physical world. The third dimension is similar in description to the holy city in the Book of Revelation with pure gold and crystal glass. The people there live in harmony, great joy and peace. The wise one instructs her to go further into the Temple and she does.

Once there, she experiences infinite knowledge and realizes her oneness with the light of God. In the light, a beautiful woman appears and asks her to gaze into her eyes. Jan realizes she is seeing into the eyes of her very own soul. She comes face to face with the glory she had from the beginning of time. As she descends back into her physical body, she is told to hold on to as much information as she can. She is sucked through a tunnel and finds herself back in her physical body. [50]

PAM REYNOLDS

Dr. Michael Sabom is a cardiologist whose latest book, Light and Death, includes a detailed medical and scientific analysis of the amazing NDE of a patient named Pam Reynolds. She underwent a highly unusual operation for a giant aneurysm in her brain. She had been referred to a doctor who had pioneered a daring surgical procedure known as hypothermic cardiac arrest, which would allow Pam's aneurysm to be removed with a reasonable chance of success. This operation, nicknamed "standstill" by the doctors who perform it, requires her body temperature be lowered to 60 degrees, her heartbeat and breathing stopped, her brain waves flattened, and the blood drained from her head. In everyday terms she is dead. As the operation was being performed, Pam's NDE began to unfold. She relates the story with remarkable detail and her observations of the surgery were later verified to be true.

Pam undergoes a surgical procedure known as a "standstill" to remove a brain aneurysm. Her body temperature is lowered to 60 degrees. Her heartbeat and breathing are stopped. Her brain waves are flattened. All the blood is drained from her head and she literally becomes brain dead. The doctors then perform the operation.

While this is happening, she leaves her body through the top of her head and floats above her physical body while the doctors operate on it. She notices only half of her head has been shaved off for the surgery. She watches as a doctor cuts open her head with an electric toothbrush-like device.

She is pulled through a tunnel and into a place of incredibly bright light. She meets deceased loved ones who prevent her from traveling all the way into the light. She realizes she has to return to her body. Her deceased relatives sprinkle her with "sparkles" to gives her strength. Afterwards, her uncle leads her back to the tunnel to return to her physical body. She is reluctant to reenter her physical body because it looks repulsive from the surgery. She is told reentering her body would be like jumping into a swimming pool. She is reluctant to do so. She falls back into her body after being given a helping push from her uncle. [51]

DR. GEORGE RITCHIE

In 1943, George was training to be a doctor while in the Army. During this time, he became ill and died of pneumonia. Nine minutes later, he returned to life to tell of an amazing NDE. His NDE so profoundly moved Dr. Raymond Moody, the so-called "father of the NDE," that he was inspired to begin to seriously investigate the NDE. George's NDE is described in his book, Return From Tomorrow.

George leaves his body and sees it lying in his bed. He is not aware the dead body in his bed is his. Wanting eagerly to travel to Richmond, Virginia to start college, he finds himself flying in the air toward a city. He is not sure how he acquired these strange powers of flight and transparency. He arrives at a city and discovers he has lost his solidness. He flies back to the hospital and sees his lifeless body in the morgue and realizes he has died.

Suddenly, Jesus appears emitting a tremendous light and love. George's entire life appears before him. Jesus asks, "What have you done with your life?" He realizes Jesus is not judging him, but he is judging himself.

Jesus gives him a tour of four different dimensions in the afterlife. They both fly toward a large city on earth where they notice a group of assembly-line workers at work. He witnesses the spirit of a woman trying desperately to obtain a cigarette from the workers who are oblivious to her presence. This woman died severely addicted to cigarettes.

In a house, Jesus shows him the spirit of a boy following a living teenage girl and begging for forgiveness – all while the girl is completely unaware of the boy's presence. Jesus tells George that the boy committed suicide and is "chained to every consequence of his act."

Jesus shows George a bar filled with sailors who are heavily drinking. Spirits try desperately and in vain to get a drink or to control the sailors' alcoholic behavior. These spirits are from humans who die severely alcoholic. He is horrified as he observes a drunken sailor pass out and an alcoholic spirit jump into the body of the sailor.

Jesus takes him to a new dimension away from earth and shows him a kind of "receiving station" where spirits would arrive in a deep hypnotic sleep because of their beliefs. These are spirits who believe they must sleep after death until Jesus returns.

Jesus shows him a dimension where angry spirits are locked in hand-to-hand combat, trying in vain to hurt each other. He hears verbal abuse going on. He observes some trying in vain to get sexual gratification from each other. He also sees spirits arguing over some religious or political point and trying to kill the ones who did not agree with them. Here, he realizes he is seeing hell. These are spirits who are locked into some earthly desire that went beyond the physical and which cannot be satisfied in the spirit.

He is then taken to a different dimension appearing like an enormous university. Here he observes people dressed as monks engaged in some form of artistic behavior or research. He is taken into an enormous library where all the important books of the universe are assembled. He asks Jesus if this is heaven. He replies that these are the people who grew beyond selfish desires while on earth. George realizes these people cannot see Jesus, just as the others could not see him in hell.

Jesus takes him into outer space toward a distant city made of brilliant light of a similar description to the city in the Book of Revelation. He speculates this is the place where people go who have become Christ-like while on earth. Here, love was the dominant focus of life. He realizes he is seeing heaven, but he is not allowed to go in. Jesus then shows him the future of the earth. He then returns to his physical body. [52]

VIRGINIA RIVERS

In 1986, Virginia had a near-fatal bout of pneumonia that caused her to have an NDE. At this time, she was extremely weak with a high fever, felt intense pressure in her ears, and had difficulty breathing. She remembers crying out inwardly, "Please, where is everybody? I must be dying." At that point, she lost consciousness, and her journey to the center of the universe and to the Source of All began. Her NDE is described in Dr. Kenneth Ring's book, Lessons from the Light.

Virginia finds herself at peace in a black void. She travels very quickly through the stars, which creates a tunnel effect. The farther she travels, the more knowledge she gains. This includes knowledge she had forgotten long ago. As she travels, her consciousness expands tremendously. Love from all the corners of the universe pours into her.

A light at the end of the tunnel gets brighter and brighter as she gets closer. At the end of the tunnel is God. All the light, love and knowledge of the universe is there. She realizes she is "home."

She hovers next to God on the ledge of a huge mountain where she sees a golden altar shining in from of her. God tells her many things she cannot remember later. She is told she has to return because there was something she had yet to accomplish. At the moment, she knew what this something was, but finds she cannot remember it upon her return.

She pleads for God to allow her to stay, but she knows she has something yet to accomplish on earth. She returns to her body in order to accomplish whatever it is she is to accomplish. [53]

DR. GEORGE RODONAIA

George holds an M.D. and a Ph.D. in neuropathology, and a Ph.D. in the psychology of religion. Before immigrating to the United States from the Soviet Union in 1989, he worked as a research psychiatrist at the University of Moscow. George was pronounced death immediately after being hit by a car in 1976 and was left for three days in a morgue. He did not return to life until a doctor began to make an incision in his abdomen as part of an autopsy procedure. When he revived, he was able to describe a very profound NDE. Prior to his NDE, he was also an avowed atheist. After his experience, he devoted himself exclusively to the study of spirituality, taking a second doctorate in the psychology of religion. He became an ordained priest in the Eastern Orthodox Church and serves as a pastor at St. Paul United Methodist Church in Baytown, Texas. His NDE is described in Phillip Berman's book The Journey Home.

George leaves his body and enters total darkness. He wonders how he could still be alive after his death. He realizes he must think positive thoughts to escape the darkness and enter into the light. As soon as he does, a bright light appears and he sees the universal form of life and nature. Afterward, he sees a holographic drama of his entire life in review. In the light, he becomes ecstatic as he becomes filled with knowledge. He travels back into time and lives in the minds of Jesus and his disciples. He does the same for other historical figures throughout history. Suddenly, he feels himself back in his physical body and is painfully aware his body is being cut open. He has returned to life after being dead for three days in the morgue. He revives to the utter shock and horror of the doctors performing his autopsy. [54]

SANDRA ROGERS

In 1976, Sandra put a gun to her heart and shot herself. Instead of the nothingness she sought from suicide, she had an NDE. Her NDE gives some insight into the process of reincarnation and reveals the choices those who commit suicide may be given. On April 28, 2000, Sandra died from complications resulting from her suicide attempt. In her book, Lessons from the Light, she describes her NDE.

Sandra commits suicide and a being of light appears. Instantaneously, her entire life is presented to her for review. She is given access to unlimited knowledge. Christ gives her two choices. The first choice is to remain in the light with the condition she must reincarnate at a future time to re-experience and overcome all that caused her to commit suicide in the first place. The second choice is to be revived and live out the rest of her life overcoming her problems. She chooses the second choice and is revived. [55]

DANIEL ROSENBLIT

As an atheist, Daniel made fun of those who believed in an afterlife. Then in 1978, after weeks of failing health, Daniel succumbed and had an NDE. It changed his life forever. For over ten years, he has been carrying on a ministry as a street preacher. He wrote a book about his experience entitled Transformed by the Light.

Daniel finds himself before the light of God. He is overcome with grief and regret because of his life of self-indulgence, atheism and persecution of religious people. The light of God crushes all his egocentric illusions. He is shown his entire life in review including every thought, word and deed. He sees he lived his whole life mostly for himself. He is in sheer agony. God pours an incredible amount of love into him that greatly comforts him. He is forgiven and in a state of ecstasy. He feels as though God has given him a second chance as he returns to physical life. [56]

THOMAS SAWYER

Thomas was an avowed agnostic when his pickup truck fell on him, crushing his chest flat. He was clinically dead for fifteen minutes and had an NDE. He was sent back to tell people about death and the unconditional love of God. He shared his NDE on such television shows as Phil Donahue, Oprah Winfrey, Unsolved Mysteries, and Good Morning America. His book, What Tom Sawyer Learned from Dying, gives a detailed account of his profound NDE.

Thomas discovers he is in total blackness taking the form of a tunnel. He travels through this tunnel toward a very brilliant light. He realizes that within the light is everything in the universe, including himself. The light is God, the light of Christ, emitting tremendous love. The light communicates with him telepathically and answers all of his questions. Afterward, he is given a choice to either return to physical life or become part of the light. He is told the instant he considers it, it will be done. In order to make his choice intelligently, he is given a life review. He decides to stay in the light and become part of it. Nevertheless, he returns to his body, not knowing how or why. [57]

PETER SELLERS

As the comic genius of a generation of actors, Peter brought brilliant characterizations to numerous films, including "The Mouse That Roared" (1959), "Dr. Strangelove" (1964), "The Pink Panther" (1964), and "Being There" (1979). He was known for his enthusiastic way of totally absorbing himself in his characters, even carrying roles offstage. He believed he drew on these characters from past lives that he had. Then in 1964, during the first of a rapid series of heart attacks, his heart stopped and he became clinically dead which led to an NDE. Peter confided in the famous actress Shirley MacLaine while shooting his last film. MacLaine writes about Peter's experience in her book, Out on a Limb. She writes how Peter was astonished she did not consider him "bonkers."

Peter leaves his physical body and watches as it is taken to the hospital where a doctor massages his heart. He sees an incredibly beautiful, bright, loving white light and wants to go to the light more than anything in his life. A tremendous amount of love from the light fills him. He knows this light is God. He observes a hand emerging from the light towards him. He tries to grab the hand, but his heart begins beating again. The light tells him it is not yet his time to die. As the hand recedes, he feels himself floating back down to his body. He wakes up bitterly disappointed. [58]

KIMBERLY CLARK SHARP

After her heart suddenly stopped, Kimberly lay on the sidewalk not breathing and without a pulse. This resulted in an NDE that changed her life profoundly. After her NDE, she became the cofounder and president of the Seattle International Association for Near-Death Studies (IANDS). Her NDE is described in her book, After the Light.

Kimberly leaves her physical body and discovers she is in a dense, dark gray fog. In this fog, the past, present and future exist simultaneously. Suddenly, an explosion of light surrounds her and fills her with love and knowledge. She learns she must return to her physical body. Against her best wishes, she does so. [59]

JAYNE SMITH

Jayne was in the hospital and in labor with her second baby. In the process, she experienced clinical death and had an NDE. Her video entitled A Moment of Truth describes in detail her profound NDE.

Jayne leaves her body through the top of her head and enters a kind of gray mist. She is ecstatic to still be alive after death. A brilliant light appears and she is cradled in rapturous love and unlimited knowledge. The rapture and ecstasy build to a point where she begins to worry she will shatter. At this point, the light recedes along with the rapture.

She discovers she is in a beautiful meadow where the colors are like nothing she has ever seen. She sees a group of people dressed in robes standing on a hill nearby. As soon as she expresses to herself she wants to join them, she is there with them on the hill.

Over the horizon, she notices a city of light representing a whole world. A man in a purple robe tells her telepathically that it isn't time for her to be there. All her questions are answered. She is prompted to look within her herself into her heart. When she does, she has a life review. She realizes the core of her being is perfect love and knows this is true for everyone. She receives knowledge long ago forgotten. She cannot understand how such important knowledge could have been forgotten. She is told that when she returns to physical life, she will not be able to remember some of the knowledge she has just learned. She hears a strange clicking sound and finds herself back in her body. [60]

JOHN STAR

One day, without any warning, John found himself face to face with the fact that life in this world is terminal. He was swimming in Lake Michigan about half a mile offshore when he got in trouble. He was swimming free style, like he had done at swimming competitions, when he turned his head to breathe and inhaled an oncoming wave. His lungs were full of water when he wondered if he could swim half a mile at top speed without breathing. He tried, but what resulted was an extraordinary NDE and a miraculous return to life. His NDE testimony was sent to me by email.

John drowns and leaves his physical body. His physical body continues to swim as he observes this from above. A tremendous light appears filling him with joy. He has a life review and discovers he is beyond the barrier of space and time. He feels as if he is waking up from a dream. Friends appear in the light to greet him. From deep within himself, a voice tells him he must return and he does. [61]

HOWARD STORM

Before his NDE, Howard was a Professor of Art at Northern Kentucky University and not a very pleasant man. He was an avowed atheist who was hostile to every form of religion and those who practiced it. He often would use rage to control everyone around him and he didn't find joy in anything. Anything that couldn't be seen, touched or felt, he had no faith in. He knew with certainty that the material world was the full extent of everything that was. He considered all belief systems associated with religion to be fantasies for people to deceive themselves with. Beyond what science said, there was nothing else. Then in 1985, Howard Storm had an NDE resulting from a perforation of the stomach. His life was so immensely changed by it, he resigned as a professor and devoted his time attending the United Theological Seminary and became a United Church of Christ minister. His NDE is documented in his book, My Descent into Death.

Howard leaves his physical body and is surprised he still exists. Strange people lead him into a dark fog until he refuses to go any further. The strange people physically and verbally abuse him. They take great delight in abusing him for their amusement. A voice deep within him tells him to pray. As he does, the strange beings scream at him and back away. He continues to pray until he finds himself alone in the darkness. He pleads to Jesus for help and immediately Jesus appears in a tremendous light that heals. Together, they leave the darkness and travel into outer space toward a great concentration of light similar to a galaxy. He feels God is at the center of this "galaxy" and feels unworthy to continue. He asks Jesus to allow him to go back. Jesus tells him he belongs there.

Other light beings join them and they review his life. He sees how self-centered he was throughout his entire life. After his life review, he asks Jesus many questions and they are answered. He learns he must return to life because of his spiritual underdevelopment. He pleads to stay but, nevertheless, returns to his body. His experience so changes him, he becomes a United Church of Christ minister. [62]

LORRAINE TUTMARC

In 1928, Lorraine became ill with blood poisoning. Because there were no antibiotics in those days, doctors sent her home and told her there was nothing more they could do for her. Her bout with blood poisoning resulted in an NDE. Her NDE appears in the book, To Heaven and Back, by Rita Bennett.

Lorraine leaves her body and floats to the upper corner of the room. She floats through the wall and finds herself up to her neck in a black river. She asks, "Where am I?" A loud, loving voice she identifies as God replies, "This is eternity. You are lost!" She asks, "What is this?" God replies, "This is the River of Death." She realizes God is revealing to her lost spiritual condition to her.

A whirlpool drags her to the bottom of the river where Christ appears to her in a brilliant light. Christ appears to be sad and has a big blotch of red on the ivory robe he is wearing. Jesus tells her, "This is the blood that I shed on the cross for your sins." Jesus tells her, "Follow me." The moment she says, "I will," the River of Death disappears and she is healed.

They both float toward a transparent, golden wall, but she cannot see all the way through it. Beyond the wall, she hears beautiful things, such as birds, choirs and musical instruments. She searches the wall to find the entrance but realizes it isn't time for her to enter yet. She turns around and discovers Jesus is not there. She then finds herself back in her body. [63]

EMMANUEL TUWAGIRAIRMANA

Emmanuel lived as a Christian in Rwanda, Africa. During the Rwanda genocide of 1994, he was seriously injured and together with ten other people hid in a school. The wounds on his body grew worse until one morning his friends realized he had died. They could not bury him because it was very dangerous to move out of the school. They hid in the school and wrapped his body in a bed cover. By now his body was beginning to decay. This situation lasted for seven days. Then he revived and, with maggots feeding on him, told his friends about an amazing NDE. His NDE testimony was emailed to me and later he sent corroborating photographs.

Emmanuel is taken to heaven where he meets an angel by the gates. The angel takes him to a beautiful garden where he meets Jesus. Jesus shows him his dead body.

He is taken to a beautiful city where he sees some of his deceased friends. Across from a beautiful lake, he sees a brilliant light. Jesus tells him he cannot approach the throne of God because it is not yet time. He is shown hell where people work as slaves. Jesus gives something to him to eat. He eats it and discovers it tastes like chocolate. He is told he just ate the whole Bible and that upon return to earth he will have the entire Bible memorized.

He returns to his maggot-infested body. He has spent several days being dead. [64]

VICKI UMIPEG

As a forty-five year old blind woman, Vicki was one of the more than thirty people Dr. Kenneth Ring and Sharon Cooper interviewed at length during a two-year study concerning NDEs of the blind. Their study appears in their book entitled Mindsight. Vicki was born blind. Her optic nerve was completely destroyed at birth because of an excess of oxygen she received in the incubator. Yet, she is able to see for the first time in her life during her NDE.

Vicki leaves her physical body and for the first time in her entire life, she can see. She observes a male doctor and a female nurse working on a body. She notices rings on the fingers of the body. She knows the body must be hers due to the unusual nature of her rings.

She floats through the ceiling of the hospital to experience a panoramic view outside. Then, she is sucked through a tunnel and out into a beautiful meadow. Here, she meets two of her deceased former schoolmates who were also blind. They appear beautiful, healthy, and no longer children. She also meets deceased family members and friends. She is overcome with a sense of complete and total knowledge.

Jesus appears and he tells her it is not her time to die yet. She is very reluctant to return until she is told she will have children to bear in the future. She is told she will and, later, she does. Jesus shows her entire life in review. Afterwards, she finds herself in her physical body again. She is blind again. [65]

RANELLE WALLACE

In 1985, RaNelle and her husband tried to fly their single-engine airplane through a snowstorm in central Utah. They became disoriented and crashed against the side of a mountain, turning their small craft into a raging inferno. She suffered severe burns and died six hours later in an ambulance. Her NDE is described in her book, The Burning Within.

RaNelle leaves her physical body and is sucked through a tunnel. At this time, she instantaneously relives every second of her life. At the end of the tunnel, she emerges into a brilliant light that heals her. Her deceased grandmother appears and RaNelle realizes for the first time she has died.

She asks about a friend who died in an accident months earlier. This friend appears, but her grandmother forbids her to embrace him because of the life he lived. He was a drug dealer in life and had caused people to suffer. The grandmother explains that not being able to embrace him was a part of his punishment.

Her grandmother leads her to a garden of astounding beauty where she is taught lessons about God's love. They fly around the landscape as knowledge pours into her. Suddenly, she has to stop because she can't handle all of the knowledge. Her grandmother reassures her and they continue on. She reunites with more deceased loved ones.

Her grandmother then takes her to a place to "teach her humility." She shows her a place where a beautiful woman is lying on her side on an altar surrounded with gold and jewels. The woman was once a queen in life and now in the spirit, she is deluded into believing there are multitudes surrounding her, bowing and worshiping her. But there is no one there. Here, she learns the full extent of what vanity can do.

RaNelle and her grandmother travel to another place where millions of people who have died are waiting for those on earth to finish their part of the work. Finally, she is shown her badly burned body and is told her mission in life is not complete. She must return, but she refuses.

In an attempt to change her mind, her grandmother introduces her to a young man named Nathaniel, who is RaNelle's future son, not yet born. Nathaniel is crying and wondering why she is there. Nathaniel tells her if she doesn't return, his mission in life would be greatly hindered. This succeeds in changing her mind and she chooses to return to life. Seven years after her NDE, she gives birth to a son and names him Nathaniel. She believes her son is the young man she saw in her NDE. [66]

ARTHUR YENSEN

In 1932, Arthur was a geologist who was involved in an automobile accident that resulted in an NDE. After seeing the afterlife, he later learned that telling others about it often brought criticism, especially from the church. But there were those who would listen and as time wore on, more and more people would ask him about it. Then in 1955, he published his NDE after public interest. His booklet, "I Saw Heaven," describes his NDE and gives many answers to questions he has been asked over the years. His NDE testimony also appears in P.M.H. Atwater's book Beyond The Light.

Arthur leaves his body through the top of his head. He discovers he is in a beautiful mountain paradise. A group of people appears singing, dancing and laughing. Four of them run over to meet him. As they converse, he realizes he is finally home as he remembers having been here before. His questions are answered and he is filled with knowledge, love and ecstasy. One of them resembles a Greek god and tells him he must return to earth. He is told he has important work to do on earth. When it is done, he can come back and stay. With this, he returns to his body. [67]

CHAPTER 3: RESEARCH CONCLUSIONS

"You would know the secret of death. But how shall you find it unless you seek it in the heart of life." -- Kahlil Gibran

The following research conclusions are the most profound insights I have found from the sixty-two NDEs profiled in this book. These conclusions have been grouped into ten categories: Pre-Existence, Life, Humanity, Religion, Spirituality, The Future, Science, God, Heaven, Hell, Spirit Guides, Music, Time, and Reincarnation. If the NDE is a real afterlife experience suggested, these insights may be the most important truths ever documented.

PRE-EXISTENCE

It is not unusual for near-death experiencers returning from clinical death to report having received information concerning their pre-existence before they were conceived in the world. Some experiencers report of learning how they chose various aspects of their lives to be predestined before they were born. Some of the choices people have reported having chosen before birth include the selection of their birth parents, choosing their mission in life, and even choosing how they will die. This knowledge received by near-death experiencers of the past and future shows how some things in life are predestined while other things are not. It shows how free will and predestination both exist and work hand in hand. It means we choose our destiny in life before our birth into the world to live it. Because reincarnation is a concept found in many cultures and religions, the metaphor of life as a river which we chose before we were our birth, shows up in many of these cultures and religions. There are many aspects to a river which make it an excellent analogy to help us understand where we came from, where we're going, who we are, why we're here, and what life is all about. The following discussion will attempt to do just that.

If our experience as a human is analogous to a journey down a river, then our experience as a spirit is analogous to the entire water cycle. Each of us is like a raindrop which fell from a cloud and ultimately entered into a river for the journey back from where it came - the sea. Then the cycle is repeated.

In the same way that a drop of water is a part of the sea and contains within itself the nature of the sea itself, so our spirit is a part of God containing within it the Whole of God itself. This concept of a something being both a part and the Whole is called in science terminology a fractal.

By becoming a droplet in the water cycle, we can experience wonderful adventures which ultimately help us to understand ourselves and the sea even more. Which river of life we choose to travel down is up to us. Once we begin the journey, we are partly at the mercy of the river and the course it takes us. How we chose to flow down the river is our decision.

This river which represents the course of our life that leads us back to God is an archetype that is familiar to us. Perhaps this is one of the reasons we feel drawn to rivers and why we regarded them as sacred. In ancient cultures, religions and even in near-death experiences, this archetype of life being a river appears. On the river, we are always moving forward from a source and toward an end. Life starts out as a small creek and grows into large river with rapids, forks, tributaries, rocks, and sometimes floods. Rivers have a history and are evolving. The river of life can take us to a variety of destinations on shore. There are many decisions and choices to make while traveling the river. Sometimes we have no choice at all but submit to the mercy of the river. At times we can relax and go with the flow. Other times we can shoot the rapids. We can row our boats gently down the stream. But if we just remain on the shore, we will never reach our destination and goal. Wisdom means knowing the best course of action to take as we travel down the river.

Someone once asked Deepak Chopra, the famous endocrinologist and spiritual guru, about the predetermination aspect of this analogy of life being a river. They asked him, "Does this mean that we are born into a pre-determined destiny and if so, why even bother cultivating free will or striving to be faithful?" His answer was:

"This connection isn't fixed or automatic, it merely represents numerical probability. Our conscious choices help determine our destiny. The deterministic world is ignorance. When we navigate from awareness, we exercise free will. It's the difference between ignorance and enlightenment. To surrender to divine intelligence, know that everything both comes from God and belongs to God. If life is a river between the banks of hope and despair, our ultimate destiny is to become independent of both, unmoved by either." (Deepak Chopra)

So the future is not fixed in stone but consists of probabilities based on current choices and trends. This answer from Deepak Chopra is another way of saying we choose our destinies.

We chose our river and destiny before we were born.

A long time ago, I read Betty Eadie's book "The Ripple Effect" (see also her website at EmbracedByTheLight.com) and read the best analogy of "life as a river" I have ever read. It concerns how we choose our destinies before our birth and how it is analogous to standing on top of a very high mountain and looking down upon a vast system of rivers and choosing which river to undertake. From the vantage point of being on top of a mountain, we can get a good view all the rivers from their beginning to their end. As in life, each river has a number of forks and branches to choose from. Some rivers are more challenging while others are less challenging. Some rivers are very dangerous and can lead to disaster. But no matter which river of life we choose before our birth, the river will always carry us back to the sea. This means we are all predestined to eventually return to God. But once we begin our journey down the river of our choosing, we have many choices which are not predetermined.

Here is the excerpt from Betty's book describing the analogy: "Our life is like a river. The destination is set, but the method of our journeying is up to us. We can cruise down the middle of the river at top speed, or we can hug the shore and spin around in eddies. We can crash over rapids or chart a safer path between obstacles. We can slum along the bottom in the mire and slime of sediment, or we can glide along the sparkling surface where the air is clean. The river is ours from birth to death. How we'll navigate it is determined by the hundreds of small choices we make each day.

"To discover our mission in life we must see challenges as opportunities for growth and then face them head on. Each challenge measures our strengths and progress. Even when trials cause pain or sorrow, we must look for new lessons in the pain and ask God for the power to learn and to grow from it. Suffering focuses our attention on what matters most, and with God's help, we can strengthen our spirits by learning patience, tolerance and love. These lessons learned, we become co-navigators with God. But when unlearned, we go into the eddies, spinning around, making little progress, even blaming God for our unremitting suffering." (Betty Eadie)

Betty then addresses how people shouldn't mistakenly believe that the circumstances of their youth can set an unchangeable course for their river of life. She states:

"But, life is dynamic, and the river stretches and bends as we go. A bad beginning does not inevitably lead to a bad ending. In fact a bad beginning can give us strength to create a good ending." (Betty Eadie)

She also describes how our past can be a springboard and a resource for accomplishment and the betterment of others. She does this by quoting from a letter someone wrote to her:

Letter to Betty: "God led me into sobriety from a life of heroin addiction, homelessness, prostitution ... In my sobriety, I've thanked God many times for these experiences. I know the pain of my clients. God gave me the gift to open the door to his love. For 39 years God was preparing me for this. I know this today because I have peace and serenity I did not know was possible."

Betty's response: "She got to know the bottom of the river - the seamy, murky side of life that swallows victims whole and never lets them see the light of day. But through unfathomable effort this woman looked up and found God. With his help she kicked addictions and self-defeating habits out of her life. She fought the undercurrents, disentangled herself, broke the surface of her troubled life and got to a place where pure air and light could provide new energy. She grew strong and rescued others from the depths. Her beginnings then became the basis for a greater good she would do in life. Her wounds became muscles. Her fears became faith. Her mistakes became experience used to benefit mankind. Like her, anyone can choose either to drown in past troubles or to fight to live."

"Each soul will attain a different level of accomplishment here. But whatever the size of the ripples we make, one thing we must learn is to be grateful for whatever trials and gifts our Father gives us in the journey ... Let us be grateful for our childhoods, even for the negative ones. Let us recognize that life is what it is, and that we are all doing our best ... We all volunteer for our positions and stations in the world, and that each of us is receiving more help than we know." (Betty Eadie)

This testimony from Betty agrees with the testimony of many other people who have also had a near-death experience as you will see below.

The following is an NDE describing the River of Life. This NDE testimony comes from P.M.H. Atwater's website. If you haven't checked out her website and all the articles she has there, you are missing out on a wealth of information. This NDE testimony involves one of P.M.H. Atwater's research subjects who is a man named Ken who was involved in a car accident which resulted in an NDE. P.M.H. Atwater calls his NDE "The River of Life" for a good reason as you will see. As Ken was dying on a gurney he moved through a tunnel and into light. He could observe his body and his surroundings and feels euphoric but he learns that he must return. When he asked the light that he be allowed to stay, he is shown a vision of a heavenly river.

"The wall beyond my gurney became transparent and I was shown what appeared to be a flowing river. It was silver and shimmering as it flowed.

"The drops in the river were each a different color yet all flowed together as one body of water. Nothing gave me the impression this was actually water or a river but this is the best descriptive example that can be given of something I witnessed for which there are no words.

"I understood (I use this term because I did not actually hear) the drops were the experiences of all who had lived. The experiences existed as separate items yet belonged to the whole. The whole was the collective knowledge of all. I understood there was no individual, just one, yet each experience was individual making up the whole. This concept of ONE is so foreign to any description I can give, there seems to be no way now of describing it. My previous understanding of "one" was a single uniqueness. In this case "one" is something else. Many being one and one being many, both exist simultaneously in the same time and space. I further understood that the collective experiences are omniscient knowledge. Everything that has been spoken, heard, and experienced.

"There was no fear, or joy from this stream. I use the term river of life to describe the stream. There was an understanding of complete peace, happiness, and contentment without need or want, coming from the river of life. I had a strong desire now to join the river of life and felt this was home.

"I understood I was not to join the river of life at that time, I was to go back. At this understanding I began to have fears and questions. I again reiterated I did not want to go. I understood I was to go back. I then was made to understand there would be great pain. I did not want to face the pain that awaited me. I understood the pain would be great and it would change and mold me. I wanted to know why and what I was to do. I was flushed with two sensations, one after the other. One sensation was of a sense of an action being right that brought a brief moment of the total peace and comfort I had experienced. The other sensation was one of an action being wrong. The sensation for wrong was a darkening of the light and cold.

"There was no explanation of why I was to go back nor was there an explanation of what I was to do. I was made to understand that my knowledge was not for everyone." (from P.M.H. Atwater's website)

Ken's vision of a heavenly river made up of drops of water representing human experiences is an excellent description of our one-ness which many near-death experiencers bring back with them. In this instance, the heavenly river represents God and each drop is a human lifetime. A drop of water is both a part of the river and within itself is the nature of the Whole River itself. Our spirit is an individualized part of the Whole (God) and yet within it is the Whole itself (the fractal concept again). Near-death experiencers describe experiencing this one-ness when they merge fully into the light during their NDE. The drop of water merges once again with the sea to become the Whole Sea again.

Perhaps a better analogy of how our spirit can exist both a part of God and yet the Whole of God is to think of our spirit as a "thought" in the Mind of God. The "thought" leaves the Mind of God to experience individuality as a human being. As a human being, our spirit is an individualized "thought" in the Mind of God but also retains its one-ness as the Whole Mind of God. When our human life is over, our "thought" returns to the Wholeness and merges into it where all the other thoughts are. The question however is this: When the thought returns to the Mind of God does it lose its individuality once it merges back into the Mind? According to Edgar Cayce, the answer is "no." The reason thoughts began leaving the Mind of God to begin with was to learn individuality while maintaining Wholeness at the same time. Otherwise, thoughts would remain as a thought in the Mind and forever by controlled by the Mind and never know individuality.

The following is about traveling down the River of Life from P.M.H. Atwater's website: "I believe my actual physical existence resides in the river of life as its natural form when not present in this reality or life. As a drop taken from a cup of water and then returned, so the individual drop exists, yet is part of the whole. I believe there is a retained knowledge of life experience that becomes part of collective knowledge yet remains intact as a unit. There is no body in the sense we know one, no love, hate, or any emotion as we know it. In a perfect existence devoid of need or want, all needs and wants, positive and negative, do not exist. The one-ness I perceived was what is referred to as God. We are of God and God is of us. The purpose of our physical existence and life is to provide every possible variation of action so an omniscient knowledge base can exist.

"There is no heaven and hell, as we perceive it. There is no punishment for wrong behaviors, nor rewards for right behaviors. There is no judgment process. This is the reason people anguish over why God would let that happen. All experience, good, bad, mixed, is part of omniscient knowledge. In our present life, we have control over our lives to create perfectly unique combinations of experience, memory, and knowledge. Some people have memory of past lives or deja vu because of our connection to the river of life. The collective knowledge knows what brings feelings of well-being, peace, and happiness as well as what brings turmoil and pain. Our reward for moving in the direction of peace and contentment is the experience we create will have more positive feelings associated with it. I note here also that no matter how horrible the action and horrible the experience, all experience must exist to make up omniscient knowledge. This is why there is no precognition. The collective knowledge is so vast, likely results can be predicted. Thus, premonition is not magic, but informed estimation. In a sense we create our own hell here in this life when we take actions which bring pain and turmoil into our lives. We can also create an existence closer to the perfect peace of after-death existence by living in such a way as to bring peace and harmony into our lives.

"There is no love in the river of life, as we know love here in this existence. Since there is no want or need and a feeling of total peace, there is a sense of perfect love in the existence. There is also not a sense of desire to be with someone nor is there anyone to be with. All are part of the whole which is the common denominator of the universal existence we call God. In that sense we are God and God is we.

"I did not wish to relate my experience for a long time. I felt very comfortable with this. It was a right action. A situation occurred 2 years later and I was suddenly compelled to tell a person. The feeling surrounding that was right also. Since that time I have come to rely on this intuition. It guides me in much of my decision making. I know when I am to tell a person about the experience when this right feeling becomes very strong. Likewise, when I logically think I should tell someone and the feeling is wrong, I do not hesitate to heed the intuition. I do not feel compelled to tell everyone about my experience. In fact, I still feel the need to be careful about whom I tell. My father developed a fear of death as he got older. I considered telling him to comfort his fears. My intuition told me not to and I heeded that feeling. At the instant of my father's death I was many miles away in route to the hospital where he lay very ill. I felt a brief return of that very peaceful feeling, devoid of want or need and I felt perfectly calm and happy. I looked at my watch. When I arrived at the hospital, the time I looked at my watch coincided exactly with the time my father died. Three years after that, I felt an overwhelming desire to tell my experience to a friend of mine at church. I also wanted to get her thoughts on sharing my experience with terminally ill patients and their families. She was head of a hospice agency. Talking to this person was an intense right feeling and I had an unexplained sense of urgency. When I related my experience the young lady cried and told me how I relieved fears and feelings of loss and grieving with the recent death of her mother. I had suggested I share my experience with terminally ill patients, but expressed concern about doing so would be a double edged sword attacking their belief systems already in place. She concurred and said the conflict may be more harmful than helpful." (from Dr. PMH Atwater's website)

The following are insights about choosing your "river" (predestined course of life) and destiny wisely. Ken's NDE fits perfectly into the whole picture of a river being a metaphor for life. Each one of us comes from the sea. Our true nature has always been the sea. Our journey began as a droplet of water from the sea, we experience land and the river, and then we return to become completely one with the sea again. Should we decide to experience the cycle again we merely become another raindrop pulled from the sea and the process is repeated.

Here are more insights:

"A central aspect of our eternal existence is continued spiritual growth through love and service. We can spend what seems like an eternity before incarnating in the flesh. During that period in the spirit world, soul growth can be attained there as well." (Nora Spurgin)

"We came to this physical realm to live the human experience and help each other rise to the higher level of love." (Sherry Gideon)

"Each one of us came to earth on a personal mission to be loved or to give love. We are to learn the value and price of love. Other parts of our mission include learning patience, humility, self-discipline, and other virtues. These attributes are parts of love." (Betty Eadie)

"Our own desire to grow and learn leads us to be born in the physical realm." (Amber Wells.

One of the reasons for the physical realm is to test our spiritual ideals to see if they are real. If a soul has a spiritual ideal and desires to know if it actually possesses that ideal, the soul can come to earth to be tested after applying this ideal in a physical life. The earth is a good school for overcoming certain weaknesses in ways that only a body of flesh can. We apply ourselves here on earth to see if those weaknesses are truly overcome. Here we can learn for sure whether we have really changed. Only by becoming subject to the physical influences of the flesh and the laws of this physical realm can a soul know for certain if they really possess that spiritual ideal. (Edgar Cayce)

"The ideal place to grow spiritually is on earth because of the influence of a physical body. The opportunity for the full range of love (child's love, marital love, and parental love) is ideally available while one is on earth. Love which has been misused or misdirected is also best corrected in the physical. On earth, there is the full range of physical and spiritual senses with which to act and communicate." (Nora Spurgin)

"One of our goals in this world is true self-realization - knowing that we are a soul, a part of God, yet also the Whole." (Thomas Sawyer)

"Our desire for soul growth in this world arises from a desire to be close to God. In the spirit world, there is an ever-increasing unity with the love of God. This is also our goal for soul growth in the physical world." (Nora Spurgin)

"We made a promise to God to accept the opportunities, challenges and responsibilities of a physical life, to make the most of this opportunity for ourselves and God, to return to God with the knowledge and experience gained such that likewise, God could be enhanced by the experience. By doing good, improving our minds, and learning to cope with physical reality, our love for God will bring us back to Him." (David Goines)

"Souls choose to be born with physical disabilities for the purpose of soul growth and to stay compassionate." (Lynn)

"There are many rewards for choosing to be born with a disability." (Mary Ellen)

"Souls who choose to be born mentally retarded are special souls who have retained more than a normal amount of their pre-birth memories and who know much more than they are able to express. Such hardships are necessary for soul growth." (Sandra Rogers)

"Some souls choose to be born for a short period of time and die as a baby or child. The purpose for this is to teach others important lessons. To love a child who is born less than perfect is an important lesson." (Sandra Rogers)

"Some parents lose a child tragically in an accident. That child was fulfilling his or her mission. The parent was fulfilling his or her mission also. The parents are in that circumstance to learn a lesson. Maybe the lesson was patience, love, acceptance, understanding, or comfort of others. It can be a number of things." (George Anderson)

"We are born to face trials and gain the experience of a physical life." (RaNelle Wallace)

Some people decide to be born into favorable conditions and some people decide to be born into unfavorable conditions. The choice has to do with satisfying divine justice and karma. (Edgar Cayce)

During our journey on the river of life, we are given many choices and opportunities along the way. But life on the river also involves situations beyond our control. At some point we may experience being unjustly mistreated or killed. Horrible things can happen. Incredible pain and catastrophe may happen to us. This causes us to ask why all the suffering? What does it mean? This is the question which has plagued humanity perhaps since the beginning of time. Western civilization knows it as the "problem of evil." How could a good God allow such evil to happen to us? This is also the same question put in different words which has plagued the East as the "problem of suffering."

The following is a description of "The River of Life" according to Edgar Cayce.

Why do good people suffer? I discovered the answer to this question many years ago when I read a book about the life of Edgar Cayce appropriately called "There is a River." Cayce discovered by accident at a young age that he could easily put himself into a particular state of self-hypnosis which is normally very difficult for most people. While in a deep trance, he could leave his body and travel through the tunnel toward the light and obtain information from the so-called "Hall of Records" in heaven. Once a woman came to Cayce requesting guidance about a very dangerous surgical procedure she was soon to have. She wanted to know if she was doing the right thing to have the surgery. While in a trance, Cayce came up with the answer.

The woman and the doctors who were planning to perform the surgery had met once before in a past life. In that past life, she was a heretic who was tortured and killed during the Inquisition. The Inquisitors who tortured and killed her then were now the doctors planning to save her life. Cayce told her to go ahead with the surgery because the doctors are paying a karmic debt owed to her for their transgressions against her. Surprisingly, Cayce guaranteed that the surgery would be successful. And it was.

So the woman and the doctors were acting on one level of consciousness as doctors and patient. But on a higher level of consciousness, they were acting as former Inquisitors saving the life of a woman they once tortured and killed.

But this insight raises a few questions? Did the Holocaust victims, for example, choose to be slaughtered or did they have a choice? Did Hitler have a choice to be a creative force or a monstrous force? If only we had the foresight to see farther down the river to see what lies ahead of us in our journey, we could avoid all catastrophes and our lives would be much better. Because NDEs and quantum physics suggests the future is based on probabilities rather than certainties, the river of life is not mechanical or deterministic. We are not "crash test dummies" on a fixed course for catastrophe. Nor does anyone force us on the river of life. NDE insights suggest we freely chose the river we're on before the journey even began. This brings us to the real question to ask: Why would anyone chose a river having a probability of turning into catastrophe?

A similar question is, "Why do people choose to float down the Colorado River in the Grand Canyon when death is possible?" The challenge? The danger? The fun? The experience? To test themselves? To discover? Reach a goal? In other words, does anyone go to the Colorado River seeking adventure while knowing they are going to die doing it?

The "River of Life" includes suffering which serves an important purpose.

So our purpose for returning to earth is to learn important lessons of love, to clean up the mess we left from previous lives, and to attain soul growth through the evolution of body and soul. People who choose to be born into a life of extreme suffering through handicaps, have decided to attain greater soul growth in a single lifetime than most people. There is also evidence that such people are actually more spiritually evolved than most, who have chosen a difficult life in order to also teach and help others attain soul growth. Even in the Bible, this principle can be found. When the disciples asked Jesus why a man is born blind, his answer was to glorify God. I have found this principle in near-death experiences as well.

Here are some examples:

"I wanted to talk with Jesus. I had a very important question to ask him. A beam of light, different from yet similar to the first one, covered me. I knew this light was Christ. I leaned against it for one moment and then asked my question. "Dear Jesus, is it true that you gave me this heart condition so that I would have a cross to carry like you did?" (Sister Agnes, my sixth-grade teacher, had told me that my heart condition was my cross to bear from Christ.) I heard the voice of Christ vibrate through me as he said, "No, this heart condition of yours is not a cross from me for you to bear. This heart condition is a challenge to help you grow and stay compassionate. Now, go back." (Lynn)

"Jesus was pleading my case. There was no conflict or argument here; Jesus' understanding was accepted without dispute because he had all the facts. He was the perfect judge. He knew precisely where I stood in relation to my need for mercy and the universe's need for justice. Now I could see that all the suffering in my mortal life would be temporary, and that it was actually for my good. Our sufferings on earth need not be futile. Out of the most tragic of circumstances springs human growth." (Angie Fenimore)

"Telepathically, he [Jesus] communicates to her: 'Isn't it wonderful? Everything is beautiful here, and it fits together. And you'll find that. But you can't stay here now. It's not your time to be here yet and you have to go back.' Vicki reacts, understandably enough, with extreme disappointment and protests vehemently, 'No, I want to stay with you.' But the Being reassures her that she will come back, but for now, she 'has to go back and learn and teach more about loving and forgiving.'" (Vicki Umipeg)

"When I was 7 years old I had an NDE as a result of measles complicated with encephalitis that resulted in a vicious high fever of 108 degrees, resulting going into a 3 day coma. I am deaf, and during the NDE experience I saw a white being and said I didn't want to go back to earth because facing a lifetime of deafness was too hard for me. The being talked me out of it and said there would be many rewards for me on the earthly realm. So I went back! The rewards did happen and continues on. I still face many difficult challenges and obstacles on a daily basis though." (Mary Ellen)

When Sandra asked why she could not take all the knowledge back with her, she was told that it would result in her appearing and being considered "abnormal" to the rest of society. She then realized that people such as the mentally retarded are special people who know much more than they are able to express. Hardships are necessary for the growth of our soul. (Sandra Rogers)

"The angel (I don't know what else to call her) said that life is an endless cycle of improvements and humans are not perfect yet. She said that most people have this secret revealed to them when they die, but that handicapped children often know this and endure their problems without complaining because they know that their burdens will pass. Some of these children, she said, have even been given the challenge of teaching the rest of us how to love. 'It stretches our own humanity to love a child who is less than perfect,' said the angel. 'And that is an important lesson for us.'" (Dr. Frank Oski)

"Between lives, with the great knowledge of our oversouls, we choose the next life we are going to live and how much karma we are going to meet and settle. For example, if you abused animals, or people, in one life your oversoul would probably cause you to reincarnate into a situation where you'd get abused to make you realize the misery you've caused others." (Arthur Yensen)

"All the suffering in our lives is actually for our good. Out of the most tragic of circumstances springs human growth." (Angie Fenimore)

"Souls who choose to be born mentally retarded are special souls who have retained more than a normal amount of their pre-birth memories and who know much more than they are able to express. Such hardships are necessary for soul growth." (Sandra Rogers)

"Souls choose to be born with physical disabilities for the purpose of soul growth and to stay compassionate." (Lynn)

"Some parents lose a child tragically in an accident. That child was fulfilling his or her mission. The parent was fulfilling his or her mission also. The parents are in that circumstance to learn a lesson. Maybe the lesson was patience, love, acceptance, understanding, or comfort of others. It can be a number of things." (George Anderson)

"God never gives us more challenges in life than we can handle. Rather than jeopardize our spiritual progression or cause more suffering than can be endured, God will bring us home where we can continue progressing." (RaNelle Wallace)

Some people decide to be born into favorable conditions and some people decide to be born into unfavorable conditions. The choice has to do with satisfying divine justice and karma. (Edgar Cayce)

"We choose the life we are going to live and how much karma we are going to meet and settle." (Arthur Yensen)

"We are born to face trials and gain the experience of a physical life." (RaNelle Wallace)

"Life's supposed to be hard. We can't skip over the hard parts. We must earn what we receive." (Angie Fenimore)

Howard Storm was given the following insights from beings of light after his life review when he was fearful of returning to earth life and afraid he would make mistakes again:

"Mistakes are an acceptable part of being human. We are here to make all the mistakes we want because it is through our mistakes that we learn. As long as we try to do what we know to be right, we will be on the right path. If we make a mistake, we should fully recognize it as a mistake, then put it behind us and simply try not to make the same mistake again. The important thing is to try our best, keep our standards of goodness and truth, and not compromise them to win people's approval. God loves us just the way we are, mistakes and all. When we make a mistake, we should ask for forgiveness. After that, it would be an insult if we don't accept that we are forgiven. We shouldn't continue going around with a sense of guilt, and we should try not to repeat our mistakes. We should learn from our mistakes. God wants us to do what we want to do. That means making choices - and there isn't necessarily any right choice. There is a spectrum of possibilities, and we should make the best choice from those possibilities. If we do that, we will receive help from the Other Side." (Howard Storm)

"Destructive earth changes are a reflection of all the social upheaval and violence happening all over the world at the moment." (Margot Grey)

"Environmentalists often refuse to interfere with nature so that evolution can continue unabated. This is the same reason why God does not interfere with our evolution." (Dannion Brinkley)

"God made a promise not to intervene in our lives unless asked." (Betty Eadie)

God does nothing to curb human freedom. However humans act, it is within God's reality. By whatever path, humans return to God. (Edgar Cayce)

"We progress at our own rate to reach the light. If we do things that take us away from the light, then we are perpetuating our time here." (Amber Wells)

"It is best to kick our bad habits while in the world. It is easier while in physical form to break those shackles than it is to undo them on the other side, where no temptations are put in our way. There is no reward for behaving correctly while in spirit, because there is nothing to tempt us otherwise. The hard school is in the physical one, and it is here that we must meet and overcome the temptations. Any habit-forming pleasure, and they are endless, traps us into the cycle of rebirth over and over, until our appetites are finally put aside while we are in the flesh." (Ruth Montgomery)

"Every act of destruction of God's environment on earth multiplies into destructive forces of nature - earthquakes, floods, pestilence, nuclear destruction and nuclear waste." (Archangel Michael to Ned Dougherty)

We must also consider whether or not retaining the memory of our destiny would be beneficial?

There are other good reasons why we come here to take on suffering and death. Some religions provide good reasons:

Buddhism: In the East, the question is about "the problem of suffering. Why do good people suffer? The answer according to Buddhism is that people suffer because of their attachments to worldly desires. Every act has a consequence called karma which basically means that when we do unto others, we do unto ourselves. Karma is the process of self-realization. The goal is to become so enlightened that all our negative karma is gone and we do not need to reincarnate to take on more karma and suffering. According to Buddhists, Buddha took on suffering in order that others attain enlightenment.

Christianity: In the West, the question is about "the problem of evil". Why does God allow evil to exist? According to the Bible, Jesus suffered at the hands of the unjust because suffering leads to perfection (Hebrews 2:10). It is through suffering that our soul learns and becomes perfected. During Biblical times, people believed that all things occurred through the will and predetermination of God. According to the Bible, people in those days did not believe in "free will" or "chance" or "accidents". For example, they believed even the outcome of a toss of the dice is determined by the will of God (Prov. 16:33, Acts 1:24-26). They believed that the evil actions of human beings are a part of God's predetermined will and they are turned into goodness. The crucifixion of Christ was viewed as the worst evil that ever happened; yet, they also believed it to be God's greatest display of divine love, goodness, and forgiveness. The Bible reveals that Christ's crucifixion by evil men was planned from eternity by God (Acts 2:22-23, Acts 4:27-28). They believed evil existed only by God's permission and that God has the forces of evil under his complete control. For example, the story of Job describes how Satan's actions are in accordance with the will of God; that is, evil can only happen if God allows it to happen. In essence, the Bible reveals that nothing can thwart the will of the Almighty and this suggest that human beings do not have free will.

However, there are a multitude of near-death experiences revealing how human beings DO have a "free will" and it is a divine trait given to us by God. Our free will is then incorporated into the will of God - we are not robots.

But would having the foresight of Jesus make our situation in life any better? Such foresight would allow us to avoid suffering if we chose to do so. But consider this: If you were ever in Jesus situation, would you allow yourself to undergo the torment of crucifixion when you could chose not to? Evidently, even Jesus wrestled with this dilemma. I must admit that I would never choose to be crucified at least not in this life. Because life is a test; and because we don't know the answers beforehand; having the foresight of Jesus would not help me in this instance.

Consider what life would be like in a world where mistakes are not permitted? It should be noted here that there is anecdotal evidence from near-death experiences that heaven is such a world where mistakes are not permitted to happen. This suggests that having the ability to choose right from wrong as opposed to automatically choosing right all the time may not be so desirable after all.

NDE insights suggest that we are souls who volunteered who chose to forget our higher knowledge. We enter the world knowing we are about to enter a realm where we are ignorance of our true selves and our missions in life for the sake of a higher purpose. We chose to forget who we are, forget where we came from, forget where we are going, and forget what the journey is about so that we can accomplish a higher purpose. But why?

So why do we choose to forget our destiny? Briefly, here are some good reasons from NDE insights on why we choose to forget our destiny:

(1) To learn more effectively and faster due to the limitations that only a physical body can achieve.

(2) To focus more on physical reality in order to better complete our missions in life so that we are not so heavenly minded we are no earthly good. If we retained all of our prior knowledge, we might not bother to experience the physical life for its fulfillment - we might decide to skip the pain and thus miss the pleasure.

(3) To make decisions out of free will without being completely influenced by our higher knowledge. Any other way would be equivalent to a student being given the answers before taking a test. It is not a good way to learn.

(4) To allow us to make mistakes out of free will for the purpose of learning and growing.

(5) To appreciate, benefit, and learn all we can from our physical life by re-discovering what we knew before - now in physical ways. Through a physical life we must re-discover how to return to God. And it is not enough to re-discover these things, we must incorporate this knowledge into our daily activities. We must make an effort to remember and find that our true selves are spirit and our spirits are one with God.

(6) To be able to succeed as a normal human beings to advance our spirits. If we retained all our pre-birth knowledge, we would seem abnormal to the rest of society.

(7) To do everything humanly possible to fulfill our missions for humanity and God.

(8) To make the most of the human experience for ourselves and God. We are spirit beings having a human experience. When we return to spirit, everyone benefits from our human experience.

(9) To prevent unpleasant and harmful past-life memories from completely influencing our lives. Imagine having a past-life memory of being Adolf Hitler. Such a past-life memory would make it very difficult to function with these memories and would seriously impede the opportunities to correct the past-life mistake of being Hitler.

(10) To help God create a human heaven on earth which only humans can build with the help of the spirit of unconditional love.

So when we are outside of our physical bodies - as when we are dreaming or having a near-death experience - we are a soul whose awareness expands to a point where we are able to hold on to these memories and our higher knowledge (the light). But while we are in our physical bodies and conscious, our soul mind plays a more subliminal role as our subconscious minds. Our spirit mind is even farther removed from our conscious awareness.

For millions of years, the human body has been evolving. Our bodies evolved from the earth. Our souls evolved from the stars and our experiences outside of our body. Our spirits do not evolve because as spirits we are already perfectly one with God (the Whole).

But at this point in history, our bodies and minds have not yet evolved to the point where we are fully "awake" as human beings. That is, humanity in general has not yet brought their higher minds fully into their conscious minds. This is evident from what near-death experiencers are telling us from the higher knowledge they learn about during their NDE. This is evident from the mystical traditions found in many ancient religions. This is also becoming evident from quantum physics. As scientists understand the universe more and more, the more they learn how reality is all in the mind.

I am convinced that until we as humans evolve into a world of beings who can walk on water and love unconditionally, we will continue to come to this physical realm. It may be as simple as that. Therefore, part of our mission is to bring this higher knowledge we have known before we were born and incorporate it into our lives. Then we will no longer be the cave men and women we are trying to evolve away from.

NDE insights reveal we come here and choose to forget our higher knowledge so we can learn more effectively and faster due to the limitations that only a physical body can achieve. We choose to forget so we can focus more on physical reality and complete our missions in life better. We choose to forget because we don't want to be so heavenly minded that we are no earthly good. If we retained all of our prior knowledge, we may try to avoid the pain, thereby avoiding any gain. We choose to forget so that we can make decisions out of free will without being completely influenced by our higher knowledge. Any other way would be equivalent to a student being given the answers before taking a test. It is not a good way to learn.

We choose to forget because it allows us to make mistakes out of free will for the purpose of learning and growing. Forgetting our higher knowledge helps us to appreciate, benefit, and learn all we can from our physical life through re-discovering this higher knowledge - now in physical ways. Through forgetting our higher knowledge, we can understand physical life better by re-discovering how to return to God. And re-discovering these things is not enough. We must incorporate and embody this knowledge into our daily activities. It helps us to make an effort to remember these things and re-discover our true selves as spiritual beings and that our spirits are one with God.

We forget our higher knowledge so that we are able to succeed as normal human beings advancing our spirits. If we retained all our pre-birth knowledge, we would seem abnormal to the rest of society. But souls do assume bodies that are retarded or crippled because they have decided to assume some of this higher knowledge in order to teach those around them lessons in love. We forget who we are because we want to do everything humanly possible to fulfill our missions for humanity and God. We forget these things so we can make the most of the human experience for ourselves and God. We are spirits having a human experience. When we return to spirit, everyone benefits from our human experience.

We also forget who were are to prevent unpleasant and harmful past-life memories from completely influencing our lives. Imagine having a past-life memory of being Adolf Hitler. Such a past-life memory would make it very difficult to function with these memories and would seriously impede the opportunities to correct the past-life mistakes of being Hitler. We forget because we want to help God create a human heaven on earth which only humans can build with the help of the spirit of unconditional love.

Here are more NDE insights on this:

"We had to take a vow not to remember anything. Then it had to pass through a gray misty-looking curtain. The reason is for us to learn more effectively and faster. The most important reason for us coming to earth is to either learn or teach. Most times both. All the bad things we go through here is either for our own learning or someone else's." (Darlene Holman)

When planning our life before birth, we do not deal with the details. Instead, we have before us our relationships to others and to situations. But some people have squandered their opportunities to such a degree that they are not completely free in their choices. (Edgar Cayce)

"We mustn't wait to find our heaven in the clouds. We must find it here because it exists here and will be whatever we make it and whatever we are willing to accept of it." (Tina)

"If we were born with our pre-birth knowledge intact, our resulting choices would be predictable and would be a violation of our free will. Free will is a highly important power given to us by God. Almost all of our choices must be made according to it." (Hal)

"We have chosen to forget most of our knowledge in order to come to earth and have human experiences." (Laurelynn Martin)

David Goines had these wonderful insights from his NDE: "Humans have a mental and spirit body. Before going through the veil, we chose our own physical body. We must forget these memories because in order to experience a physical life, we must experience the physical things, be physically challenged, make choices of free will, and make mistakes so that we can learn from them in ways that only a physical life could impart. If we retained all of our prior knowledge, we might not bother to experience the physical life for its fulfillment - we might decide to skip the pain and thus miss the pleasure. We promised God that upon accepting the opportunity, challenges and responsibility of a physical life, we would make the most of this opportunity for ourselves and God, return to God with the knowledge and experience gained so that God will be enhanced by our experience. The reason we need to experience a separation of our total reality when we took on a physical body is because in order for us to appreciate, benefit, and learn all we can from our physical life, we must re-discover what we knew before - in physical ways. Through our physical life we must discover how to return to God. By the good that we do to each other here, by the ways we improve our minds, and by the ways that we learn to cope with a physical body and physical life, we earn our right of safe passage back to God; and in doing so, we honor God. It is God's love that sends us on the journey and it is our love for God that will allow us to return to God's loving arms." (David Goines)

So, should we know our higher purpose within the "River of Life?" Do we really want to know what our higher purpose in life is? Consider what Dr. George Rodonaia and Dr. P.M.H. Atwater have to say about it:

"The point is to live the questions now, and perhaps without knowing it, someday we will live into the answers. Live the questions and the universe will open up its eyes to you." (Dr. George Rodonaia)

"The drama of creation is unbounded and is neither limited by our perception of it, nor by our ability or inability to comprehend it. This drama is as stupendous as it is terrifying, as awesome as it is wonderful, as miraculous as it is mysterious, as beautiful as it is the ultimate act of all-consuming love. To witness even a glimpse of such glory, to know the Real Truth of it, leaves a mark so deep and so profound you are forever uplifted and transformed." (P.M.H. Atwater)

According to information obtained from the human experience with the universe in the realms of science, religion, metaphysics, and near-death experiences, the universe is waiting right now for us to open our eyes and see the answer that will help us attain our goals on the River of Life. From what I can gather, the story resembles a modified version of the parable of the prodigal son who left his father to experience life on his own and to discover new worlds.

As a soul, we come to this world to have a life experience as a human being. Everyone has been doing this for millions of years. We are bringing God into this garden called earth. We are bringing light into darkness and peace into chaos. We come to help our loved ones within our soul group and humanity in general evolve and learn lessons that only a human experience can give.

Millions of years ago, the human experience began when souls, like pilgrims and prodigals, began exploring the universe. We came to earth and began influencing and eventually inhabiting the bodies of a particular species of humanoid. Through evolution we influenced these creatures to come out of the trees create societies. Throughout the course of human evolution, as a soul, we could come here and have a human experience, fulfill whatever mission we came to do, then death would free us to return as a soul back to where we came from which is our true home in non-physical realms.

Living in this world is analogous to experiencing on-the-job training. We come here to attain growth as a soul (an individualized aspect of spirit). As a spirit, we are already perfectly one with God. But with every human body and life we experienced on earth over the millennia, we create a different soul body to be the vehicle for our spirit as it experiences the world in the vehicle of a human body. At the physical level, our body is conscious. At the soul level, our mind is subconscious. At the spirit level, we are superconscious. We are multi-dimensional and exist in three different worlds at the same time. There are many abodes and many dimensions. We are working our way back up "Jacob's ladder" of success toward the goal of perfected individuality as a soul to go along with our already perfect Wholeness as a spirit. We are evolving into an individualized version of the Whole which is "God" consciousness.

As a human being, we seem like such a small creation in an infinite universe, but this is really only an illusion. As individuals, we are the human and soul part of God. We are extensions of thought in the Mind of God (the collective Whole). We are bringing this higher universal consciousness into this tiny world called earth while at the same time we are developing individual consciousness. We are the Mind of God becoming human. We are the body, mind and spirit of God evolving into a perfect individual-divine unity. We have examples of this human-divine unity in the lives of Jesus and Buddha and others. The goal in human evolution is for us to attain a human-divine consciousness which can overcome the limitations of the body, walk on water if we choose, or even live forever on this planet as a human if we choose to. We are powerful spiritual beings with a oneness of the Whole and the wholeness of the One. On a higher level, we are gods just as Jesus said. This is another way of saying we are "godlings" or "children." We are growing up to be like our Parents. The core of our being, our spirit, is perfect love and perfect "God consciousness." We travel this River of Life to bring the "kingdom of God" to this world.

Now we can understand how the "River of Life" is the "River of God-realization."

When Mellen-Thomas Benedict entered into the light during his NDE, the light responded to him by saying: "This is the RIVER OF LIFE. Drink of this manna water to your heart's content."

When he did, he said it was ecstatic. He asked the light to see the whole universe and beyond. The light told him that he could "go with the Stream." He was then carried through the light at the end of the tunnel. While in the light, Mellen-Thomas learned our higher purpose. Here are some of his and other NDE experiencers insights:

"Creation is God exploring God's Self through every way imaginable, in an ongoing, infinite exploration through every one of us. Through every piece of hair on your head, through every leaf on every tree, through every atom, God is exploring God's Self.

"The interesting point was that I went into the void, I came back with this understanding that God is not there. God is here. That's what it is all about. So this constant search of the human race to go out and find God ... God gave everything to us, everything is here - this is where it's at. And what we are into now is God's exploration of God through us. People are so busy trying to become God that they ought to realize that we are already God and God is becoming us. That's what it is really about.

"In this expanded state, I discovered that creation is about absolute pure consciousness, or God, coming into the experience of life as we know it." (Mellen-Thomas Benedict)

Here are more insights into this subject:

"Through our physical life we must discover how to return to God. By the good that we do to each other here, by the ways we improve our minds, and by the ways that we learn to cope with a physical body and physical life, we earn our right of safe passage back to God; and in doing so, we honor God. It is God's love that sends us on the journey and it is our love for God that will allow us to return to God's loving arms." (David Goines)

"Our life in this world is a preparation for a fuller, freer and richer spirit world. It can be compared to life in the womb being a preparation for a fuller, freer and richer existence in the physical world." (Nora Spurgin)

"The conquering of self is truly greater than were one to conquer many worlds." (Edgar Cayce)

"Everyone who passes through this world must learn their final lessons in this world, where our free will is called into play in a fashion different from existence in other realms of reality." (Edgar Cayce)

"If we choose to clean up the mess we create on earth, we will not contribute to the mess of others and this will contribute to the healing of the earth. Reincarnation is the process which allows us to return to earth to "clean up our mess." (David Oakford)

"Everyone's gain or loss affects everyone else to some degree because we are all connected. (Dr. P.M.H. Atwater)

"In order to return to God we have to come to ourselves and realize that our lower nature is leading us down the road of materialism and of living only for ourselves. This causes us to turn away from God and our divine destiny. This caused us to forget who we are and it caused our spiritual death." (Dr. George Ritchie)

Now let's turn our attention to our life before birth into the River of Life. There are a number of good reasons why people believe they have lived before they were born. Here is a list of them:

(1) During a near-death experience, people such as Betty Eadie have received forgotten memories of a life in heaven before they were born. Such memories have been called "pre-birth" memories. Other experiencers have also re-remembered such memories during an NDE.

(2) Some experiencers, such as RaNelle Wallace and Plato's account of the NDE of Er, see people in heaven who are yet to be born during an NDE. Sometimes people are even seen preparing for being born into the world.

(3) A relatively small number of people, such as Roy Mills, were permitted to retain vivid pre-birth memories when they were born. As such people grow older, they usually forget these memories.

(4) Some people, such as Jeffrey Keene, are inspired by their day-to-day life experience to remember past-life memories. In Jeffrey Keene's case, he has very compelling circumstantial evidence identifying him as a particular individual in history. People can also recover past-life memories through such means as near-death experiences, hypnosis, meditation, hallucinogens, and dreams, just to name a few.

(5) The eastern religions of Buddhism and Hinduism teach reincarnation. In ancient times, Christianity and Judaism held a belief in reincarnation. In such countries were these religions are dominant, very young children have vivid memories of past-lives. There is evidence that such memories appear in young children born in the West as well; but, because reincarnation is generally considered an alien concept in western society, young

children are often told these memories are imaginary and that they are encouraged to not entertain these thoughts and feelings. As they grow up, these thoughts and feelings are forgotten.

(6) There exists compelling circumstantial evidence concerning the possible reincarnation of some individuals such as President Kennedy and Jeffrey Keene.

And there are a multitude of rivers to choose from because we choose our destiny. Before we were born, we had an opportunity to see all the possibilities for our life. Using an analogy, it is like standing on a mountain top looking at a large river below. We saw all the possibilities like a person can see all the branches and tributaries of the river. Our mission is to float this "river" of life. All the branches (opportunities) eventually return to the river (our mission) and to the sea (God). Returning to the sea is predestined, but how we decide to float the river it is based on our own free will.

"Everyone assisted in planning the conditions on earth, including the laws of mortality which would govern us. These included the laws of physics as we know them, the limitations of our bodies, and spiritual powers that we would be able to access." (Betty Eadie)

"A heavenly process exists in the spirit realm that is designed to help us choose our destiny." (Dr. Allen Kellehear)

The heavenly process determines the number of destinies a soul can choose from. This process is an astrological process. This astrological process is connected to the various realms of the afterlife. (Edgar Cayce)

A cosmic matrix of rainbow light exists around the earth. This matrix provides souls with a number of earthly destinies from which to choose from. Then, before we are born into the world, we are required to forget these memories. (Plato)

"We choose the life we are going to live and how much karma we are going to meet and settle." (Arthur Yensen)

"Before we were born, we choose our stations in life based upon the objectives of completing our missions." (Betty Eadie)

"We choose which body we to enter before birth." (Sandra Rogers)

When planning our life before birth, we do not deal with the details. Instead, we have before us our relationships to others and to situations. But some people have squandered their opportunities to such a degree that they are not completely free in their choices. (Edgar Cayce)

"Because our spirits remember the plan we chose for this life, we are often drawn to people or situations that impact us in important ways. This is often the force behind 'chance' encounters. I was told there are no coincidences. However, making the most of these opportunities is up to us as we exercise our free will." (Betty Eadie)

According to Dr. Michael Newton, author of Journey of Souls, the decision to be born into this physical world is not an easy one. Our souls left a world of total wisdom, where they exist in a blissful state of freedom, for the physical and mental demands of a physical body. Dr. Newton writes:

The rejuvenation of our energy and personal assessment of our soul takes longer for some souls than others, but eventually the soul is motivated to start the process of being born. While our spiritual environment is hard to leave, as souls we also remember the physical pleasures of life on earth with fondness and even nostalgia. We feel the pull of having a physical expression for our identity.

Training sessions with our counselors and peer groups have provided a collaborative spiritual effort to prepare us for life in the flesh. Our soul takes action based upon three primary decisions:

(1) Am I ready for a new physical life?

(2) What specific lessons do I want to undertake to advance my learning and development?

(3) Where should I go, and who shall I be in my life for the best opportunity to work on my goals?

Once the decision has been made, we are directed to the place of life selection. We then consider when and where we want to go on earth before making a decision on whoever we will be in life. We then entered a heavenly building which resembles a movie theater to allow us to see ourselves in the future, playing different roles in various settings. In this place of life selection, our souls preview the life span of more than one human being within the same time cycle. When we leave this area, most souls are inclined toward one leading candidate presented to us for soul occupation. However, our spiritual advisors give us ample opportunity to reflect upon all we have seen in the future before making a final decision.

After we completed our consultations with guides and peers about the many physical and psychological ramifications of entering the physical realm, the decision to come was made. Afterward, we underwent a significant amount of preparation in a place called the recognition class. This heavenly class is where we prepare ourselves for entry into the physical realm in a manner that is similar to cramming for a final exam.

One of the last requirements before being born is that we went before the Council of Elders. The Elders reinforce the significance of our goals for life. Once we were ready for entering the physical realm, we were like battle-hardened veterans girding ourselves for combat. This was our last chance for us to enjoy the omniscience of knowing just who we are before we adapt to a physical body. (Dr. Michael Newton)

"We are given teachings, training, and anything we need to help us prepare for entering the physical realm. We choose our own pace and need not be hurried through the realms of the next dimensions. It may take what might feel like eons of time before our soul knows what is best for our development while in the flesh." (Betty Bethards)

"As part of our training, we are allowed to watch people on earth to see how they handle situations in life. When we are ready, we can choose to be shown our past lives. If we don't believe in reincarnation it may take a long period of time before we are able to deal with this. Reviewing our past lives helps us recognize all the strengths we have built and all the karmic debts we have created which must be dissolved." (Betty Bethards)

"After integrating the knowledge learned from our past lives, we have reached a state of total objectivity. We feel no remorse or condemnation, but see it as merely a review of why situations occurred and had to be worked through." (Betty Bethards)

When we made the decision to enter the physical realm for soul growth, we first planned with the members of our soul family the karmic considerations because our relationship with them is vital to what we desired to accomplish in earthly life. (Edgar Cayce)

There was a vast amount of planning that was done before we were born. When planning for entering into the physical realm, we do not have physical details before us. Instead we have before us relationships to others, to situations, and to those forces which have prepared us. (Edgar Cayce)

"God not only prepares us to do his will, he also gives us all that we need to do it. He sends to our path the right people when we need them, whether we realize it or not." (Betty Eadie)

In our decision-making process about the life we currently lead, we dealt largely with two factors:

(1) We worked with our motivation for entering, then with the potential we had for entering.

(2) The rest was left for the great adventure of life. (Edgar Cayce)

"Any habit-forming pleasure can trap them into the cycle of reincarnation over and over, until their appetites are finally put aside while they are in the flesh. This is a lesson for those souls who would like to break the cycle of reincarnation." (Ruth Montgomery)

So the evidence shows that we are all on a mission from God. Information gleaned from many near-death accounts provides us with a wealth of information concerning concepts such as destiny, predestination, free will, missions and how they relate to our lives. Here are some of them:

The purpose for our earth lives includes the opportunity to pay and receive karmic debts from family members. We plan to connect once again with members of our soul family on earth because of our love for them. (Edgar Cayce)

"Our stations in life are based upon the objectives of completing our missions. We bonded with family and friends to help us in completing them." (Betty Eadie)

"We are here to learn. Our mission in life has to do with love." (Kimberly Clark Sharp)

"The fact that we are born here shows that we are on the path to developing an individual consciousness. Ultimately, we will find God within ourselves because this is our true identity." (Mellen-Thomas Benedict)

"If we were born with our pre-birth knowledge intact, our resulting choices would be predictable and would be a violation of our free will. Free will is a highly important power given to us by God. Almost all of our choices must be made according to it." (Hal)

"Our missions mainly have to do with love, but the purpose of life is also to experience joy, gain spiritual understanding and self-awareness, play with the joyful abandon of a child, absorb ourselves in the delight of each moment, let go of obligation and duty, and live for the pure joy of being." (Jan Price)

LIFE

The NDE reveals our universe to be merely one dimension out of many. The universe is a part of a vast university of discovery where we come to learn important lessons for soul growth. Experiencers learn from their experience this profound fact: life is God. Everything of which life consists is God. To know that life is God, is to know how very special life is. We must be very careful how we treat things in life because how we treat things in life is how we treat God. Do we destroy life or do we respect it? Do we nurture life or do we abuse it? Do we value life or do we take it for granted?

The following are insights from many NDEs concerning life and our relation to it.

"The reason we are here in this physical world is for soul growth. This physical world is the ideal place for this. Spiritual growth in the spirit realms is more difficult. The reason is that the influence of our physical bodies gives us the opportunity for a full range of love (a child's love, marital love, and parental love) which is ideally available here. Love that is misused or misdirected is best corrected in the here. In this physical world, there is the full range of physical and spiritual senses with which to act and communicate." (Nora Spurgin)

"Our behavior on earth provides a teaching ground for those in the spirit world." (Betty Bethards)

"Life in this world exists for us to test our ideals and learn from them. Learning our lessons here in the physical world is the fastest way to learn." (David Oakford)

"As long as we have life here, we are learning, our spirits are growing, and we are coming closer to the divine, even by the things we suffer. We may not always know what to do in our lives, we may be troubled and in pain, but be assured, as long as we are here, we are growing." (Betty Eadie)

"Life in this world is the ultimate experience for our souls. It is ultimate because our souls evolve faster here than anywhere else. The lessons we need to learn are difficult to learn without having a physical form." (David Oakford)

"Trouble is nature's way of teaching lessons that won't be learned otherwise. If we learn from the troubles of others, we can avoid most of our own." (Arthur Yensen)

"Life in this world is a place for us to overcome certain weaknesses by applying ourselves to see that those weaknesses are truly overcome. Here we can learn for certain whether we have really changed." (Edgar Cayce)

"Life is a boot camp and school for our soul's spiritual education, and as such, it's tough." (Karen Brannon)

"This world is only a temporary place for our schooling. Our true permanent home is the spiritual universe." (Betty Eadie)

"This world is only one realm of learning; there are many." (Sandra Rogers)

"When we die, we will realize that we have been living behind a veil our whole lives. The veil will be lifted and the floodlights will shine on us. Everything in life is really veiled spirit. We are literally on display our whole lives. Every thought, word, and deed has been recorded since birth and will be fully exposed. Everything we have ever done in secret will be brought out into the light for review in front of God and all the heavenly hosts. Our entire life is one huge test and we will be graded on everything." (Daniel Rosenblit)

"Life is a test. If you pass the test you'll look back upon them as good experiences." (Peace Pilgrim)

"None of us will fully fathom the great truths of life until we finally unite with eternity at death. But occasionally we get glimpses of the answer here in the world and that alone can be enough." (Dr. George Rodonaia)

"The highest spiritual values of life can come from the study of death." (Elisabeth Kubler-Ross)

"The universe runs according to a perfect plan. All the so-called injustices we see in life really has no meaning. The perfect plan is working itself out in its perfection." (Jayne Smith)

"Life in this world is like a rigged roulette wheel in a casino. As much as we try, we can never be able to fully satisfy our selfish desires. It's virtually impossible." (Daniel Rosenblit)

"Nothing in life or death is an accident." (Lynnclaire Dennis)

"There are no accidents in the universe. Everything that happens in life has a purpose." (George Anderson)

"From the vantage point of the spirit world, there is no problem or disharmony on earth that will not be corrected." (Margaret Tweddell)

"Life is about people, not pursuits." (Laurelynn Martin)

"The most important thing in life is love." (Dr. Raymond Moody)

"Anyone who has had such an experience of God, who has felt such a profound sense of connection with reality, knows that there is only one truly significant work to do in life, and that is love; to love nature, to love people, to love animals, to love creation itself, just because it is." (Dr. George Rodonaia)

"A life of piety without a life of love (which occurs only in this world) is not a spiritual life. Rather, it is a life of love, a life of behaving honestly and fairly in every task, from a more inward source that leads to a heavenly life. Such a life is not hard." (Emanuel Swedenborg)

"We are to leave the world a little better than we found it." (David Oakford)

"If we learn to give what we have, we will receive more. This is a spiritual law. We will be given all that we are prepared to receive." (Betty Eadie)

"The gift of life God gives us comes with a catch: We are to give the gift back." (P.M.H. Atwater)

"Half the gain in coming into earth life is merely showing up." (Edgar Cayce)

"One little girl summed up what she learned from her NDE as: 'Life is for living and the light is for later.'" (Dr. Melvin Morse's research)

"The point is to live the questions now, and perhaps without knowing it, someday we will live into the answers. Live the questions and the universe will open up its eyes to you." (Dr. George Rodonaia)

"All the suffering in our lives is actually for our good. Out of the most tragic of circumstances springs human growth." (Angie Fenimore)

"God never gives us more challenges in life than we can handle. Rather than jeopardize our spiritual progression or cause more suffering than can be endured, God will bring us home where we can continue progressing." (RaNelle Wallace)

"Life's supposed to be hard. We can't skip over the hard parts. We must earn what we receive." (Angie Fenimore)

"Our ability to accept truth, to live by it, governs our progress in the spirit, and it determines the degree of light we possess." (RaNelle Wallace)

"Our missions mainly have to do with love, but the purpose of life is also to experience joy, gain spiritual understanding and self-awareness, play with the joyful abandon of a child, absorb ourselves in the delight of each moment, let go of obligation and duty, and live for the pure joy of being." (Jan Price)

"We are sent here to live life fully, to live it abundantly, to find joy in our own creations ... to use our free will to expand and magnify our lives." (Betty Eadie)

"Life is a joyful game to be played and everything works out perfectly. Sooner, if played joyfully with love. Later, if not." (Dee Rohe)

"We mustn't wait to find our heaven in the clouds. We must find it here because it exists here and will be whatever we make it and whatever we are willing to accept of it." (Tina)

"How we lived our lives in this world determines which afterlife realm we have earned and travel to after death." (Betty Bethards)

"If we develop along the lines of unselfish love while in this world, we make it better for us when we die. It's what we are that counts!" (Arthur Yensen)

"Our life in this world is a preparation for a fuller, freer and richer spirit world. It can be compared to life in the womb being a preparation for a fuller, freer and richer existence in the physical world." (Nora Spurgin)

"Day by day we are building for eternity. Every gentle word, every generous thought, every unselfish deed will become a pillar of eternal beauty in the life to come. (Rebecca Springer)

"Our life matters and is significant in determining how far we can go into the light." (Grace Bubulka)

"The general rule of thumb is this: hellish life, hellish afterlife - heavenly life, heavenly afterlife. Death will not change a hellish life into a heavenly afterlife, nor does it change a heavenly life into a hellish afterlife." (Dr. Melvin Morse)

"If we educate ourselves as much as possible about the spirit world, it makes our transition there even better. Even if we gain the smallest impression that there is life after death, we are able to obtain enlightenment and understanding. (Nora Spurgin)

"We are preparing for death throughout our whole lives." (Edgar Cayce)

"Life in this world corresponds to our external nature handling external resources. Life in the spirit world corresponds to our internal nature handling spiritual resources." (Nora Spurgin)

"It is best to kick our bad habits while in the world. It is easier while in physical form to break those shackles than it is to undo them on the other side, where no temptations are put in our way. There is no reward for behaving correctly while in spirit, because there is nothing to tempt us otherwise. The hard school is in the physical one, and it is here that we must meet and overcome the temptations." (Ruth Montgomery)

"Our quality of life in the spirit world is directly affected our heart and activities in the physical world." (Nora Spurgin)

"Life is love is God. If you add any more to this definition then you are not making it any better." (Chuck Griswold)

"In each atom, in each corpuscle, is life. Life is what you worship as God ... and earth is only an atom in the universe of worlds." (Edgar Cayce)

"To know that life is God, is to know how very special life is. We must be very careful how we treat things in life because how we treat things in life is how we treat God. Do we destroy life or do we respect it? Do we nurture life or do we abuse it? Do we value life or do we take it for granted?" (Elsie Seachrist)

"Life tries out different shapes and then returns to where it came." (John Star)

"Creation is about absolutely Pure Consciousness coming into the experience of life." (Mellen-Thomas Benedict)

"Life is light itself." (Dr. John Jay Harper)

God is life. (1 John 5:20)

HUMANITY

Every human being is a very, very special person. One proof of this can be found in the reproductive process which led to our birth. Everyone begins life by winning a race against 40 million to 1.2 billion other sperm cells. This alone is evidence that everyone is literally one in a million. As a part of life, we are a part of God. People who have a near-death experience often realize this fact first-hand in a very profound way. There is more to humanity than meets the eye. Beyond our visual reality, there exists a higher reality where our true self resides. This reality exists within us.

The following are insights from many NDEs regarding humanity.

"From the light we have come, and to the light we all shall return." (Josiane Antonette)

"It is God's love for us that sends us on our journey and it is our love for God that allows us to return to God's loving arms again." (David Goines)

"We are all-knowing. But we have chosen to forget most of our knowledge in order to come to earth and have human experiences." (Laurelynn Martin)

"Jesus' parable of the prodigal son is the cosmic tale of each and every human being. We have all forgotten that we are children of God and that our spiritual side needs to return to God." (Dr. George Ritchie)

"We are like babies crawling around, trying to learn how to use the forces within us. They are powerful forces and are governed by laws that will protect us from ourselves. But as we grow and seek the positive all around us, even the laws themselves will be revealed. We will be given all that we are prepared to receive." (Betty Eadie)

"We are immortal and indestructible. We have always been alive, we always will be, and there is no way in this world that we can ever be lost. It is impossible for anyone to fall into a crack in the universe somewhere and never be heard from again. We are utterly safe and we have always been forever and ever." (Jayne Smith)

"Upon receiving the plan of creation, we [as spirits] sang in rejoicing and were filled with God's love. We were filled with joy as we saw the growth we would have here on earth and the joyous bonds we would create with each other." (Betty Eadie)

"Earth is not our natural home and we did not originate here. Earth is only a temporary place for our schooling and everyone has cultivated a certain degree of light (knowledge) here." (Betty Eadie)

"The reason we need to experience a separation of our total reality when we take a physical body is because in order for us to appreciate, benefit, and learn all we can from our physical life, we must re-discover what we knew before - now in physical ways. We must also discover how to return to God. By the good that we do to each other here, by the ways we improve our minds, and by the ways that we learn to cope with a physical body and physical life, we earn our right of safe passage back to God; and in so doing, we likewise honor God." (David Goines)

"We are to make the most of our opportunity for ourselves and God. We will return to God with the knowledge and experience we have gained and God is enhanced by it." (David Goines)

Our bodies evolved from the earth. Our minds evolved from the stars. Our spirits evolved from God. We are evolving into the image of God in body, mind and spirit." (Edgar Cayce)

"Humans are educated at a higher level by spirit beings who bring us into heaven. We grow and increase, and grow and increase, and shed the concerns, desires, and base animal stuff that we have been fighting much of our life. Earthly appetites melt away. It is no longer a struggle to fight them. We become who we truly are, which is part of the divine." (Rev. Howard Storm)

"Humans are immortal beings who have been alive forever. Our bodies come from an unending stream of life, going back to the Big Bang and beyond. Humans are part of a natural living system that recycles itself endlessly." (Mellen-Thomas Benedict)

"Humanity is progressing up the spiral of evolution. There is no problem, no pain, no ill, no disharmony in the whole universe that eventually will not be made into harmony." (Margaret Tweddell)

"Life is a cycle for humans to improve and become perfected." (Dr. Frank Oski)

"Humans have a potential that is so far beyond our wildest dreams. Whatever we want to be we can be. It may take a hundred lifetimes of learning but if we want it we can get it." (Darren Corlett)

"It is possible that the near-death experience is an evolutionary device to bring about a transformation in all humanity over a period of years ... By transforming ourselves we transform the world around us, and so, by stages, the whole future of humanity." (Dr. Ken Ring)

"Each person's Higher Self is connected to each other to form a single matrix around the planet which is called the Higher Self matrix. It a sacred circle of human souls existing within everyone. It is a direct connection to God that makes us all one being." (Mellen-Thomas Benedict)

"A cosmic matrix of rainbow light exists around the earth. This matrix provides souls with a number of earthly destinies from which to choose from. Then, before we are born into the world, we are required to forget these memories." (Plato)

"Everyone has a light connection to their Higher Self which is an extension of our lives. Everyone is interconnected, forming a light grid. We are all one. Our oneness is interconnected by love and this love is connected to the grid. Our love connection to each other is available for us to access." (Linda Stewart)

"Everything is united by a transparent net, or web, and each thread shines with great radiance. Everything pulses with the same luminosity a magnificent light of unparalleled brilliance." (Josiane Antonette)

"Within the light, I knew that everyone and everything is connected to the light. God is in everyone, always and forever. Within the light is the cure for all diseases." (Dr. Dianne Morrissey)

"Humans are actually different aspects of the same being. This being consists of love - the kind of love that cures, heals and regenerates. This is the core of our being. We are all beautiful in our essence, our core. We are very beautiful creations." (Mellen-Thomas Benedict)

"We all have the innate ability to heal ourselves, if only we have the desire and determination to enable this gift. Life has meaning and we are all connected. It is in finding those connections that we find the secret to good health and a long life." (Dr. Melvin Morse)

"Everyone's gain or loss affects everyone else to some degree because we are all connected." (P.M.H. Atwater)

"We are all connected and we know each other. All things are of the LOVING light." (Kathy Oros)

"We are all collectively bonded to each other while on earth, united in this one supreme purpose: to learn to love one another." (Betty Eadie)

"Humans are really children of the cosmos - not just children of this world. The deeper part of us travels the entire universe and we chose to dwell in this solar system." (Edgar Cayce)

"We affect each other because we are all a part of each other. We affect all parts of the universe because all parts of creation interweave and interrelate with all other parts. (P.M.H. Atwater)

"The fact that we are here on earth, shows that we are on the path to developing an individual consciousness that is part of the group consciousness of humanity. There are racial personality clusters, national personality clusters, municipal personality clusters, family personality clusters. Our individual identity is evolving like branches of a fractal. This is the group soul exploring in our individuality." (Mellen-Thomas Benedict)

"So the problems of individuals, groups, races, and nations, are dealt with from one lifetime to the next through a person's free will until they are solved. Then the soul is free to move on to other worlds, other solar systems, other universes, and other dimensions." (Edgar Cayce)

"No matter who we are, we are all joined under one God. Our souls are all one. All living things in the universe are connected to one another." (May Eulitt)

"There is a hierarchy in the universe that is dedicated to preserving the harmony of the universe. Humans are an integral part of this harmony." (David Oakford)

"We are multi-dimensional beings. We can access our other dimensions through lucid dreaming. This universe is God's dream." (Mellen-Thomas Benedict)

"The solar system we live in is our larger, local body. This is our local body and we are much bigger than we imagine. The solar system is our body. The earth is this great created being that we are, and we are the part of it that knows that it is." (Mellen-Thomas Benedict)

"The earth, the sun, the moon, the darkness, the light, the planets, and all forms of life plants, rocks, animals, people are interconnected; they come from the same source of light." (Josiane Antonette)

Everyone is influenced by their body and, in many ways, the influence of the body determines a person's level of spiritual development. Our body is a temple for the divine spirit. We can find God within us by awakening the spiritual centers of our body to higher spiritual dimensions and realms. (Edgar Cayce)

"There is no evil in any human soul. We seek love to sustain us and it is the lack of love that distorts people. We were designed by God to self-correct, just like the rest of the universe. No one is lost because everyone is already 'saved.'" (Mellen-Thomas Benedict)

Howard Storm was given the following insights from beings of light after his life review when he was fearful of returning to earth life and afraid he would make mistakes again: "Mistakes are an acceptable part of being human. We are here to make all the mistakes we want because it is through our mistakes that we learn. As long as we try to do what we know to be right, we will be on the right path. If we make a mistake, we should fully recognize it as a mistake, then put it behind us and simply try not to make the same mistake again. The important thing is to try our best, keep our standards of goodness and truth, and not compromise them to win people's approval. God loves us just the way we are, mistakes and all. When we make a mistake, we should ask for forgiveness. After that, it would be an insult if we don't accept that we are forgiven. We shouldn't continue going around with a sense of guilt, and we should try not to repeat our mistakes. We should learn from our mistakes. God wants us to do what we want to do. That means making choices - and there isn't necessarily any right choice. There is a spectrum of possibilities, and we should make the best choice from those possibilities. If we do that, we will receive help from the Other Side." (Rev. Howard Storm)

"God knew we would make mistakes. Life is all about mistakes. It is constant change and growth. Our greatest challenges in life will one day be known to us as our greatest teachers." (Betty Eadie)

"Humanity saves, redeems and heals themselves. We always have and we always will." (Mellen-Thomas Benedict)

"The more we exercised our individual consciousness and free will for self-interest, self-gratification, self-glorification, and self-consciousness, the more we heightened our sense of self apart from the Whole." (Edgar Cayce)

"The greatest enemy we can face is ourselves." (George Anderson)

"The conquering of self is truly greater than were one to conquer many worlds." (Edgar Cayce)

"Within every human being is perfect love. That is our core - this love, this perfection, this God-ness." (Jayne Smith)

"God is within us and we are an inseparable part of God. We are perfect love as a creation of God. We and God are one - Creator and created." (Linda Stewart)

"We must stop trying to become God because God is becoming us." (Mellen-Thomas Benedict)

"Humans are the true essence of God. We are God creating God. God lives within us and through us. God experiences it all, right along with us." (Sherry Gideon)

"We were conceived in love spiritually, and love is the center of our beings. It is the energy of our souls, the spark of our divine nature. Being made of love, we cleave to it and seek it in all that we do. When we do not have it, or when we have lost it, we grieve. Its presence or absence colors our every action. It is life. It is happiness. It is salvation itself." (Betty Eadie)

"We are the human part of God." (Mellen-Thomas Benedict)

"The human soul has the same power as God. We have exactly the same intensive power as God. We have the same potential as God within the human condition. The oneness of the Whole, or the wholeness of the One, being God, is ultimately powerful and unconditional love." (Thomas Sawyer)

"God is expanding through us." (Mellen-Thomas Benedict)

"We call ourselves children of God and co-creators made in the image of God. But it would be closer to the truth if we called ourselves extensions of God or thoughts in the Mind of God." (P.M.H. Atwater)

"We are an individualized portion of God who has attained a perfect oneness with God - which is also our goal." (Arthur Yensen)

"God is exploring Self through us in an infinite Dance of Life by every way imaginable, in an ongoing exploration through every one of us, through every piece of hair on our head, through every leaf on every tree, through every atom." (Mellen-Thomas Benedict)

"The greatest gift we were ever given was the free will to create our own reality and experience the biggest, grandest version of ourselves." (Sherry Gideon)

"God made a promise not to intervene in our lives unless asked." (Betty Eadie)

"God does nothing to curb human freedom. However humans act, it is within God's reality. By whatever path, humans return to God." (Edgar Cayce)

"We are supposed to do whatever we want to do. That means making choices where there isn't necessarily any right choice. There exists a spectrum of possibilities, and we should make the best choice we can from these possibilities. If we do that, we will receive help from above." (Rev. Howard Storm)

"An important purpose for mortality is to help us learn to recognize and to choose the positive even though the negative more fully surrounds us. We make this choice consciously or unconsciously in every moment of the day, and these millions of tiny choices create the foundation of our identity. We are what we think. We are what we say, what we do, what we fill our lives with. Ultimately, every being creates himself by these countless, crucial choices." (Betty Eadie)

"The freedom of one person is enough to change the whole universe." (David Oakford)

"Everyone's life is shaped to some extent by their karma. But karma is not greater than free will because with free will, anything is possible." (Edgar Cayce)

"Our ability to accept truth, to live by it, governs our progress in the spirit, and it determines the degree of light we possess. Nobody forces light and truth upon us, and nobody takes it away unless we let them." (RaNelle Wallace)

"The hell fire of purification mentioned in many traditions is symbolic of the divine energy that dwells within the seven chakras of human beings. The struggle between our higher and lower selves grows until finally the destructive elements are completely overcome." (Betty Bethards)

"Our body is constantly in opposition to our spirit. The flesh is weak but persistent. Although the spirit must battle constantly to overcome the flesh, and this battle strengthens the spirit's influence over the body." (Betty Eadie)

"In order to return to God we have to come to ourselves and realize that our lower nature is leading us down the road of materialism and of living only for ourselves. This causes us to turn away from God and our divine destiny. This caused us to forget who we are and it caused our spiritual death." (Dr. George Ritchie)

"Our Father in Heaven created man in his own image -- which is that of a perfect and multifaceted man. Women, too, are in the image of God and are multifaceted. Women's bodies are co-creators of mortal life, and this makes us Godlike in a literal sense. In heaven, women and men are perfectly balanced in their roles and are equal. Standing side by side, they are perfect complements of each other." (Betty Eadie)

"During my experience, I learned that there are two parts to every person. They can be described in various ways: male and female, intellectual and emotional, protective and nurturing, right brain and left brain. Often we go through life being one way or the other, but we can learn to balance both parts. Being off balance, too far one way or the other, keeps the spirit away from where it needs to be to achieve its greatest growth." (Betty Eadie)

"Our individual actions and thoughts make an impact on the Universal Mind - the Whole." (Edgar Cayce)

"The small inner voice in our thoughts is the voice of God." (Sandra Rogers)

"God is aware of the consciousness of every person." (Edgar Cayce)

"Day by day we are building for eternity, every gentle word, every generous thought, every unselfish deed will become a pillar of eternal beauty in the life to come." (Rebecca Springer)

"Our thoughts in this world become real things in the spirit world." (Edgar Cayce)

"There is power in our thoughts. We create our own surroundings by the thoughts we think. Physically, this may take a period of time, but spiritually it is instantaneous. If we understood the power of our thoughts, we would guard them more closely. If we understood the awesome power of our words, we would prefer silence to almost anything negative. In our thoughts and words we create our own weaknesses and our own strengths. Our limitations and joys begin in our hearts." (Betty Eadie)

"Truth comes to us in stages. As we assimilate and understand a layer, the next layer is peeled away for us to ruminate." (Lauren Zimmerman)

"We are given knowledge only as we are ready to receive it." (Betty Bethards)

"We must be ready to accept the possibility that there is a limitless range of awareness that can expand beyond our egos and range of everything we have learned, beyond your notions of space and time, beyond the differences which usually separate people from each other and from the world around them." (Dr. Timothy Leary)

"We are made up of three different levels of consciousness: mind, soul and spirit. Our conscious mind is our personality. Our subconscious mind is our soul. Our superconscious mind is our spirit. When we "awaken" our superconscious mind, we attain at-one-ment with God." (Edgar Cayce)

RELIGION

Heaven is not about religious beliefs, but about spiritual actions. It is not true, as some people believe, that we get to heaven by giving verbal assent to belief in God. It is love, not religious doctrines, that creates spiritual growth. Religions are cultural institutions but love is universal. Those religions which claim superiority over other religions or exclude people for various reasons go against God's law to love others as we love ourselves. Although religion, in itself, is not important to God, all religions are necessary because there are people who need what they teach. For this reason, all religions are precious in the sight of God. All religions refer to the same God. All religions are different ways of trying to describe the same God. After death, if you insist upon searching for an old man on a throne as God, you will do this for a while until you get the idea that you are following an illusion. These insights into religion, and more, come from people who have experienced heaven through near-death experiences (NDEs) which you will discover in the article below.

An example of the spiritual change that often takes place in near-death experiencers can be found in Tom Harpur's excellent documentary entitled Life After Death. In it, he profiles a minister named Ken Martin who had a near-death experience. Upon his return from his experience, he discovered that everything he had previously known - his ministry, his calling, everything - was insignificant in comparison to his experience with the afterlife. (Life After Death)

"Doctrine and creed and race mean nothing. No matter what we believe we were all children joined under one God. The only rule is God's true law: Do unto others as you would have them do unto you." (May Eulitt)

"God does not care which religion is best. God does not care what religion people practice. They are all a blooming facet of the whole. All religions refer to the same God." (Mellen-Thomas Benedict)

"One man who had a near-death experience realized that the "God" of his religious background wasn't anything like the reality. He learned that it doesn't matter if people call him God, Allah, Great Spirit or whatever, he is one and the same." (Dr. Liz Dale)

"Everyone, religious or not, believing in God or not, transitions to the spirit world as part of the natural process of life. Just as one does not need to be religious to live in the physical world, one does not need to profess a particular faith to live in the spirit world." (Nora Spurgin)

"Heaven is about deeds, not creeds. Therefore, persons of many cultures and religions form the societies of heaven." (Emanuel Swedenborg)

"Religious beliefs have little to do with what we experience in the transition from one realm to another, except that we are allowed to see briefly the teacher or guru that we followed. Regardless of cultural or religious beliefs, we have the same basic experience at death." (Betty Bethards)

"God is not dependent on our belief, for our belief or disbelief in God does not affect God - only us." (P.M.H. Atwater)

"God cares little about our religious affiliation or church membership. Love is not limited to any one religion or even religion at all. Religions are cultural institutions but love is universal." (Kevin Williams)

Kenneth Hagin was born and raised a Southern Baptist. As a child, he first made his commitment to Christ and was baptized with water. He was a member of the church all his life. He was saved, on the path toward heaven, a believer, a follower of Jesus, and he knew this assured him a place in heaven. Nevertheless, he had an NDE and it sent him straight to hell. (Rev. Kenneth Hagin)

"God is not a member of any church or religion. It is the churches and the religions that are members within the vastness and the glory that is God. There is no one religion just as there is no chosen people or person, nor any single way of regarding what cannot be fully comprehended. We are all sons of God in the sense that we are all souls of God's creation,

95

without gender, without form, without nationality, complete and whole and perfect as we explore the never-endingness of God's wonderment." (P.M.H. Atwater)

"Having faith IN Christ doesn't matter as much as having the faith OF Christ. It is foolish to think that Jesus will carry your cross for you because he taught people that they must take up their own cross. Having the faith of Christ means practicing unconditional love." (Kevin Williams)

"There is a lot of solid evidence in the Bible itself that the Bible has serious and devastating errors in it." (Kevin Williams)

"I asked the light, which I call Christ, how people from other religions get to heaven. I was shown that the group, or organization, we profess alliance to is inconsequential. What is important is how we show our love for God by the way we treat each other. This is because when we pass to the spiritual realm we will all be met by him, which substantiates the passage, 'No one comes to the Father, but by me.' The light showed me that what is important is that we love God and each other, and that it isn't what a person says, but the love in their being that is examined in the afterlife." (Sandra Rogers)

"What is truly important is love, not religion." (Beth Hammond)

"The best religion is the religion that brings you closest to God." (Rev. Howard Storm)

"There are only two true religions - the religion of love and the religion of fear." (Sandra Rogers)

"Your religion is where your love is." (Henry David Thoreau)

"How are we saved? By unselfish love. When we love unselfishly, our vibrations are so high that the only place we'll fit into is heaven. There is no other place we can go if we want to. This is divine justice because it gives all the people who ever lived, as well as all the higher animals who know right from wrong, an equal chance to eventually attain internal harmony which will fit them into some kind of heaven - regardless of their intelligence, education, indoctrination, ignorance, wealth or poverty." (Arthur Yensen)

"The central message that Buddhist near-death experiencers bring back from their journey is that the most important qualities in life are love and knowledge, compassion and wisdom." (Lingza Chokyi)

"People who truly practice the religion of love will find themselves in a universal sphere where everyone understands that true religion is to love others as ourselves." (Nora Spurgin)

"There is light that can be found in many, many other faiths. All faiths which stress love have this focus. All have their own paradise, but the devoted eventually learn the tremendous experience that all is one under God and that there is no division in purpose. There is one God of us all." (Margaret Tweddell)

"Near-death accounts suggest that unconditional love is the highest form of religion there is." (Kevin Williams)

"Jesus didn't come to preach a new religion. Jesus was a Jew who preached unconditional love." (Kevin Williams)

"I wanted to know why there were so many churches in the world. Why didn't God give us only one church, one pure religion? The answer came to me with the purest of understanding. Each of us, I was told, is at a different level of spiritual development and understanding. Each person is therefore prepared for a different level of spiritual

NOTHING BETTER THAN DEATH

knowledge. Each church fulfills spiritual needs that perhaps others cannot fill. No one church can fulfill everybody's needs at every level." (Betty Eadie)

"The different religions just have different ways of explaining the same Creator." (Dr. Liz Dale)

"God created differences in religion because of the different lessons we all need to learn." (Sandra Rogers)

"All religions are necessary because there are people who need what they teach." (Betty Eadie)

"Religions have a place and any one person in that religion is on the path of learning what is important for that soul." (Darlene Holman)

"The most important thing is to really live what our religion teaches. Even if we have the greatest religion of all, it won't do us any good if we don't put it into practice in our lives. Whatever we practice becomes a part of us." (Daniel Rosenblit)

"Religion is used as a stepping stone to further knowledge. As an individual raises his level of understanding about God and his own eternal progress, he might feel discontented with the teachings of his present church and seek a different philosophy or religion to fill that void. When this occurs he has reached another level of understanding and will long for further truth and knowledge, and for another opportunity to grow. And at every step of the way, these new opportunities to learn will be given." (Betty Eadie)

"One does not have to be religious to dwell in the spirit world, but one inevitably will benefit from a thorough understanding and practice of a particular tradition." (Nora Spurgin)

"We have no right to criticize any church or religion in any way. They are all precious in God's sight. Very special people with important missions have been placed in all religions that they might touch others." (Betty Eadie)

"It is possible for the uneducated and unbelieving spirit to be a virtual prisoner of this earth. Such spirits may not recognize the energy and light which draws one toward God. Lacking the faith and power to reach for the light, unenlightened spirits may actually stay on earth until they learn of the higher power which surrounds, and is available to them." (Betty Eadie)

"One of the truths about NDEs is that each person integrates their NDE into their own pre-existing belief system." (Jody Long)

"The Beings of Light found in NDEs usually conform to the predominant religion the person was exposed to, but not always. Jesus has appeared in near-death scenarios of Jewish people, for instance; a Muslim man once told me he was met by Buddha." (P.M.H. Atwater)

"Some experiencers find joining a church to be helpful. Others find quitting their church to be helpful. Near-death experiences tend to make people less religious and more spiritual." (IANDS FAQ)

"Experiencers tend to become more spiritual - though not necessarily more involved in organized religion." (Dr. Kenneth Ring)

"No matter what the nature of the NDE, it alters some lives. Atheists embrace the existence of a deity, while dogmatic members of a particular religion report feeling welcome in any church or temple or mosque." (P.M.H. Atwater)

"After having an NDE, people tend to exhibit a significant shift in their beliefs on a wide range of subjects including a general tendency toward an increased openness to the idea of reincarnation." (Dr. Kenneth Ring)

"After having an NDE, religious observance may increase or lessen, but a deepened belief in God, or a Higher Power, is almost certain. People say, 'Before, I believed; now I know.'" (IANDS FAQ)

"Religious orientation is not a factor affecting either the likelihood or the depth of the NDE. An atheist is as likely to have one as a devoutly religious person. Regardless of their prior attitudes - whether skeptical or deeply religious - and regardless of the many variations in religious beliefs and degrees of skepticism from tolerant disbelief to outspoken atheism - most of these people were convinced that they had been in the presence of some supreme and loving power and had a glimpse of a life yet to come. Almost all who had an NDE find their lives transformed and are changed in their attitudes and values, and in their inclination to love and to help others." (Dr. Kenneth Ring)

"An experiencer's religious beliefs do not prevent the expansion of psychic abilities resulting from their experience." (P.M.H. Atwater)

"Death does not suddenly turn a non-religious person into a religious person." (Margaret Tweddell)

"I saw that we could literally call down thousands of angels in our aid if we ask in faith." (Betty Eadie)

"NDErs are not more or less religious than in the cross-section of the population. They come from many religious backgrounds and from the ranks of agnostics and even atheists." (IANDS FAQ)

"Religious backgrounds do not affect who are most likely to have an NDE." (P.M.H. Atwater)

"Many people are turned off by religion. Any complete body of knowledge is like a spoke in a wheel - pointing to the center of ultimate truth. Science, art, music, philosophy and religion run into trouble because they are not yet complete bodies of knowledge even though religion is advertised and sold as such." (Arthur Yensen)

"Evil and the devil do not exist. What people consider evil is really ignorance. Hitler was not an evil man. He was just so incredibly ignorant of spiritual realities that he was practically retarded at a spiritual level. Such people are to be pitied and our unconditional love should extend even to him because it is hard to hate a retarded person." (Kevin Williams)

"There is no such thing as sin. There are only mistakes. Everything is a learning experience. We are here to make mistakes in order to learn and grow from them." (Jayne Smith)

"If you read the Bible with the idea of finding contradictions and problems, you will find them. The Bible contains spiritual truth and it has to be read spiritually in order to understand it. It should be read prayerfully. When read prayerfully, it talks to you and reveals itself to you." (Rev. Howard Storm)

"Religious figures including the founders of world religions, the saints and prophets, exist in various spirit realms. The similarity of one's life, heart and knowledge to a particular figure determines one's closeness to these religious figures." (Nora Spurgin)

"The Being of Light seen in near-death experiences can change into different figures, such as Jesus, Buddha, Krishna, mandalas, archetypal images and signs. Our beliefs shape the kind of feedback we get from this Being. If we were a Buddhist or Catholic or Fundamentalist, we would get a feedback loop of our own beliefs." (Mellen-Thomas Benedict)

"In the spirit realms, you are able to go back in time and live in the minds of Jesus and his disciples. You can hear their conversation, experience them eating, passing wine, smells, tastes - as pure consciousness. Any time in history, you can go there." (Dr. George Rodonaia)

"There is no difference between scrubbing floors and praying, between balancing your checkbook and praising God. It's all the same energy from the same Source. The only difference is how we choose to manifest that energy at any given moment in time and space." (P.M.H. Atwater)

"Outward worship does not accomplish anything, but rather it is the inner elements from which the outward ones come that really count." (Emanuel Swedenborg)

"I saw the Christian heaven. We expect it to be a beautiful place, and you stand in front of the throne, worshiping forever. I tried it. It is boring! This is all we are going to do? It is childlike." (Mellen-Thomas Benedict)

"Life is what you worship as God." (Edgar Cayce)

"Then I thought about Jesus and he came. There was never any feeling or need to worship him. No awe or fear. Rather, it was a feeling of seeing a beloved elder brother after being apart for so long." (P.M.H. Atwater)

"Worship God within others through love and you will be following the commandment of Christ." (Kevin Williams)

"Hindu near-death experiences often consist of someone reading a person's record of their life. In some Christian near-death experiences, it is the Book of Life that is read." (Pasricha and Stevenson)

SPIRITUALITY

The words "religious" and "spiritual" have historically been used interchangeably to describe a variety of concepts concerning religion. But the consensus among people having a near-death experience (NDE) reveals a striking difference between religion and spirituality. The modern phrase "spiritual but not religious" is commonly used by experiencers to express this difference. For example, a religious person may go to their place of worship regularly, have an understanding of their interpretation of their organized religion and scriptures, and identify themselves as being "spiritual." They may believe their particular religion is the only means to further "spiritual" growth and be justified in the eyes of their God or Gods. They may even severely persecute or kill people of different religions because of this narrow religious mindset. But information gleaned from near-death experiencers (NDErs) reveal how spirituality is a very different concept than being religious. Perhaps the best way that NDErs distinguish between "being religious" and "being spiritual" is to define religion as the outward practice of guiding people inwardly into the spiritual force of love and compassion for others. In fact, the difference between religion and spirituality are so great, you probably know somebody who is so religious that they are not very spiritual at all. As you will understand in this article, religions are cultural institutions only; but love is universal. This universal concept of loving and accepting everyone, no matter what they believe to be true for themselves or their God(s), is what NDErs reveal to be the universal way to inward spirituality.

"We came into this world to have trouble and to learn from it. Unfortunately many people don't realize this and complain about their bad luck and spend their lives chasing pleasure, fame and money. Then they die without making any spiritual progress. And so they waste life after life. It should be obvious that all we'll take with us is our character, our karma and our abilities, and that we'll have to live with people like ourselves. Therefore, our highest success would be to rise into the highest heaven through unselfish love." (Arthur Yensen)

"The desire for spiritual growth arises from a desire to be close to God." (Nora Spurgin)

"We cannot dwell in the higher spiritual realms until we have perfectly qualified for it by a change of heart and mind, a significant amount of preparation, and by completing our mission." (Dr. Craig Lundahl)

"God has a job for us. We don't have to know what it is. We just have to trust and follow our heart. That's because our heart knows more than our head does." (P.M.H. Atwater)

"All souls come to earth to test their spiritual ideals to see if they are real. Only by becoming subject to the physical influences of the flesh and the laws of the earth realm can a soul know for certain if they really possess that spiritual ideal. Through this process, the soul is tested and the result is self-realization. This is the purpose of the earth realm." (Edgar Cayce)

"In order for us to appreciate, benefit, and learn all we can from life, we must re-discover what we knew before we were born - now in physical ways." (David Goines)

"In order to become one with God, work must be done to remember and find the truth. The truth is this: our true self is a spirit and our spirit is one with God." (Sandra Rogers)

"While the ideal place to grow spiritually is on earth (this is the reason for life on earth), growth in the spirit world remains a possibility. There, however, in the absence of a physical body, growth is more difficult. The opportunity for the full range of love (child's love, marital love, and parental love) is ideally available while on earth. Love which has been misused or misdirected is best corrected in a physical life." (Nora Spurgin)

"If we worship the God within others through love, we will find the kingdom of heaven within." (Kevin Williams)

"We are souls visiting and experiencing the physical realm in order to grow and evolve into ultimate light beings, our true origin and final destiny." (Juliet Nightingale)

"[The light] showed me that God is love. By spreading love, you make God stronger. By making God stronger, He can, in return, help you. He told me your love has to be unconditional. That is the only rule here ally has." (an anonymous NDEr)

"I heard the words, "Remember, pray without ceasing. Play, love, laugh, live for the joy of it. Have fun. Happiness is holy. The purpose of life is joy. Savor fully the loveliness of each experience. Self-awareness is the prayer of the heart. To pray without ceasing is to play. Play with the joyful abandon of the child, absorbed in the delight of each moment. Let go of obligation and duty. Live for the pure joy of being." (Jan Price)

"Life is for living and the light is for later." (a child in Dr. Melvin Morse's research)

"Our lives are a golden opportunity to live a spiritual life in a world of darkness." (Daniel Rosenblit)

"The highest purpose of our earthly connections is love." (Lynnclaire Dennis)

"Humanity has to think of life everlasting, manifested now in the present. This is very important. Life has been held very cheaply. Millions of people have been killed through devastation, torture, war, and man's inhumanity to man. This has brought spiritual pollution on all levels." (Margaret Tweddell)

"If we live true to the spirit we came to earth with, we can progress more quickly. We do that by expressing the love of God that is within us, and we do that by loving God, ourselves, and each other. It is that simple." (Betty Eadie)

"When we leave ourselves open to God to learn more about unconditional love, he readily sends us the people we need to learn to love without judgment. Put to the test, our spirits expand with greater love, God's pure love, and it shines brighter within us." (Betty Eadie)

"Life is God, everything that exists. Light is God, what everything is made of. Love is God, the power holding everything together. This is the same message coming from people who have had near-death experiences. It's the same message from Jesus, Buddha, Krishna, Moses, Muhammad, Zoroaster, etc.." (Kevin Williams)

"Our ultimate purpose for existing is to be a companion to God." (Edgar Cayce)

"Love is really the only thing that matters. Love is joy! It all seemed so simple. If we're kind, we'll have joy." (Betty Eadie)

"The absolutely only thing that matters is love. Everything else, our achievements, degrees, the money we made, how many mink coats we had, is totally irrelevant. It will also be understood that what we do is not important. The only thing that matters is how we do what we do. And the only thing that matters is that we do what we do with love." (Elisabeth Kubler-Ross)

"There is only one truly significant work to do in life, and that is love; to love nature, to love people, to love animals, to love creation itself, just because it is. To serve God's creation with a warm and loving hand of generosity and compassion - that is the only meaningful existence." (Dr. George Rodonaia)

"He who understands nature walks close with God." (Edgar Cayce)

"I was shown that love is supreme. I saw that truly without love we are nothing." (Betty Eadie)

"Since love is supreme, opportunities for the practice of love will continue after death." (Nora Spurgin)

"Love, being God, is too immense and profound to ever be fully understood or experienced in the physical world. To have an abundance, do what you do with Love, and Love what you do. In the search for truth and understanding, all paths lead to Love. The only thing that lives forever is Love.God's paradise for us is Love. We can create paradise again if we learn to Love one another as ourselves. Life is a road full of lessons teaching Love. When Love is learned, you will forever be home. God transforms the results of man's sins into opportunities to learn Love. When we work for God, we create Love. Love at its best is Love motivated to action. Every action of Love has a reaction of joy. The greatest joy is to share Love. Where Love dwells, God is there. Forgiveness is the capacity to give Love in the most difficult circumstances. Forgiveness shows God's Love in action. It is as close as we get to God's nature in this physical world. Love in the physical world is a reflection of Love throughout eternity. Indifference is the opposite of Love." (Sandra Rogers)

"What all people seek, what sustains them, is love, the light told me. What distorts people is a lack of love." (Mellen-Thomas Benedict)

"Without feelings of self-love, the love we feel for others is counterfeit. We must love all others as ourselves." (Betty Eadie)

"Above and beyond anything else, we must first learn to love ourselves non-judgmentally and unconditionally. Then we will actually love all people and all things the same way." (Laurelynn Martin)

"Happiness is love of something outside of self. It may never be obtained, may never be known by loving only things within self or self's own domain." (Edgar Cayce)

"Our ultimate goal is not the complete loss of self-identity; rather, it is to know ourselves to be ourselves, yet one with the Whole." (Edgar Cayce)

"How are we saved? By unselfish love. If we do only good things we will eventually run out of bad karma and only good things will happen to us, and vice versa. The purpose of karma is to force us to learn life's lessons whether we want to or not. The only way to bypass karma is to develop so much unselfish love that paying for bad karma will serve no purpose - much like a college student challenging a course he already knows. We evolve faster through unselfish love." (Arthur Yensen)

"Our minds are led by the spirit we are entertaining, the spirit of God or the spirit of self. People are led astray through self-centeredness, self-gratification, self-righteousness, self-glorification, self-condemnation, self-interest, and self-consciousness. The greatest enemy we will ever face is self - the false god. Jesus' mission was to demonstrate to humanity how self-sacrifice and self-denial can overcome these selfish desires and how it leads to our complete restoration with the divine nature within us." (Edgar Cayce)

"The conquering of self is truly greater than were one to conquer many worlds." (Edgar Cayce)

"If everyone completely understood the afterlife, they'd quit trying to keep up with the Joneses and start learning how to live unselfishly. Here [in the world] we can change ourselves quite easily and should use this life to make ourselves into the kind of people we want to be in the hereafter. [The spirit world] is a miserable place for anyone who hasn't learned internal harmony - characterized by unselfish love." (Arthur Yensen)

"Our earthly selves, however, are constantly in opposition to our spirits. Although our spirit bodies are full of light, truth, and love, they must battle constantly to overcome the flesh, and this strengthens them. Those who are truly developed will find a perfect harmony between their flesh and spirits, a harmony that will bless them with peace and give them the ability to help others." (Betty Eadie)

"In the earth realm, as in spiritual realms, until we turn our attention from ourselves, we cannot in any way change our estate." (Edgar Cayce)

"Not all people are lovable, but when we find someone difficult for us to love, it is often because they remind us of something within ourselves that we don't like." (Betty Eadie)

"The minute we judge others for their faults or shortcomings, we are displaying a similar shortcoming in ourselves. We don't have the knowledge to judge people accurately here. Only God knows the heart of man, and only God can judge perfectly. He knows our spirits; we see only temporary strengths and weaknesses. Because of our own limitations, we can seldom look into the heart of man." (Betty Eadie)

"We don't have any knowledge or right to judge anybody else in terms of that person's heart relationship to God. Only God knows what's in a person's heart. Someone whom we think is despicable, God might know as a wonderful person. Similarly, someone we think is good, God may see as a hypocrite, with a black heart. Only God knows the truth about every individual." (Rev. Howard Storm)

"Love is the power of life. I know that love between people here can be eternal. The key is love." (RaNelle Wallace)

"Everyone is in the circle of God, Love. The Kingdom of God is within us. But more important, we are in the Kingdom of God. The Spirit of God is within us, but more important, we are in the Spirit of God. The love of God is within us, but more important, we are in the love of God. All there is - is God." (Jan Price)

"The meaning of the terms Christ, Christ Consciousness, and Mind of Christ, has little to do with the personality known as Jesus. These terms refer to the spiritual condition of human-divine unity or at-onement. This unity is the ultimate goal of everyone and is spiritually possible for all. Jesus became a Christ in that he attained perfect human-divine unity. It is God's desire for everyone to attain Christhood; or Buddhahood if you live in the East (same concept)." (Edgar Cayce)

"The truth of who I am, indeed, who we all are, is perfect love as a creation of God." (Linda Stewart)

"The very core of our essence is love, nothing else. Our core is perfect love, loving perfection." (Jayne Smith)

"When humanity recognizes the divinity within them as the controlling force in the world and turns away from their own selfish pattern of living for self alone, the old pattern disappears and the Christ pattern emerges." (Edgar Cayce)

"All it takes to change the world is to change one person (ourselves) which, in turn, will cause a chain reaction of change from one person to another." (Rev. Howard Storm)

"The quickest way to change the world is to be of service to others. Show that your love can make a difference in the lives of people and thereby someone else's love can make a difference in your life. By each of us doing that and working together we change the world one inner person at a time." (Dannion Brinkley)

"Those whose hearts have been awakened to God have a responsibility to share his love with others. That is the nature of service and of love; all of our lights shine brighter when we pass them along." (Betty Eadie)

"The positive, as well as the negative, impact of one decision has the capacity to be felt throughout the world." (Angie Fenimore)

"I saw myself [in a life review] perform an act of kindness, just a simple act of unselfishness, and I saw the ripples go out again. The friend I had been kind to was kind in turn to one of her friends, and the chain repeated itself. I saw love and happiness increase in others' lives because of that one simple act on my part. I saw their happiness grow and affect their lives in positive ways, some significantly." (Betty Eadie)

"I saw [in a life review] that I had sent out waves of goodness and hope and love when I had only meant to smile or to help in a small way." (RaNelle Wallace)

"A chain is only as strong as its weakest link. As humans, we are all linked together. What one person does to another person affects everyone else. This is why it is important to help people. We are not only helping them, we are helping ourselves and everyone else. And this is why powerful spirit entities on the other side are trying to help us. Until we all progress spiritually, the powerful spirit entities on the other side cannot fully progress. But, a simple smile has within it the power to alter the whole course of world history, change the balance of power, and save the universe." (Kevin Williams)

"As we find one person with whom to share our light, a wonderful miracle begins to take place: we find the Lord answering our individual prayers and preparing us to become the light, the answer, to yet many others." (Betty Eadie)

"The good that we have done for others, all of our good deeds and kind words, will come back to us and bless us a hundred fold after this life. Our strength will be found in love." (Virginia Rivers)

"We are all one. I comprehended that our oneness is interconnected by love and is an available, much higher level and means of communication than we normally use but to which we have access. This love is available to anyone who is willing to do the hard spiritual work that will allow us to open our hearts and minds and eyes to Spirit." (Linda Stewart)

"They want every person to consider every other person greater than their own flesh. They want everyone to love everyone else, completely; more, even, than they love themselves. If someone, someplace else in the world hurts, than we should hurt we should feel their pain. And we should help them." (Rev. Howard Storm)

"This is the simple secret to improving humanity: The amount of love you received during your life is equal to the love you gave. It is just that simple." (Dannion Brinkley)

"If we learn to use what we have, we will receive more. This is a spiritual law. We will be given all that we are prepared to receive." (Betty Eadie)

"By giving love, we receive and experience a tremendous love from the universe." (Laurelynn Martin)

"We are here to help each other rise to the higher level of love." (Sherry Gideon)

"I asked, 'How do I know right from wrong?' He replied, 'Right is helping and being kind. Wrong is not only hurting someone but not helping when you can.'" (Cecil, age 11)

"Whatever we become here in mortality is meaningless unless it is done for the benefit of others. Our gifts and talents are given to us to help us serve. And in serving others we grow spiritually." (Betty Eadie)

The Being of Light told Dannion, "Humans are powerful spiritual beings meant to create good on the earth. This good isn't usually accomplished in bold actions, but in singular acts of kindness between people. It's the little things that count, because they are more spontaneous and show who you truly are." (Dannion Brinkley)

"They never gave me a direct mission or purpose. Could I build a shrine or cathedral for God? They said those monuments were for humanity. They wanted me to live my life to love people not things." (Rev. Howard Storm)

"Life is not about pursuits but about people." (Laurelynn Martin)

"If we look after others, God will look after us - and do a lot better job of it than we can." (Arthur Yensen)

To know about love is not enough. We must express that knowing. How we do that is up to us. (P.M.H. Atwater)

"Love unconditionally as much as you can, by all the means you can, in all the ways you can, at all the places you can, during all the times you can, for as many people as you can, for as long as you can." (Kevin Williams)

"The guides taught us that doctrine and creed and race meant nothing. No matter what we believed we were all children joined under one God, and that the only rule was God's true law - do unto others as you would have them do unto you. We should treat all people as if they were a part of our soul because they were." (May Eulitt)

"It is love, not religion, which creates spiritual growth. Where religion teaches love, there is growth. Where religion impedes love, there is stagnation." (Nora Spurgin)

"What counts most is what comes from the heart, not what one professes to believe. The most difficult thing for a person who has been deeply steeped in a particular religious tradition is to realize that the form alone is not what elevates a person; it is the heart." (P.M.H. Atwater)

"It is not true, as some people think, that if we only give verbal assent to belief in God, well, that's fine -that is our passport to heaven and everything will be all right. What we have to remember is that Jesus showed us the path by which it will be all right. He doesn't say, "It's all right, brother, come along in. Sit down now and relax and do nothing." He says, "It's all right. You are on my way. There are a lot of stones in it, but you are on my way. If you ask me, I'll help you over the stones." The old teachings that "as you strive, so you'll be helped" are right. The Lord helps those who help themselves." (Margaret Tweddell)

"The Golden Rule is the governing principle in the spirit world: do unto others as you would have them do unto you. People who truly practice the religion of love will find themselves in a universal sphere where everyone understands that true religion is to love others as ourselves." (Nora Spurgin)

"God is love in all religions, so the more we live love the closer we are to God." (Betty Bethards)

"Because our opportunities on earth for spiritual growth are limited time-wise, we should realize that indoctrinating children before they are old enough to reason can spoil the learning value of their lives. In some cases this is worse than murder because it may spoil their whole lifetime instead of just a few years." (Arthur Yensen)

"When I asked what a person should do while on earth to make it better for him when he dies, he answered, 'All you can do is to develop along the lines of unselfish love. People don't come here because of their good deeds, or because they believe in this or that, but because they fit in and belong. Good deeds are the natural result of being good, and bad deeds are the natural result of being bad. Each carries its own reward and punishment. It's what you are that counts!'" (Arthur Yensen)

"God is really only concerned about what is within us, our heart and spirituality. The way to heaven is through love. We do not go to heaven by worshipping Jesus, or by believing in his name, or by believing in the cross, or by accepting Jesus as our Savior. We grow to heaven by creating heaven within us by practicing unconditional love." (Kevin Williams)

"You'll not be in heaven if you're not leaning on the arm of someone you have helped." (Edgar Cayce)

"Love in action is what lasts. After death, a person is his love. This is the person's life." (Emanuel Swedenborg)

"Our state in the spirit realm is determined by our level of spiritual maturity. If not mature, we may find that an understanding of the knowledge available through the various religious traditions may help to begin the process." (Nora Spurgin)

"The more knowledge of the spirit world we acquire while on earth, the further and faster we will progress in the spirit after death." (Nora Spurgin)

"There are only two things we can take with us at death: love and knowledge. This is why it is best to learn about both as much as possible." (Virginia Rivers)

"No one can truly fathom the great truths of life until they finally unite with eternity after death." (Dr. George Rodonaia)

"In the spiritual universe, sin is not seen in the same way as it is here. In the spirit world, all things are learning experiences. We are here in this world to make mistakes, to learn and grow from them." (Jayne Smith)

"I heard the voice of Christ vibrate through me as he said, 'No, this heart condition of yours is not a cross from me for you to bear. This heart condition is a challenge to help you grow and stay compassionate.'" (Lynn)

"Hardships are necessary for soul growth." (Sandra Rogers)

"We need negative experiences as well as positive experiences in life because before we can feel joy, we must know sorrow. Every experience is a tool for you to grow by. Negative experiences allow you to obtain greater understanding about yourself until you learn to avoid those experiences." (Betty Eadie)

"The angel (I don't know what else to call her) said that, 'Life is an endless cycle of improvements and that humans are not perfect yet. She said that most people have this secret revealed to them when they die, but that handicapped children often know this and endure their problems without complaining because they know that their burdens will pass. Some of these children, she said, have even been given the challenge of teaching the rest of us how to love. It stretches our own humanity to love a child who is less than perfect,' said the angel. 'And that is an important lesson for us.'" (Dr. Frank Oski)

"It cannot be stated too often that the spiritual perspective is inward and not outward. Once we leave the physical realm we will view reality inwardly and not outwardly. All that we have placed inside ourselves will act as a lens, a filter. All that we see will be seen through and be distorted by these things we have stored within ourselves. This is why it is important to remove as much clutter as possible so as not to obscure our reality. We not only take our attitudes with us into death, but we inhabit them. They will, however, become much, much larger in death, much harder to bear, with no way to set them aside easily." (Edgar Cayce)

"If, during our lifetime on earth, we matured in a spiritually rich and beautiful way, we will come to dwell in an environment that corresponds with these qualities. Conversely, if one has been stunted in his spiritual growth through an undeveloped or misdirected lifestyle, has led a purely self-centered life or has hurt other people, their spiritual environment will reflect something of these realities. A self-centered life on earth places one in an area of the spiritual world with like-minded people who have yet to learn the value of unselfishness for the advancement of the soul. Environments distant from God are said to be dark, cold and inhospitable. Indeed, they reflect the spirits of those dwelling therein. In between these extremes are many levels representing different stages of spiritual growth. The central factor determining our level is the degree to which we have lived for the sake of others, and the extent to which we have been able to influence others likewise to follow paths of service and love. In this respect, the actions of loving, serving and teaching others carry the highest spiritual value." (Nora Spurgin)

"The spiritual state of being you have on earth is the spiritual state you take with you to the world beyond when you die. There is no sudden metamorphosis from an idle person into an active person, from a nonreligious person into a religious person, from a money-centered person into a God-centered person. This is not an automatic thing." (Margaret Tweddell)

"According to Edgar Cayce, death in the physical world means birth in the spirit world; and death in the spirit world means birth in the physical world. Because of this, everyone is born with a spiritual void within them. Throughout our lives, we fill our void with a multitude of things. Then when we die, we step into the spiritual void we have filled. This is why having love within us is so important when we die. Giving and receiving love from the heart creates a heavenly paradise within us which is manifested in the spirit world and becomes realized at death." (Kevin Williams)

"Since we know that we enter the spiritual world at the same level of spiritual development we have gained while on earth, then it makes sense that those who have had much give and take with selfishness, revenge and maliciousness will continue such acts in the spirit world." (Nora Spurgin)

"Our ability to accept truth, to live by it, governs our progress in the spirit, and it determines the degree of light we possess. Nobody forces light and truth upon us, and nobody takes it away unless we let them." (RaNelle Wallace)

"The higher one's soul development, the brighter the light will shine from their spirit. What determines what one looks like in the spirit world is the person's quality of heart and life. One's inner quality is perceived as light. One's features are visible but the light that comes from their very essence is the identifying feature. For example, because they lived totally for other people, Jesus and other religious leaders emanate brilliant light." (Nora Spurgin)

"Spiritually, we are at various degrees of light - which is knowledge - and because of our divine, spiritual nature we are filled with the desire to do good." (Betty Eadie)

"Heaven and hell are not places - they are spiritual states of being. They are not static states but are states in which there can be growth and progress toward ultimate wholeness of being." (Margaret Tweddell)

"You grow to heaven. You don't go to heaven." (Edgar Cayce)

"The only thing you take with you when you die is the love you give away." (Laurelynn Martin)

"A soul is given the time it needs to turn away from its selfish ways and, like the prodigal son, return home to a feast of joy and welcome from its Father in heaven. Reincarnation is the method that allows the soul enough time to correct its mistakes and develop itself." (Edgar Cayce)

"We progress at our own rate to reach the light. If you do things that take you away from the light, then you are perpetuating your time here." (Dr. Kenneth Ring's research)

"The chief purpose for reincarnation is instruction. We return to earth, not because of any external pressure, but because we desire spiritual growth. This is a universal process that prevails throughout all of nature. All living things are evolving through the use of a physical form in order to gain physical experiences. When we have learned the lessons we need from the physical world, we need not return unless we come back of our own accord to act as teachers or helpers in the glorious plan of evolution." (Dr. Kenneth Ring's research)

"God loves and suffers for those in spiritual darkness, ignorance and misery. Based on their desire and willingness, such souls are given opportunities for advancement." (Nora Spurgin)

"After we die, we may realize that we haven't learned everything we should. So, we return and are born again. As we transform into another personality, our soul is maintained throughout. Our soul does not get bigger or smaller. We carry with us the characteristics of our former personalities. The phrase "burning off bad karma" means that we have characteristics that we have to deal with." (Thomas Sawyer)

THE FUTURE

Many people were given visions of the future during their near-death experience (NDE). Generally, these visions foretell a future of catastrophic natural disasters and social upheaval leading to a new era of global peace and enlightenment. Some of these prophecies did not occur when they were foretold to occur; and there are good reasons for this which will be explained. Many of these apocalyptic visions have been predicted to occur within the next few decades. Remarkably, these visions of the future agree with prophecies of the Bible, Edgar Cayce, Nostradamus, and the Virgin Mary visitations of Fatima, Garabandal, Medjugorje and Zeitoun. The following are insights from many NDEs dealing with the future.

During his NDE, Ned Dougherty was given a vision of the future involving a terrorist attack. He wrote about it in his book, Fast Lane to Heaven, six months before 9/11 occurred. Here is what he wrote: "A major terrorist attack may befall New York City or Washington, DC, severely impacting the way we live in the United States." This description of Ned Dougherty's vision of a future terrorist attack is a perfect description of what happened six months later in New York and Washington.

Dannion Brinkley received a psychic vision of the September 11th terrorist attack before it happened. On September 1st, ten days before the New York terrorist attacks, Dannion announced that the world is on the verge of a "spiritual awakening which calls for deep self-examination." On September 1, 2001, Dannion Brinkley also called for a global Day of Truth to occur on September 17 where people could "take time before this date to personally examine our own lives and priorities as citizens of earth in this time of transition. This is a wake-up call ... For it is only as we are willing to see and to embrace all of our deeply human fragmented realities that the light of grace can shine upon us." Brinkley gave this announcement ten days before the September 11th terrorist attack. Something certainly provoked Dannion Brinkley to make this announcement.

Almost every day, several times a day, for more than forty years, Edgar Cayce would induce himself into a unique out-of-body state identical to an NDE. Through his sojourns he would reveal profound information on various subjects. But it was the information that he revealed about the future that he is most known for. The following is an listing of his prophecies which have already happened: (1) The Stock Market Crash of October 1929; (2) The Great Depression; (3) The rise and fall of Adolf Hitler; (4) The beginning and end of World War II; (5) America's entry into World War II; (6) The death of Franklin D. Roosevelt; (7) India's independence from Britain; (8) The re-establishment of the nation of Israel; (9) The discovery of the Dead Sea Scrolls and Essenes; (10) The death of John F. Kennedy; (11) The Civil Rights Movement and 1960's civil unrest; (12) The fall of the Soviet Union and communism; (13) The U.S. and Russia alliance; (14) New technological discoveries; (15) The existence of the planet Pluto; (16) A shift of earth's magnetic poles; (17) The day of his own death. Edgar Cayce's prophetic visions yet to happen include: (1) Armageddon will be a battle in the spirit realm to prevent souls from the hell realms to reincarnate for 1000 years. It is also a battle within everyone between their higher nature and their lower nature; (2) The possibility of a World War III; (3) Catastrophic natural disasters; (4) A dramatic rise in the level of the ocean.

Dannion Brinkley's major prophetic visions which have already happened include: (1) The demoralization of America from the Vietnam War; (2) The presidency of Ronald Reagan; (3) Turmoil in the Middle East. (4) The 1986 Chernobyl nuclear plant disaster; (5) The collapse of the Soviet Union; (6) The Desert Storm war against Iraq in 1990; (7) The existence of chemical weapons in the Middle East. Dannion Brinkley's major prophetic visions yet to happen include: (1) Oil used as a weapon to control the world economy; (2) The economic collapse of the world economy; (3) A war between China and Russia; (4) Democracy in Egypt overthrown and fanatics rule; (5) An alliance between the Chinese and Syrians; (6) Catastrophic natural disasters in America; (7) The fall of America as a world power; (8) The rise of an environmental religion beginning in Russia; (9) A leader from Russia to become a U.N. leader; (10) The possibility of a World War III; (11) A scientific discovery to alter DNA and create a biological virus that will be used in the manufacture of computer chips. Concerning Dannion's visions of the future, the Being of Light told him the following: "Watch the Soviet Union. How the Russian people go, so goes the world. What happens to Russia is the basis for everything that will happen to the economy of the free world."

The following prophecies of the future were given to Dr. George Ritchie during his NDE: (1) Increasing natural disasters on the earth hurricanes, floods, earthquakes, volcanoes); (2) Families are splitting and governments are breaking apart because people are thinking only of themselves; (3) Armies will march on the U.S. from the south; (4) Explosions will occur over the entire world of a magnitude beyond our capacity to imagine. If they continue, human life as we have known it will not exist.

The following prophecies of the future were given to Ned Dougherty during his NDE: (1) Wars will continue to spread from the Eastern Hemisphere to the Middle East, Africa, Europe, Russia and China; (2) A great threat to global peace will come from China which is preparing itself for a global war; (3) The U.S. government will collapse because a staggering national debt will cause it to fail to meet its financial obligations; (4) U.S. banking institutions will collapse due to natural disasters; (5) The U.S. will be thrown into political, economic, and social chaos; (6) Terrorist activities and wars will occur first in the Middle East, then in Italy the Vatican and Rome); (7) A shift of the earth's axis will result in massive earthquakes, volcanic and tidal waves disasters; (8) America will lose its ability to defend itself, leaving the country vulnerable to invasion by foreign troops, particularly by China. Concerning the future of the world, the Lady of Light specifically told Ned Dougherty: "Pray for the conversion of China. The conversion of China to God is necessary for the salvation of the world."

The following prophecies of the future were given to Ricky Randolph during his NDE: (1) The earth will drastically change because of turmoil, wars and death; (2) A giant explosion in the earth's atmosphere will cause much land to be destroyed; (3) The U.S. government will collapse; (4) A volcano will explode which will result in many cities in the U.S. being put in darkness; (5) People will kill over food and water; (6) Cities will fall and new ones will be built; (7) Few cities will be left, but people will be content.

The following prophecies of the future were given to David Oakford during his NDE: (1) Humans have fallen away from the balance of nature and allowed themselves to be affected by what they create which violates the natural laws of the universe; (2) Humans must restore the harmonic balance of the earth if they want to survive as a race and live on the earth forever; (3) The next overall goal for humanity is to learn about this harmonic balance; (4) Before humans realize they must restore the harmonic balance, great damage will be inflicted on the earth; (5) The earth is very strong but has been weakened considerably ever since humans have chosen to use its resources in a manner inconsistent with the laws of the universe.

The following prophecies of the future were given to Elaine Durham during here NDE: These catastrophic earth changes upon America will come about by natural and man-made disasters. Unless Americans begin to make better choices, these changes will certainly come to pass: (1) North America will be completely divided by a large body of water. A large part of both eastern and western shorelines will be lost. Icebergs and polar icecaps will melt significantly. America will be ravaged by earthquakes, hurricanes, fierce storms, massive fires burning huge areas of the country, explosions in some areas, and the western coastline will change causing California, Oregon, and Washington to become submerged. Much of the eastern coastline will be gone, though not as bad as the western coastline. The southern half of Florida will be under water. The oceans of the entire world will rise significantly; (2) The seat of power will move away from Washington, D.C because there will be so much turmoil and warfare on the eastern side of America. America will come to the very edge of destruction because Americans have chosen to seek worldly things rather than loving or serving others, and because they refused to care for their precious natural resources, and because their greed and selfishness. The U.S. government will lose most of its power and no longer govern completely and lawlessness will reign on the eastern side of America as well as tremendous anarchy and crime. There will be less turmoil on the western side of America and even a certain amount of prosperity. A new seat of power will rise near present-day Kansas City. From this location, a true spiritual force will become the governing power over the whole land -- a power such that emanates from Christ; (3) Native Americans will be partially responsible for the peacefulness that will exist in western America. Their knowledge of how to live from the land, or how to be in harmony with it, will bring forth an abundance. Their spiritual knowledge will be taught to the people and everyone will start to learn to live in harmony with each other. Prosperity will come by becoming harmonious with nature or the natural elements upon which they depended.

The following prophecies of the future were given to Reinee Pasarow during her NDE: (1) There will be tremendous upheaval in the world as a result of humanity's general ignorance of true reality; (2) Humanity is breaking the laws of the universe and, as a result of this, humanity will suffer. This suffering will not be due to the wrath of God, but rather like the pain one might suffer by arrogantly defying the law of gravity; (3) Humanity is being consumed by the cancers of arrogance, materialism, racism, chauvinism, and separatist thinking; (4) Sense will turn to nonsense, and calamity, in the end, will turn to providence; (5) An inevitable educational cleansing of the earth will occur because of humanity's transgressions.

The following prophecies of the future were given to Lou Famoso during his NDE: (1) People from different nations, different religions, with different weapons, will kill each other which will result in hundreds of thousands of dead people; (2) Man will prey on man until man will pray for man; (3) Floods will spill across the earth on different continents in different seasons; (4) Hundreds of lives and acres upon acres of crops will be lost as well as hundreds of animals; (5) Volcanoes from around the world will erupt; first one then another; (6) Earthquakes will destroy sections of almost every continent. One massive earthquake will occur in America. Most of the others will be in Europe and Asia and thousands of people will be killed; (7) There will come a time when these things will happen all at once. It will come at the same time of humanity's greatest sins; (8) Millions of people will cry because of the devastation of portions of New York City. Webmaster's note: This could be a reference to the New York City terrorist attack; (9) A huge earthquake of magnitude 8.6 will happen at a place called Eureka (Eureka, California?); (10) Thousands of people will migrate from areas of frequent disasters to places of safety; (11) Missiles will be fired simultaneously into space from several nations; (12) Eruptions on the sun will interfere with the earth - more than it ever has; (13) A large mass from space will pass by the earth and cause it to wobble wildly like a spinning top; (14) The oceans will rise, first along the Pacific Ring of Fire then others; (15) A space station will fall from the heavens because of an internal explosion. Note: This could be a reference to the doomed Space Shuttle Columbia disaster of 2003; (16) Landmasses will start to sink under the pressure of the ocean on it; (17) These earth changes will result in a newer, cleaner, more beautiful planet. The archangel Gabriel gave Lou Famoso the following message to take back to let others know that there is little to fear because the earth will go on forever: "Look to Orion (the constellation) and you will know when the new world will come."

Lou Famoso was also told of a future event known as "The Gathering" involving sudden, catastrophic earth changes and sudden tremendous loss of life. Surprisingly, there are other credible sources mentioning a similar future event also called "The Gathering," such as by the OBE pioneer Robert Monroe, and the near-death experiencer Natalie Sudman. These sources appear to be in agreement: The Gathering is a future event where alien intelligences from other areas of universe (extraterrestrials) and other beings from other dimensions (afterlife realms) gather to observe the sudden upcoming earth changes. This event may also satisfy those who believe the second coming of Jesus will involve UFOs. It is also possible this event is part of the so-called "the Rapture" described by Christians when millions of souls are instantly translated into spirit -- possibly when they are suddenly killed by the coming catastrophe. I believe "The Gathering" will be the "revelation" about the existence of UFOs and spirit beings. The higher beings who started life on this planet will finally stop monitoring Earth's evolutionary progress and will intervene to help humanity to the next evolutionary level.

The following prophecies of the future come from Dr. Kenneth Ring's NDE prophecy research conclusions: (1) An increasing incidence of earthquakes, volcanic activity and generally massive geophysical changes; (2) Disturbances in weather patterns and food supplies; (3) The collapse of the world economic system; (4) The possibility of nuclear war by accident (respondents are not in agreement on whether a nuclear catastrophe will occur); (5) Dramatic climate changes, droughts, food shortages. Dr. Kenneth Ring says that near-death accounts sometimes involve a sense of having total knowledge and some are given a view of the entirety of the earth's evolution and history from the beginning to the end of time.

The following prophecies of the future come from Margot Grey's NDE prophecy research conclusions: (1) There are going to be a lot of upheavals such as earthquakes and volcanoes occurring in the next few years, which are going to get increasingly worse. I was given to understand that these activities are a reflection of all the social upheaval and violence that is going on all over the world at the moment; (2) Among the many volcanic eruptions that are going to occur, I saw the one that just occurred in Hawaii. As I saw the pictures on the television, it was really quite uncanny, as I had already seen it taking place during the vision I had seen at the time of my NDE; (3) There are going to be serious food shortages around the world due to droughts in many places. This will push the price of food up so that many people will have to start going without things that they have always taken for granted; (4) There are going to be very severe droughts in many countries. Others are going to suffer from freak storms that will cause tidal waves or flooding to happen as a result of unnaturally heavy rainfalls ... All in all, the weather is going to be very unpredictable from now on. In fact these disturbances in the weather patterns have already started.

The following prophecies of the future were given to Arthur Yensen during his NDE: "You have more important work to do on earth, and you must go back and do it! There will come a time of great confusion and the people will need your stabilizing influence. When your work on earth is done, then you can come back here and stay."

According to NASA's Goddard Space Flight Center, in 1998 something changed the earth's gravitational field which moved the magnetic poles closer together. The NASA article explained that as the ice on the poles melted, ocean currents moved water toward the equator, which factors researchers believe to be partly responsible, in conjunction with shifts in atmospheric patterns, for this ongoing shift in the earth's magnetic field. This finding by NASA is verification of NDE prophecies that predicted this to occur. Here are some of them:

In the late 1920's and early 1930's, Edgar Cayce was the first to describe the concept of pole shift as a result of the crust of the earth moving independently from the core of the earth to bring different a surface area over the spin axis. During the past 30 years, this concept has received more and more attention by geophysicists, some of whom now seriously argue that the crust does move independently. Some geophysicists now also argue that the best way to explain a variety of paleo sea-level and other data is that it moves and shifts fairly frequently and more rapidly than previously imagined. Cayce predicted changes to the earth surface to begin some time between 1958 and 1998. The cause of these dramatic earth changes will be the shift in the world's magnetic poles. He stated: "There will be upheavals in the Arctic and Antarctic that will cause the eruption of volcanoes in the torrid areas, and pole shift. There will be the shifting then of the poles, so that where there has been those of a frigid or the semi-tropical will become the more tropical, and moss and fern will grow."

"A shift of the earth's axis will result in massive earthquakes and tidal waves." (Ned Dougherty)

"There may be a pole shift ... there are going to be polar changes ... it's not going to kill all the races off, but we're going to have to start again from square one ... There's going to be a larger land mass." (Dr. Kenneth Ring's NDE research subject)

"The poles are going to shift." (Margot Grey's NDE research subject)

"Practically no coastal areas will be safe during the shifting of the earth's poles because of the tidal waves. Many people will not survive this shift, but others will, because after a period of churning seas and frightful wind velocities, the turbulence will cease, and those in the north will live in tropical clime, and vice versa." (Ruth Montgomery)

The following prophecies of a future "Golden Age" were given to Howard Storm during his NDE: (1) No nuclear holocaust will occur (but possibly 1 or 2 bombs go off); (2) There will be almost no technology in the future; (3) Children to be the most precious commodity in the world; (4) Raising children is will be the highest priority; (5) A euphoric future with no anxiety, no hatred, no competition, enormous trust and mutual respect; (6) Love and prayer will become a stronger force on earth; (7) People will garden more in the future with almost no effort; (8) Gardens will grow by the power of prayer; (9) Groups of people praying together will be able to control the climate; (10) Animals will live in harmony with people; (11) Wisdom will be more important than knowledge; (12) All knowledge can be accessed through prayer; (13) People will be able to communicate telepathically with everyone else in the world; (14) There will be greater insight into life after death; (15) It will be like the Garden of Eden; (16) God will usher the paradise on earth within the next 200 years; (17) For paradise to come, God will have to restrict some of humanity's free will; (18) This world will resemble some near-death descriptions of heaven; (19) Travel will be instantaneous; (20) The need for clothing and shelter will be eliminated.

The following prophecies of a future "Golden Age" were given to Mellen-Thomas Benedict during his NDE: (1) The second coming of Jesus is about self-correction because we are already saved; (2) Science will soon quantify spirit and discover what holds the universe together. They will have to call it God; (3) Religions are about to become more enlightened because more light is coming into the world; (4) There will be a reformation in spirituality that is going to be just as dramatic as the Protestant Reformation; (5) There will be many religious people fighting against other religious people because they believe that only they are right; (6) The world will become a safer place; (7) The clearing of the rain forest will slow down and in fifty years there will be more trees on the planet than in a long time; (8) The earth is in the process of domesticating itself and it will never again be as wild of a place as it once was; (9) There will be great wild reserves where nature thrives; (10) Gardening will be the thing in the future; (11) The population increase will reach an optimal range of energy to cause a shift in consciousness. That shift in consciousness will change politics, money, and energy; (12) Humans will soon be able to live as long as we want to live in our bodies. After living 150 years or so, there will be an intuitive sense that it is time to change channels; (13) Humanity will eventually see the wisdom of life and death.

Howard Storm was also given an important message from the Beings of Light concerning the future of humanity: "They want every person to consider every other person greater than their own flesh. They want everyone to love everyone else, completely; more, even, than they love themselves. If someone, someplace else in the world hurts, than we should hurt we should feel their pain. And we should help them. Our planet has evolved to the point, for the first time in our history, that we have the power to do that. We are globally linked. And we could become one people."

The following prophecies of a future "Golden Age" were given to George Ritchie during his NDE: (1) The world will grow more peaceful - both humanity and nature; (2) Humans will not be as critical of themselves or others; (3) Humans will not be as destructive to nature; (4) Humans will begin to understand what love is.

"After the darkest hour had passed away, during which time all the former things of this world had disintegrated and decayed, I saw a new consciousness emerging and humanity evolving in a new form. Thereafter I beheld a Golden Age in which people would live in love and harmony with each other and all of nature." (Margot Grey's research subject)

"At the end of this general period of transition, humanity was to be born anew, with a new sense of his place in the universe. The birth process, however, as in all the kingdoms, was exquisitely painful. Mankind would emerge humbled yet educated, peaceful, and, at last, unified." (Dr. Kenneth Ring's research subject)

"The disastrous earth changes will be followed by a new era in human history, marked by human brotherhood, universal love and world peace." (Dr. Kenneth Ring's research subject)

"After the global disasters, the planet will become more peaceful. Humanity and nature will both be better. Humanity will not be as critical of themselves. Humanity will not be as destructive of nature and will begin to understand what love is. It is up to humanity which direction they will choose." (George Ritchie)

"I saw the earth stretching and groaning while giving birth to a new consciousness. I saw that every so often in the history of the world this happens and is inevitable in order for the earth to bring forth a new state of evolution." (Margot Grey's research subject)

"Humanity will mature enough to assume a higher place in the universal scheme of things. But before this, humans must learn acceptance and tolerance and love for each other. There will come a new age of tolerance will come where the hearts and souls of humanity will be joined as all religions and doctrines will be joined. People will not be able to endure seeing others homeless and hungry. Only by helping each other could we truly help ourselves." (May Eulitt)

"Within the next two hundred years a new era of peace, love and harmony will rule the world." (Howard Storm)

"After the coming earth changes, the harmonic balance of nature on earth will finally be restored." (David Oakford)

"Eventually, humanity will become more peaceful. A new type of human being will emerge with a younger and peaceful nature." (Ricky Randolph)

"The world is on the verge of a spiritual awakening." (Dannion Brinkley)

"People will be happier and more content although living like the native populations of old. There will be no more wars and true peace and happiness will finally come to humanity." (Lou Famoso)

"A profound spiritual awakening will occur to everyone on earth. People will be able to perform supernatural events and miraculous healings." (Ned Dougherty)

"Humanity will be born anew with a new sense of their place in the universe. This birth process will be painful, but humanity will emerge humbled yet educated, peaceful, and, at last, unified." (Reinee Pasarow)

"A great Awakening has begun. People around the world are opening their eyes to their own spiritual natures. They are beginning to see who they truly are and what they have always been -- beings with an eternal past and a glorious future." (Betty Eadie)

SCIENCE

Ultimately, all materialistic explanations for NDEs must fail because they cannot explain the paranormal components of the phenomena, such as shared near-death experiences where multiple people share a near-death experience, and veridical near-death experiences where the experiencer remembers verifiable information that could not have been perceived with his normal senses even if he were conscious. The Spiritual Development Blog has discussed these types of cases and provided examples on their website and elsewhere on their blog. Even claims that veridical perceptions are due to ESP do not contradict the conclusion that near-death experiences represent out-of-the-body consciousness and evidence for the afterlife because ESP is not produced by the brain and ESP during near-death experiences is best explained as out-of-the-body consciousness. However it is interesting to see how weak the materialists' hypotheses are on their own ground. It shows that these materialistic hypotheses are proposed by people who are incredibly ignorant of near-death experiences. It says something sad about the current state of the scientific profession that scientists would make such reckless proposals without investigating the subject they are discussing.

The Dying Brain Theory: According to this skeptical theory, because NDEs have many common core elements, this shows they are not spiritual voyages outside of the body, but are a function of the dying brain. All brains die in the same way and this is why all NDEs have essential core elements which are the same. They are the result of neurotransmitters in the brain shutting down which creates lovely illusions. However, because NDEs have many common core elements, this suggests they are spiritual voyages outside of the body. Also, if the dying brain creates NDE illusions, what is the purpose for doing it? If our brains are only a high-tech computer-like lump of tissue which produces our mind and personality, why does it bother to create illusions at the time of death? If everything, including the mind and personality, are about to disintegrate, why would the brain produce a last wonderful Grand Finale vision? Even if NDE elements can be reduced to only a series of brain reactions, this does not negate the idea of NDEs being more than a brain thing. Read this article on the errors of the pseudo-skeptics of NDEs.

The Lack of Oxygen Theory: Neurologist Ernst Rodin offers cerebral anoxia as a possible cause of NDEs of the dying brain. Such anoxia produces a confusing dream-like state of delusions and hallucinations. However, according to cardiologist Dr. Michael

Sabom, the NDE involves a clear awareness and a more mystical content, and NDEs have also occurred in people without anoxia. Pim van Lommel led a study concerning NDEs during cardiac arrest. In our study all patients had a cardiac arrest, they were clinically dead, unconsciousness that was caused by insufficient blood supply to the brain, and the EEG has become flat. In patients cardiac arrest (ventricular fibrillation) is sometimes induced for testing internal defibrillators. In these patients the EEG becomes usually flat within 10-15 seconds from the onset of syncope due to the (reversible) total loss of function of the brain. According to the physiologic theory, all patients in our study should have had NDE, but only 18% reported NDE.

The Right Temporal Lobe theory: Neurologist Dr. Michael Persinger argues that instability and activity in the brain's right temporal lobe is responsible for religious experiences of deep meaningfulness, early memories, and out-of-body experiences. However, Dr. Melvin Morse agrees with the right temporal lobe showing NDE-like activity, but he sees it as the mediating bridge for a spiritual experience, not reductionistically as nothing but brain activity (Morse, 1992). Also, the characteristic emotions resulting from temporal lobe stimulation are fear, sadness, and loneliness, not the calm and love of an NDE. While scientists may be discovering a mechanism associated with NDEs, this does not mean NDEs are strictly produced by this mechanism. A mechanical function associated with NDEs does not negate the idea of NDEs being more than a mechanical function.

The Cortical Disinhibition theory: NDE skeptic Susan Blackmore interprets the tunnel and the light as an optical illusion created by the effects of anoxia and drugs, creating cortical disinhibition, with the effect of random light spots radiating from the center of a dark internal visual field. However, Dr. Michael Sabom tested and rejected this brain-only argument. While brain neurology is obviously a part of NDEs, he says, it is not a sufficient explanation because of the verified or veridical aspects found in some NDEs. This aspect is suggestive of the possibility of consciousness existing outside of the body.

The Hallucination theory: The psychiatrist Dr. Ronald Siegel interprets NDEs and similar imaginative visions of the afterlife as hallucinations, similar to the effects of psychedelic drugs or anesthesia. However, Psychologist John Gibbs states, "NDE accounts from varied times and cultures were found to be more orderly, logical, defined and predictable than comparable accounts from drug or illness-induced hallucination. Impressive data from Tart, Moody and Carl Becker also argue for the objective elements of an NDE, including returning with knowledge later verified and third-party observations of odd death-bed phenomena (such as luminosity or apparitions). Peter Fenwick, a neuropsychiatrist, notes drug induced hallucinations taking place while the subject is conscious. During an NDE the subject is unconscious. While in the state of unconsciousness, the brain cannot create images. Even if they did, the subject would not be able to remember them. NDEs involve clear, lucid memories. Also, drug induced hallucinations distort reality while NDEs have been described as "hyper-reality."

The Depersonalization theory: Noyes and Kletti theorizes a defense of the nervous system stalling off mental disorganization during the death crisis by presenting an altered passage of time, vivid and accelerated thoughts, a sense of detachment, unreality, automatic movements, and revival of memories. However, Dr. Michael Sabom argues depersonalization fails to account for all the elements of NDEs. Some NDE elements do not fit into the depersonalization mode, such as the strong spiritual and mystical feelings, and the increased alertness and awareness. Also, the vast majority of experiencers reject the idea of their NDE being the result of depersonalization. To reduce what was a profound and transforming experience to nothing more than a set of neurotransmitters going on the blink is a bit like seeing Michelangelo's statue of David as nothing more than several tons of marble.

The Memory of Birth theory: Otto Rank proposed birth trauma being behind all neuroses, for all anxiety-producing experiences of separation reactivate the separation from the mother at birth (Brown, 52-53). This theory has been modified to explain the NDE. The cosmologist Carl Sagan proposed the tunnel and light are a reliving of the infant's descent down the birth canal (Sagan, 353-68). However, Carl Becker asserted that infants descending the birth canal have their eyes closed and brains too undeveloped to allow memories of birth (Becker, 1982). Similarly, Susan Blackmore proved that people born by caesarian section have the tunnel experience and OBEs in equal proportion to those born naturally (Blackmore, 1983). Birth is also often an unpleasant experience for babies. In contrast, NDEs are often described as extremely pleasurable.

The Endorphins theory: The brain's naturally produced narcotics, such as the endorphins, have been offered by endocrinologist Daniel Carr to explain why, at the very moment when the body's death would be expected to bring incredible pain and terror, the NDE surprises us with pleasure, calm, and peace. However, Dr. Melvin Morse responds that patients receiving prescribed narcotics similar to the endorphins experienced no NDEs (Morse, 1989).

The Denial of Death theory: The NDE is seen by some Freudians as a denial of death, a hallucinatory wish fulfillment defending the ego from its impending annihilation. However, a large number of people who have NDEs are initially not even aware they have died. In these cases death is not even considered or denied (e.g., Dr. George Ritchie, Rev. Howard Storm).

The Dissociative (Fear of Death) theory: Severe anxiety and stress at the time of death creates a dissociative state. However, Pim van Lommel led a study concerning NDEs during cardiac arrest. Only a very small percentage of patients said they had been afraid the last seconds preceding the cardiac arrest. Also, the medication given to them made no difference.

Darwin's Evolution theory: This theory holds that NDE reports are a deliberate ploy of humans to help the human race to adapt better to the inevitable end of their lives. This is based on the survival of the fittest which means that every species has the primary urge to struggle to increase its hold on the planet and guarantee the survival of its descendants. However, this theory of evolution, which NDEs support, does not explain why NDEs are erratic, or why we shunted down an evolutionary sidetrack for years by making NDEs something that people are reluctant to talk about.

Too Much Carbon Dioxide (Hypercarbia) theory: This theory holds that NDEs are tricks of the mind triggered by an overload of carbon dioxide in the bloodstream. During cardiac arrest and resuscitation, blood gases such as CO_2 rise or fall because of the lack of circulation and breathing. Patients who experienced the phenomenon, blood carbon-dioxide levels were significantly higher than in those who did not. (Zalika Klemenc-Ketis of the University of Maribor in Slovenia). However, according to neuropsychiatrist Peter Fenwick of the Institute of Psychiatry at Kings College London, "The one difficulty in arguing that CO2 is the cause is that in cardiac arrests, everybody has high CO2 but only 10 percent have NDEs. What's more, in heart attack patients, there is no coherent cerebral activity which could support consciousness, let alone an experience with the clarity of an NDE."

Rapid Eye Movement (REM) Intrusion theory: Dr. Kevin Nelson of the University of Kentucky suggests near-death experiences are akin to dreaming and they use the same rapid eye movement (REM) mechanism associated with sleep. In other words, near-death experiences are a part of the dream mechanism and the person having the experience is in a REM state. However, Dr. Jeffrey Long from the Near-Death Experience Research Foundation (NDERF.org) disagrees with Nelson on a number of points. First of all, he states that Nelson's comparison group - the non-NDErs - is not typical and many were medical professionals and colleagues of Nelson. Secondly, Nelson's research questionnaire was poorly designed. Thirdly, Nelson failed to recognize dramatic differences between NDE and REM intrusion. Hallucinations stemming from REM intrusion - just before waking or while falling asleep - are often "bizarre and unrealistic" such as seeing objects appear through cracks in a wall or movement in a painting on the wall. By contrast, memories from an NDE are lucid and rooted in the real world. NDErs almost uniformly don't say, "Oh, that must have been a dream." About 75 percent say they were more alert, more conscious than normal. There's also a consistency of elements in NDEs which hallucinations don't have. Fourthly, 98 percent of NDErs encounter deceased relatives, as opposed to dreams where it's common to encounter living people. NDErs also encounter deceased relatives whom they didn't know at the time were dead. Fifthly, the totality of evidence shows there's something going on that's outside the medical evidence. NDEers almost always say that it wasn't a hallucination or dream; it was some different realm, some different aspect of their existence. And finally, REM intrusion - whether sleep paralysis or hallucinations - tends to be frightening or deeply unsettling. By contrast, most people who go through an NDE say the experience is almost supernaturally calm and peaceful, even joyful. Not only anecdotes, but real evidence does support this. In a 2001 study in the medical journal The Lancet, of 62 cardiac attest patients who reported an NDE, more than half said the main emotions they experienced were "positive." Long says these distinctive, positive emotions are powerful evidence that an NDE is not just REM intrusion in disguise.

The "Sharp Increase of Brain Activity After Heart Stops" theory: Dr Jimo Borjigin of the University of Michigan suggests that the dying brain does not shut down as might be expected, but instead, becomes much more active during the dying process than even the waking state. He bases his findings on a study involving rats where it was discovered that in the 30-second period after the rodents' hearts stopped beating, there was a sharp increase in high-frequency brainwaves. However, in a paper entitled, "Seeing Dead People Not Known to Have Died: Peak in Darien Experiences," Dr. Bruce Greyson from the Division of Perceptual Studies at the University of Virginia argues that in his collection of 665 NDEs, 138 (21%) included a purported meeting with a deceased person. People on their deathbeds see and often express surprise at meeting a recently deceased person whose death neither they nor anyone around them had any knowledge. This excludes the possibility that the vision was a hallucination related to the experiencer's expectations. Such NDEs are termed "Peak in Darien" cases, after a book by that name published in 1882 by Frances Power Cobbe. The title is taken from a John Keats poem describing the shock of the Spaniards, who, after scaling a peak in Darien (in what is now Panama), expect to see a continent, but are confronted instead with another ocean. Bruce Greyson reports in his paper, published in the academic journal 'Anthropology and Humanism', many examples, including that of Physician K. M. Dale who related the case of 9-year-old Eddie Cuomo, whose fever finally broke after nearly 36 hours of anxious vigil on the part of his parents and hospital personnel. As soon as he opened his eyes, at 3:00 in the morning, Eddie related that he had been to heaven, where he saw his deceased Grandpa Cuomo, Auntie Rosa, and Uncle Lorenzo. Then Eddie added that he also saw his 19-year-old sister Teresa, who told him he had to go back. His father became agitated, because he had spoken with Teresa, who was attending college in Vermont, just two nights ago. Later that morning, Eddie's parents learned that Teresa had been killed in an automobile accident just after midnight, and that college officials had tried unsuccessfully to reach the Cuomos at their home. Bruce Greyson relates many other examples, including cases in which the deceased person seen was someone whom the experiencer had never known. For example, Greyson reports cardiologist Maurice Rawlings describing the case of a 48-year-old man who had a cardiac arrest. In an NDE he perceived a gorge full of beautiful colors, where he met both his stepmother and his biological mother, who had died when he was 15 months old. His father had remarried soon after his biological mother's death, and this person had never even seen a photo of her. A few weeks after this episode, his aunt, having heard about this vision, brought a picture of his mother with a number of other people. The man picked his mother out of the group, to the astonishment of his father.

The Consciousness Survives Bodily Death (Afterlife) theory: There exists strong circumstantial evidence of consciousness surviving bodily death. While this evidence does not constitute conclusive scientific proof, it does make survival after bodily death a possibility which can be upheld in a court of law. The evidence for survival can be found in science, philosophy, history, metaphysics, religion, and anecdotal testimony. Quantum physics (see above) makes some scientific theories of the NDE outmoded while supporting elements of NDEs. Scientific studies support the possible validity of NDEs elements such as being out of the body, the retention of mental images during brain death, veridical experiences of autoscopic events, the ability to accurately foresee the future, receiving information that leads to new scientific discoveries, people born blind being able to see, groups of people sharing a single experience, unbiased children having similar experiences as adults, causing experiencers to be drastically changed and convinced of survival after death, the evidence supporting the objectivity of NDEs, and the affirmation of ancient religious concepts found around the world. Some of the skeptical arguments against the survival theory are often not valid and the burden of proof against survival has shifted to the skeptics.

The following is evidence supporting NDEs as the survival of consciousness:

Quantum physics makes some materialistic theories of the NDE outmoded. New developments in quantum physics show that we cannot know phenomena apart from the observer. Arlice Davenport challenges the hallucination theory of NDEs as outmoded because the field theories of physics now suggest new paradigm options available to explain NDEs. Mark Woodhouse argues that the traditional materialism/dualism battle over NDEs may be solved by Einstein. Since matter is now seen as a form of energy, an energy body alternative to the material body could explain the NDE. This is supported by

Melvin Morse who describes how NDEs are able to realign the charges in the electromagnetic field of the human body so that somehow the brain's wiring is renewed. He reports on patients who have NDEs and who recover from such diseases as pneumonia, cardiac arrest, and cancer (1992, 153-54). Perhaps the brain is like a kind of receiver such as a television, radio, or cell phone. What is received (i.e., signals, music, voice) is not produced by the receiver, but exists separately as electromagnetic waves that are processed by the receiver to make them visible or audible to the senses.

Quantum physics support elements found in NDEs. Similarities can be found between elements of NDEs and in quantum field concepts of non-locality, universal interconnectedness, a non-material dimension without our time-space relationship, and in the concept of subjectivity. All events are related and influence each other instantaneously and in reciprocity, and only subjectivity remains.

Scientific studies support the out-of-body aspect of NDEs. Pim van Lommel led a study concerning the NDEs of research subjects who had cardiac arrest. The findings of this study suggest research subjects can experience consciousness, with self-identity, cognitive function and memories, including the possibility of perception outside their body, during a flat EEG. Those research subjects who had NDEs report that their NDE was a bona fide preview of the afterlife.

Memories and images are produced and retained by standstill patients. See Dr. Michael Sabom's groundbreaking Atlanta study.

People see and hear verifiable events far from their bodies during an NDE. See (a) Dr. Charles Tart's research subject, (b) Pam Reynolds, (c) Dr. George Rodonaia, (d) Dr. George Ritchie, and (e) various NDE experiencers.

Strange aspects to NDEs cannot be explained by brain chemistry alone. If NDEs are merely hallucinations, why do the vast majority of experiencers report being told an identical and unusual message? This unusual message is that they must return because their time for death hasn't come, or some variation of this. Assuming that NDEs are merely hallucinations, it is odd that people are having mass hallucinations of receiving similar unusual messages.

People born blind are able to see during an NDE. See Vicki Umipeg's NDE account.

Groups of people can share the same NDE at the same time. NDE research Arvin Gibson documented the account of a group of firefighters who succumbed to a forest fire. During their NDEs they saw each other outside of their bodies and had a most interesting experience. See thee Group NDE web page involving May Eulitt and Jake.

People are able to successfully foresee future events during an NDE. Some of these events were the Second World War, Desert Storm, and the September 11, 2001 terrorist attack.

People are declared dead and left for dead for several days during an NDE. A Russian scientist was declared dead and put in the morgue for three days during which he had an NDE. See Dr. George Rodonaia's and Emanuel Tuwagirairmana's NDE accounts.

Unbiased children have NDEs that are similar to adult NDEs. See P.M.H. Atwater's research on childhood NDEs.

Scientific discoveries have been made from the direct result of NDEs. See the list of scientific discoveries above.

NDEs can be viewed to be archetypal initiatory journeys. Dr. Ken Ring stated that NDEs can be viewed psychologically as archetypal initiatory journeys involving a death of one's old ego and a rebirth of a new self. An adequate interpretation must incorporate the spiritual realm of kundalini experiences, the imaginal realm, and the mind at large. As Ring envisions in an essay in this book, this paradigm can deconstruct our traditional Western worldview. It may lead to a dramatic next step in the evolution of a more ecological and more compassionate consciousness.

People are dramatically changed as a result from having an NDE. The philosophy of Positivism, founded by A. J. Ayer, is the philosophy that anything not verifiable by the senses is nonsense. And since NDEs mark the end of the senses, the survival of the senses after death is nonsense. But this philosophy is challenged by its founder A. J. Ayer himself. Later in life, Ayer had an NDE where he saw a red light. His NDE made him a changed man: "My recent experiences, have slightly weakened my conviction that my genuine death...will be the end of me, though I continue to hope that it will be." (Ayer, 1988 a,b).

People are absolutely convinced they were out of their body during an NDE.

NDEs can be considered an objective experience: The philosopher Carl Becker examined four ways in which NDEs may be considered objective: examined four ways in which NDEs may be considered objective: (a) Paranormal knowledge that is later verified; (b) The similarity of deathbed events in different cultures; (c) Differences between religious expectations and visionary experiences; (d) Third-party observations of visionary figures, indicating that they were not merely subjective hallucinations (Becker, 1984).

Other paranormal phenomena supports NDEs to be experiences of the survival of consciousness including: (a) Deathbed visions, (b) Quantum physics, (c) Dream research, (d) Out-of-body research, (e) After-death communications research, (f) Reincarnation research, (g) Hypnosis, (h) Synchronicity, (i) Remote viewing, and (j) Consciousness research.

NDEs have been happening for thousands of years and are not a modern phenomenon: See the NDE accounts associated with (a) Plato, (b) the Apostle Paul, and (c) the Tibetan Book of the Dead.

Skeptical arguments against the survival theory of NDEs are often not valid. Sociologist Dr. Allan Kellehear states that some scientific theories are often presented as the most logical, factual, objective, credible, and progressive possibilities, as opposed to the allegedly subjective, superstitious, abnormal, or dysfunctional views of mystics. The rhetorical opinions of some NDE theories are presented as if they were scientific (Kellehear, 1996, 120). Many skeptical arguments against the survival theory are actually arguments from pseudo-skeptics who often think they have no burden of proof. Such arguments often based on scientism with assumptions that survival is impossible even though survival has not been ruled out. Faulty conclusions are often made such as, "Because NDEs have a brain chemical connection then survival is impossible." Pseudo-skeptical arguments are sometimes made that do not consider the entire body of circumstantial evidence supporting the possibility of survival or do not consider the possibility of new paradigms. Such pseudo-skeptical claims are often made without any scientific evidence.

Memories of near-death experiences are more real than reality: Researchers at the Coma Science Group, directed by Steven Laureys, and the University of Liege's Cognitive Psychology Research, headed by Professor Serge Bredart and Hedwige Dehon, have demonstrated that the physiological mechanisms triggered during NDE lead to a more vivid perception not only of imagined events in the history of an individual but also of real events which have taken place in their lives! These surprising results - obtained using an original method which now requires further investigation - are published in PLOS ONE. The researchers looked into the memories of NDE with the hypothesis that if the memories of NDE were pure products of the imagination, their phenomenological characteristics (e.g., sensorial, self-referential, emotional, etc. details) should be closer to those of imagined memories. Conversely, if the NDE are experienced in a way similar to that of reality, their characteristics would be closer to the memories of real events. Their results were surprising. From the perspective being studied, not only were the NDEs not similar to the memories of imagined events, but the phenomenological characteristics inherent to the memories of real events (e.g. memories of sensorial details) are even more numerous in the memories of NDE than in the memories of real events.

The burden of proof has shifted to skeptics of the survival theory of NDEs. All neurological theories that conclude NDEs to be only a brain anomaly must show how the core elements of the NDE occur subjectively because of specific neurological events triggered by the approach of death. These core elements include: the out-of-body state, paranormal knowledge, the tunnel, the golden light, the voice or presence, the appearance of deceased relatives, and beautiful vistas. Perhaps the final word should go to Nancy Evans Bush, a NDEr with the International Association for Near-Death Studies, who said: "There is no human experience of any description that can't simply be reduced to a biological process, but that in no way offsets the meaning those experiences have for us-whether it's falling in love, or grieving, or having a baby."

A significant amount of support suggestive of consciousness surviving bodily death exists. Although this has not been proven conclusively using the scientific method, the open-minded skeptic include this significant amount of evidence as well as taken into consideration the testimonies of millions of people who have had both objective and subjective NDEs and OBEs constituting very strong circumstantial evidence.

GOD

People having NDEs know the light they have seen during their NDEs is what religions refer to as "God". Once people enter into this light, the consensus among experiencers is that they never want to return to their body. They are also told it is not their time to die and so they return having this experience of the light of God seared into their soul. They carry this experience back with them to share with others, but they sometimes find difficulty doing so. But their experience with the light and the lessons they learned are just too important to keep to themselves. For example, one particular experiencer said he was told the time is now for humanity to know for certain there is life after death. Many aspects of the NDE are now considered common knowledge among the public such as the light, the tunnel, the being of light, etc. Clearly, NDE testimonies are bringing information about God and heaven to Earth. In this article, experiencers describe how God is life, light, time and space, the pattern for all life, the energy of all matter, the heart of all that matters, the very essence of all being, the source behind every sun, the source of all light and love, the core of all things, the single point of infinite light and absolute love, and the very life force of the universe.

The following NDE insights show that God is Light:

"Within the Light of God, we realize that everyone and everything is connected to God ... Within the Light was the cure for all diseases; within the Light was all the knowledge of every planet, every galaxy, every universe. Indeed, the Light was Wisdom and Love beyond all comprehension." (Dr. Dianne Morrissey)

"The closer one gets to God, the closer one comes to all the light, love and knowledge in the universe." (Jayne Smith)

"The joy of being in the light of God can be so intense, we may think we are going to shatter. But God will not let us shatter. We are not permitted to take in more of this bliss and joy than we are able to handle at a time." (Jayne Smith)

Bible Verse: "This is the message we have heard from him and declare to you: God is light; in him there is no darkness at all." (Apostle John, 1 John 1:5)

Bible Verse: "For everyone practicing evil hates the light and does not come to the light, lest his deeds should be exposed. But he who does the truth comes to the light, that his deeds may be clearly seen, that they have been done in God." (Jesus, John 3:20-21)

The following NDE insights show that God is Love.

One of the best NDE revelations concerning God, the universe and everything in it comes from Larry Hagman of the Dallas television series whose NDE testimony is described in my list of NDEs of the Rich and Famous. Here is the revelation he learned: "Everyone has within them a unique "celestial song" - an inner melody wanting to burst forth. The inner vibration within us connects us to the deep, modulating, harmonious music of the "celestial orchestra." This cosmic orchestra is the collective energy of everything that's ever lived and everything that's ever going to live. It is the life force. It is the power of the universe. It is ecstatically happy. The culmination of this energy is love. Love abounds with its feelings of ecstasy and deep bliss. It is the love holding every atom, every sparrow, every galaxy, everything together. Everyone has forever been a part of this life force and always will. We are already familiar with this at a deep level. We know it. The problem is we bury it under so much apprehension and worry. Don't worry. Be happy and feel good. There are an infinite number of levels of existence and each level adds to the hum of the cosmic orchestra. It's as if we're always spiraling upward until we reach a state of atomic bliss. Life continues. The show goes on in ever varied and unfolding settings." (Larry Hagman)

"God is love in its purest form ... To be in his presence and share his love, we must become as he is and learn to love without judgments or conditions." (Betty Eadie)

"God's standard is pure love. Our lives will be compared to this standard in the light of God. Pure love is serving God and others without any self-centered motives. Self-centered motives are what makes our acts (as the scriptures say) "dirty rags" before God." (Daniel Rosenblit)

Bible Verse: "Dear friends, let us love one another, for love comes from God. Everyone who loves has been born of God and knows God. Whoever does not love does not know God, because God is love... And so we know and rely on the love God has for us. God is love. Whoever lives in love lives in God, and God in them." (Apostle John, 1 John 4:7-8; 1 John 4:16)

The following NDE insights show that God is Life:

"God is everywhere because nothing exists that is not a part of God. God is neither a man nor a woman nor a thing. Life itself is God." (P.M.H. Atwater)

"All creation is God exploring God's very being through every way imaginable, through every one of us." (Mellen-Thomas Benedict)

"The Biblical name for God, 'I AM,' really has a question mark behind it. 'I AM? WHAT AM I?'" (Mellen-Thomas Benedict)

Bible Verse: "From one man he (God) made all the nations, that they should inhabit the whole earth; and He marked out their appointed times in history and the boundaries of their lands. God did this so that they would seek him and perhaps reach out for him and find him, though he is not far from any one of us. 'For in him we live and move and have our being.' [1] As some of your own poets have said, 'We are his offspring.'" [2] (Acts 17:26-28). Notice in this Bible verse how the Apostle Paul references the Greek philosopher poets Epimenides [1] who lived in the 7th or 6th century BC, and Aratus [2] who lived from 310 BC - 240 BC.

The following is Edgar Cayce's description of God as paraphrased in Thomas Sugrue's book, There Is A River:

People usually demand a beginning, so in the beginning there was a sea of Spirit and it filled all of space. The Spirit was static, content, and aware of itself. It was a giant resting on the bosom of its thought and contemplating what it is. Then the Spirit moved into action. It withdrew into itself until all of space was empty. In the center, the sparkling Mind of the Spirit shone. This was the beginning of the individuality of the Spirit. This was what the Spirit discovered itself to be when it awakened. This Spirit was God. God desired self-expression and desired companionship; therefore, God projected the cosmos and souls. The cosmos was built with music, arithmetic, geometry, harmony, system, and balance. The building blocks were all of the same material - the life essence - God simply changed the wavelength and rate of vibration of these building blocks thereby creating the patterns for multitudes of life forms. This action resulted in the law of diversity which supplied endless patterns. God played on this law of diversity as a pianist plays on a piano - producing melodies and arranging them in a symphony.

Each design carried within it the plan for its evolution - both physical and spiritual. This plan corresponds to the sound of a note struck on a piano. The sounds of several notes unite to make a chord; chords in turn become phrases; phrases become melodies; melodies intermingle and move back and forth, across and between and around each other, to make a symphony. Then in the end, the music will stop and the physical universe will be no more; but between the beginning and the finish of the music, there was glorious beauty and a glorious experience. The spiritual universe will continue on. Everything assumed its design in various forms and their activity resulted in the laws of attraction and repulsion. All forms would attract and repel each other in their evolutionary dance. All things are a part of God and an expression of God's thought. The Mind of God was the force which propelled and perpetuated these thoughts. All minds, as thoughts of God, do everything God imagined. Everything which came into being is an aspect of this One Mind. All things, including the souls of individuals, were created as "fractals" of God for companionship with God - the "Whole." This revelation from Cayce revealed the astonishing fact of how self-similar the universe is on every scale: from the atom to biological organisms, from human beings to the planet Earth, from solar systems to galaxies, from the universe(s) to God. (Edgar Cayce)

The following NDE insights show that God is Everything.

"The only reality is God and God is love. God loves without limit. God is everything." (Linda Stewart)

"God is everything." (Dr. George Rodonaia)

Bible Verse: "He (God) is before all things, and in him all things hold together." (Colossians 1:17)

"God is in everyone, always and forever ... Being one with the Light was like suddenly knowing every grain of sand on every planet, in every galaxy, in every universe, and at the same time knowing why God had put each grain of sand in its particular place. The Light held within it the knowledge of every book in every language, from the beginning of creation to the end of time. The Light knew why every author had put every word exactly where it was. The Light conveyed the message that each gain of sand, each plant, rock, animal, and human being has a purpose and that nothing ever dies because after death, there is a new life on the Other Side." (Dr. Dianne Morrissey)

The following NDE insights show that God is Darkness:

"God is more than light. God is also the darkness." (Dr. George Rodonaia)

Bible Verse: "I form the light and create darkness, I bring prosperity and create disaster; I, the Lord, do all these things." (Isaiah 45:7)

The following NDE insights show that God is Energy:

"The Master-Vibrational energy of God controls the universe and seems to regulate everything except the ignorance within the minds of people on Earth." (Arthur Yensen)

"God is the creative energy of the universe, expressing itself as us and everything else. Wherever we are, God is. Like God, we are constantly expressing ourselves in some way." (Jan Price)

One of the major laws of physics states that energy cannot be created or destroyed. $E = mc2$ (or Energy is the product of mass times the speed of light squared, shows how important the properties of light are to energy.) (Albert Einstein)

The following NDE insights show the Nature of God:

"God has a vantage point we can never perceive. He sees into our eternal pasts and futures and knows our eternal needs. In his great love he answers prayers according to this eternal and omniscient perspective. He answers all prayers perfectly." (Betty Eadie)

"God is Love, Light, and energy in all. God is the source of perfect Love and all; life. Everything is a part of God. Just as the smallest atom of your physical body is part of you, you are a part of God. God is in all places at all times. Our soul is a part of God and God is a part of us; therefore, our souls are immortal and eternal. Listen to that small inner voice in your thoughts; it is the voice of God. All you do and think is known to God, and God understands everything perfectly, and loves everyone just the same. God loves and forgives you, and expects you to love and forgive others. We are all one with God, and to hurt even the smallest part of God hurts us all. God does not punish, He only loves. He has given us free will to grow in knowledge and find happiness. Every thought or action causes a reaction by which we must live with the consequences. As an example, if I choose evil over good I suffer the natural consequences which I may perceive as God punishing me. Light is the single source through which all are united. God sends truth through many channels to those who ask." (Sandra Rogers)

"God wants us to become as he is, and has invested us with godlike qualities. I understood that he wants us to draw on the powers of heaven, and that by believing we are capable of doing so, we can." (Betty Eadie)

"The little voice inside us that prompts us to do good things comes from God. It is the light of love inside each of us." (Kerry Kirk)

"God doesn't force anyone to heaven, hell, or anywhere. We are free to choose and build our destiny. All paths lead back to God." (Edgar Cayce)

"God perfectly understands our lack of knowledge. He knows that most of us do not remember our commitments to him. In his eyes we are like little children: susceptible and even expected to make mistakes." (Betty Eadie)

"In the light of God, it is impossible to lie to yourself, or to others or to God. There is no place for secrets to hide." (Dr. George Ritchie)

"God does not judge us when we die. In the clear light and understanding of God, some people may judge, condemn and punish only themselves. There is no judgment except the judgment one levels at oneself. And self is the worst enemy we will ever face." (Kevin Williams)

"God has promised not to intervene in our lives unless we ask." (Betty Eadie)

"It is God's love for us that sends us on our journey and it is our love for God that allows us to return to God's loving arms again." (David Goines)

"God feels the pain we feel and inflict on others." (Sandra Rogers)

"One of the grandest mysteries of God is his foreknowledge. Truth is knowledge of things as they were, as they are, and as they are to come. God, possessing all truth, has the ability to know all things in advance. This being the case, we can trust him to give us only that which will be good for us in completing our life's mission successfully." (Betty Eadie)

"God's overriding desire is to purify the darkness of our souls, irrespective of the suffering it puts us through to achieve that end. If we learn to accept our situations in life, instead of getting angry, then our suffering is greatly minimized." (Daniel Rosenblit)

"God never uses his love to hurt us. To do so would countermand his own law of judgment. "Do unto others as you would have them do unto you." So he will never let us down, and will never forsake us. His love is extended to all, and he knows exactly how to reach each person." (Betty Eadie)

The following NDE insights show how God encompasses all religions:

"God does not care about theology. God cares mostly about your heart." (Rev. Howard Storm)

"It doesn't matter what you call God. The different religions have different ways of explaining the same God." (Mellen-Thomas Benedict)

"Your beliefs shape the kind of feedback you get from God." (Mellen-Thomas Benedict)

"God is not concerned about a person's sexual orientation whether gay or straight." (Kerry Kirk)

P.M.H. Atwater, L.H.D., Ph.D. (Hon.) survived three near-death experiences in 1977. She is one of the original researchers of the near-death phenomenon, having begun her work in 1978. Today, her contribution to the field of near-death studies is considered on par with those of Raymond Moody and Ken Ring. Her first two books, Coming Back to Life and

Beyond the Light, are considered the "Bibles" of the NDE. Here she explains the concept of God learned from her experiences and her research:

"God IS. God is the one presence, the one power, the one force and source of all. There are no competitors to God, no reality existent outside of God. God is omnipotent (all powerful), omniscient (all knowing), and omnipresent (present everywhere). There is no place where God is not, simply because nothing exists outside of God.

"God is neither a man nor a woman nor a thing. God is no one's father or mother or benefactor. These terms are used only to help us understand relationships -- ours to God -- not to establish a more human type of parentage. We use such terms as a matter of convenience or because it is comforting to do so. We call ourselves children of God because we do not know what else to call ourselves, and it seems as good a term as any to use. We are made in the image of God, not in the sense of physical appearance, but with respect to the power of our souls and the potential of our minds. God is the Creator; we are co-creators. It would be more appropriate and more in line with Truth, if we called ourselves extensions of God or, perhaps, thoughts in the Mind of God. It would even be appropriate to use another name for God, like The Force, The One, The All, The Is-ness, The One Mind, The Source, or whatever conveys that sense of deity that is without limitation or boundary, beyond what can be comprehended.

"While God is more than any name, protocol, hierarchy, concept, or grandiosity could describe or define; God truly is as near as our next breath - as close as our next thought. We are part of God and existent with God. A belief in separation, that we could possibly exist and have our being apart from God, is the only real sin. This belief is of our own making. God has not decreed separation; this we did ourselves by our own perception that somehow, some way, we could transcend That Which Cannot Be Transcended.

"God is not dependent on our belief, for our belief or disbelief in God does not affect God -- only us. God is not a member of any church or religion. It is the churches and the religions that are members within the vastness and the glory that is God. There is no one religion just as there is no "chosen" people or person, nor any single way of regarding what cannot be fully comprehended. We are all "sons" of God in the sense that we are all souls of God's creation, without gender, without form, without nationality, complete and whole and perfect as we explore the never-endingness of God's wonderment. A spark from the essence of All God Is resides in each and every one of us has an unbreakable connection, that thread or cord that ensures we remain a part of That Which We Could Never Leave.

"The splendorous joy of recognizing and acknowledging our special-ness, our greatness, as creations of God and as co-creators with God, is akin to being engulfed by overwhelming floodtides of God's Glorious Love." (P.M.H. Atwater)

HEAVEN

Where is heaven? Is it up in the sky somewhere? From the beginning of recorded history, humans have expressed in various ways their desire to attain heaven - as a paradise on earth and after death. But history shows how searching for a heaven on earth is like searching for an illusion. Religions have been created to help people find heaven after death. The overall consensus of the major religions is that heaven as a society cannot be found on earth; but rather, heaven is a state of mind and condition of the heart. Skeptics unknowingly agree with this when they claim heaven to be merely a figment of the human mind and imagination. By focusing within ourselves through meditation, dreams, prayer, and even quiet reflection, we connect with the heaven we seek within us. When we are in love, we say we're "in heaven." When we are separated from love, it may feel like "hell." Religious figures such as Jesus and Buddha have helped humanity understand how loving others is the way to heaven and that this heaven can be found within us. Near-death experiences (NDEs) describe a hierarchy of afterlife realms of which the physical realm is just one of them. The following presents revelations about heaven from the perspective of NDE testimony and research.

"God doesn't force anyone to heaven, hell, or anywhere. We are free to choose and build our destiny. Nevertheless, all destinies eventually lead back to God." (Edgar Cayce)

"If I lived a billion years more, in my body or yours, there's not a single experience on earth that could ever be as good as being dead. Nothing." (Dr. Dianne Morrissey)

"Life on earth is a preparation for a fuller, freer and richer eternal existence in heaven; much like a baby in a womb preparing to be born." (Nora Spurgin)

"The earth is the only place where God can determine if you want to go to heaven or hell." (Mihbond)

"We mustn't wait to find our heaven in the clouds. We must find it here because it exists here and will be whatever we make it and whatever we are willing to accept of it." (Tina)

"Love is a sign from the heavens that you are here for a reason." (J. Ghetto)

"There may be a good reason why relatively few people have NDEs. Perhaps too many glimpses of heaven might destroy our freedom. Forcing people into heaven would be like turning them into robots. And nobody loves a robot because they are incapable of love." (Kevin Williams)

Sandra Rogers asked the light, whom she identified as Jesus, how people from other religions get to heaven. She was shown that the group, or organization, that people profess alliance to is inconsequential. What is important is how we show our love for God by the way we treat each other. (Sandra Rogers)

"Doctrine, creed and race mean nothing in heaven. No matter what we believed we were all God's children. The only rule is to do unto others as you would have them do unto you." (May Eulitt)

"Heaven is about deeds, not creeds. Therefore, persons of many cultures and religions form the societies of heaven." (Emanuel Swedenborg)

"Heaven is not sitting down and casting down your golden crowns and singing Hallelujah. However, there is a tendency among certain religious people in heaven to congregate in their little groups and have their little sessions of what they feel are "heaven." Eventually, they become very bored with this narrowness, and then their own helpers and teachers will try to give them another thought and another idea and help them to break away from this narrow approach." (Margaret Tweddell)

"I saw the Christian heaven. We expect it to be a beautiful place, and you stand in front of the throne, worshipping forever. I tried it. It is boring! This is all we are going to do? It is childlike. I do not mean to offend anyone. Some heavens are very interesting, and some are very boring. I found the ancient ones to be more interesting, like the Native American ones, the Happy Hunting Grounds. The Egyptians have fantastic ones. It goes on and on. There are so many of them." (Mellen-Thomas Benedict)

"The most difficult thing for a person who has been deeply steeped in a particular religious tradition is to realize that the form alone is not what elevates a person; it is the heart. Still, those who cling to an external form of religion will be most comfortable with others who practice the same rituals, whatever they may be. In this sense, congregations may continue centered around the particular religious traditions they practiced while on earth." (Nora Spurgin)

"In heaven, Buddhists can experience their own path and Christians can experience their own path. Same with Hindus, Muslims, and any religious group. All have their own paradise, goals, aims, and objectives until they suddenly have a tremendous experience of knowing that all is one under God and that there is no division in purpose. There is one God of us all." (Margaret Tweddell)

"It is said that the Golden Rule is the governing principle in the spirit world: do unto others as you would have them do unto you. People who truly practice the religion of love will find themselves in a universal sphere where everyone understands that true religion is to love others as ourselves." (Nora Spurgin)

"It is within the simple principles of the gospel that the mysteries of heaven are found." (RaNelle Wallace)

"Genesis is the symbolic account of the soul's journey from heaven. Revelation is the symbolic story of the soul's return to heaven. It is the story of paradise lost and paradise found." (Edgar Cayce)

"The purpose of religion is not so much to get us into heaven, or to keep us out of hell, but to put a little bit of heaven into us, and take the hell out of us." (E. Stanley Jones)

"People who have spiritual love will enter heaven. People who do not have spiritual love will enter hell." (Emanuel Swedenborg)

"God's paradise for us is love. We can create paradise again if we learn to love one another as ourselves." (Sandra Rogers)

"When we love unselfishly, our vibrations are so high that the only place we'll fit into is heaven. There is no other place we can go if we want to. This is divine justice because it gives everyone an equal chance to eventually attain the harmony to fit into some kind of heaven - regardless of their intelligence, education, indoctrination, ignorance, wealth or poverty." (Arthur Yensen)

"A heavenly existence is created by how we live on earth, including the truths we have lived, taught, and believed in life; and the love, peace, and compassion we have known for ourselves and those we have touched. Everything else is associated with a hellish existence." (Tina)

"It is a life of love, a life of behaving honestly and fairly in every task, that leads to a heavenly life. This life is not hard." (Emanuel Swedenborg)

"The heavenly realm we enter into after death is determined by how we have lived our lives on earth. We must earn our citizenship into the various heavenly realms and we do so at our own pace." (Betty Bethards)

"Everyone is born with a spiritual void within them. Throughout our lives, we fill our void with a multitude of things. Then when we die, we step into the spiritual void we have filled. This is why having love within us is so important when we die. Giving and receiving love from the heart, creates a heavenly paradise within us which is manifested in the spirit world and becomes realized at death." (Kevin Williams)

"The general rule of thumb is this: hellish life, hellish afterlife - heavenly life, heavenly afterlife. Death will not change a hellish life into a heavenly afterlife, nor does it change a heavenly life into a hellish afterlife." (Dr. Melvin Morse)

"We do not go to heaven. We grow to heaven here on earth." (Edgar Cayce)

"The spiritual state of being we have on earth is the spiritual state we take with us to heaven. There is no sudden metamorphosis from an idle person into an active person, from a nonreligious person into a religious person, from a money-centered person into a God-centered person." (Margaret Tweddell)

"Day by day we are building for eternity. Every gentle word, every generous thought, every unselfish deed will become a pillar of eternal beauty in the life to come." (Rebecca Springer)

"When we die, we take this heaven of love with us to the level of heaven that corresponds to the love within us." (Kevin Williams)

"All you may know of heaven or hell is within your own self." (Edgar Cayce)

"If we are willing to suppress our self-centered nature so that our higher spiritual nature can gain control, it will bring about a resurrection and ascension of the transformed self, which can create heaven on earth." (Dr. George Ritchie)

"No heaven can come to us unless our hearts find rest in it today." (Fra Giovanni)

"The best way to get to heaven is to take it with you." (Henry Drummond)

"People don't go to heaven because of their good deeds, or because they believe this or that, but because they fit in and belong. It's what you are that counts." (Arthur Yensen)

"To love is to receive a glimpse of heaven." (Karen Sunde)

"Jesus taught people that the way to heaven is through love and that this heaven of love is within us. And because love is God, we manifest this heaven on earth when we love others. But when we refuse to love, we create a hell within us which also becomes manifested on earth. Being without love is absolute hell. But if we give love, we are already in heaven." (Kevin Williams)

"As much of heaven is visible as we have eyes to see." (Ralph Waldo Emerson)

"You'll not be in heaven if you're not leaning on the arm of someone you have helped." (Edgar Cayce)

"Children who have NDEs sometimes report having to visit an animal heaven before they can go to the adult heaven. (P.M.H. Atwater)

"From the light we have come and to the light we all shall return." (Josiane Antonette)

"Paths are visible in the spirit realm. Some lead to heaven and some to hell. Good people travel only along paths that lead to heaven according to their own desire. They do not see paths leading in other directions. Evil people follow only paths that lead to hell according to their own desire. They do not see paths leading in other directions; and even if they do, they do not want to follow them." (Emanuel Swedenborg)

"In heaven you feel much more alive than you will ever feel here. Our lives on earth are for just a short time, like a vacation. You visit, try to find your way around, and just when you think you've got it down, it's time to go home. When you go home to heaven, you know exactly where you are, what you're doing. It's just a wonderful place. There's no hatred, just love, kindness, and mercy. It's one huge family there." (Roy Mills)

"Some experiencers meet people in heaven who are yet to be born or preparing to be born into the world." (Kevin Williams)

"To appreciate heaven well it is good for a man to have some fifteen minutes of hell." (Will Carleton)

"From an endless dream we have come. In an endless dream we are living. To an endless dream we shall return." (Michio Kushi)

"As the two beings approached us, I could also feel the love flowing from them toward us. The complete joy they showed at seeing the Christ was unmistakable. Seeing these beings and feeling the joy, peace and happiness which swelled up from them made me feel that here was the place of all places, the top realm of all realms. The beings who inhabited it were full of love. This, I was and am convinced, is heaven." (Dr. George Ritchie)

"Turning back to the interior of the temple, I saw that creative activities were taking place in different areas. There were a number of individuals sitting at easels painting, and I saw one man playing a flutelike instrument that emitted the sweetest of sounds. Farther on, dancers moved with ethereal grace, performing with a lightness impossible to the physical human form. As I watched in utter delight, I became aware that the musical background for this visual feast came from what I would call a celestial choir - an orchestra of voices creating heavenly music for the dance. This Music of the Spheres was indeed singing the praises of the Creator." (Jan Price)

"Instead of allowing me to enter, the angel stationed me before the gates, slightly to one side. He instructed me to stay there and watch as the saints were permitted to enter into heaven. As the saints were allowed into heaven, I noticed a strange thing. They were permitted to enter only one at a time. No two were permitted to enter those gates at the same time. I wondered about this but it was never explained to me." (Rev. Howard Pittman)

"The experience of merging with the light of God is like having your body explode in a pleasant way and becoming a million different atoms. Each atom can think its own thoughts and have its own feelings. You feel all at once what it feels like to be everything and everybody." (Nora Spurgin)

"Jesus said that I would never quite be the same as I was before I visited heaven. He said that some of the power of the light would remain within me. And he told me to let the love that I would feel in my heart express itself to all people. He said that I should never worry if people doubted my story or could not understand what I was telling them. 'One day,' Jesus said, 'everyone will come to see for themselves what you have seen.'" (Randy Gehling)

"A little girl who died in a swimming pool said to Dr. Melvin Morse, 'Don't worry, Dr. Morse, heaven is fun!'" (Dr. Melvin Morse)

"It seemed like the dawn of a new day; day was just breaking! It was a beautiful experience. I heard little birds singing, tiny birds, and they got louder and louder. People have said there are no birds in heaven, but I heard them." (Lorraine Tutmarc)

"Then, as if I had eyes all around my head, I saw saints, souls that were in heaven - multitudes. There was no way to count them. Whether there were millions or billions, I have no idea. As far as I could see in every direction were people of all sizes dressed in white robes. The people were transparent; I could see through them. They were behind me, across from me, all around me. They were floating on what appeared to be a crystal mirror or cloud or smoke. It is hard to describe these things in earthly terms, but I am trying to show you what my spirit saw. Each person was holding a crown in his or her hand. The saints were saying, 'We were waiting for you.'" (Dr. Gerard Landry)

"The angels told me that all who enter the third heaven must remain there until brought back to this physical world by Christ himself." (Rev. Howard Pittman)

"Because in heaven only the best in each person survives and good is all anyone wants to do there, this allows a freedom and happiness that people on earth cannot imagine. On earth we need thousands of laws to keep order, but in heaven restrictions are not needed." (Arthur Yensen)

"Negative thoughts cannot be expressed in the heavenly realms - only positive ones." (Ned Dougherty)

"Humans are educated at a higher level by spirit beings who bring us into heaven. We grow and increase, and grow and increase, and shed the concerns, desires, and base animal stuff that we have been fighting much of our life. Earthly appetites melt away. It is no longer a struggle to fight them. We become who we truly are, which is part of the divine." (Rev. Howard Storm)

"In heaven, we can remember our real identity and know what possibilities exist for soul growth. We do not move forward until we choose to do so." (P.M.H. Atwater)

"Heaven is a joyous condition and a state of expanded awareness, of perceiving more and more of the grand plan of creation." (Emanuel Swedenborg)

"Knowledge beyond our deepest dreams exists in heaven and in the hearts of those who dwell there." (Betty Eadie)

"What people call 'heaven' is really our true home and destination. It is where we go for recess or to be rewarded by assessing our progress as a soul, evaluating our lives, and to remember all truths, including our real identity. We stay there for however long best serves our development." (Nora Spurgin)

"Everyone in the realms of light knows that there is a Creator. It is said that this presence is so obvious it cannot be denied." (Nora Spurgin)

"Once in heaven, a person may feel as if they had been there before. They may remember that heaven is their real home. They may remember that on earth, people are visitors and homesick strangers." (Arthur Yensen)

"We tend to feel that when we die, heaven is as we thought it-and it certainly is. We can be received exactly the same way we always thought we would be received. People can remain in narrowness if they want -they don't need to change unless they wish. There is perfect freedom of spirit in heaven." (Margaret Tweddell)

"Some people have high hopes that everything is going to be different for them in heaven. However, nothing can be different for them because they have brought with them what they are. There is so much harmony in heaven that if anyone brings a disharmonious personality with them, they will find it very difficult to link in with the harmonious existence that exists." (Margaret Tweddell)

"In heaven there is no way to get ahead of others. This is because there is no place in heaven for discontent or personal ambition." (Arthur Yensen)

"Heaven is a world much like our own except there is neither time nor space as we think of them here. Heaven exists in a higher dimension of energy. The higher realms are a world of inexpressible beauty. They are realms where it is possible to be fully alive, where, for example, the whole body perceives. They are realms of endless possibilities for creativity and full realization of self; and they are where the love of God is like the air we breathe. As air is the atmosphere on earth, God's love is the atmosphere in the spirit world." (Nora Spurgin)

"Heaven is very hard to describe because words are inadequate to describe it. Heaven is a place of imagination. Heaven is exactly what our imagination needs it to be. It is a lively hilarious place that's unbelievably sweet, serene and melodious. It is characterized by its vivid greenness, its crystalline cleanliness, its newness, its all-pervading music and its overall beauty - all of which are maintained by God. It's a vigorous, lively place with an outflowing happiness that's uncontainable. It's not a place of rest because no one there gets tired. It's more like a new lease on life. Everything in heaven is pure. The elements don't mix or break down as they do on earth. Everything is kept in place by God's all-pervading Master-Vibration which prevents aging. That's why things don't get dirty, or wear out, and why everything looks so bright and new." (Arthur Yensen)

"Heaven and hell are spiritual states of being. They are not static states but are states in which there can be growth and progress toward ultimate wholeness of being." (Margaret Tweddell)

"Think of stepping on the shore and finding it heaven, of touching a hand and finding it God's, of breathing new air and finding it celestial, of waking up in glory and finding it home." (Don Wyrtzen)

"To me, the valley appeared to be Heaven, but at the same time I knew that James and Rashad were seeing it differently. James saw it as the Gulf of Souls. Rashad saw it as Nirvana, and somehow we knew all this without speaking." (May Eulitt)

"The people in heaven are like uninhibited, carefree children. Heaven is where all people really love each other. There are no inhibitions, or need for them. Everyone does exactly as they please; which works out well because only the best in each person survives, and good is all anyone ever wants to do. This allows a freedom and happiness that people on earth can't imagine." (Arthur Yensen)

"Heaven is a realm where we recognize and enjoy our worth, talents, abilities, joys, courage, generosity, caring, empathy, giving-ness, virtue, cheer, diligence, thoughtfulness, patience, loving kindness, or whatever else reveals the power of our own light. We stay in heaven (and there are many divisions to this vibratory level) for however long best serves our development. There is a sense of benefit here, as if one has found their true home. In heaven, we have the opportunity to assess our progress as a soul, to evaluate pros and cons and outcomes, to remember all truths including our real identity. We experience the glory of love and the power of forgiveness." (P.M.H. Atwater)

"What we do in the spiritual world depends on where we are in the spirit world. The higher realms of the spirit world is truly heaven; a world of enjoyment and recreation. People do things they enjoy, and keep company with people they enjoy. It is a world of joyful activity. The skills, interests, and abilities developed on earth may be reflected in the roles chosen in eternity. Each of us will contribute uniquely toward the goodness and beauty in our realm." (Nora Spurgin)

"Plans, paths, and truths await us in heaven, some of which are eternities old, and some of which we have yet to make." (Betty Eadie)

"Everyone in heaven is enjoying themselves and they do not have to work in order to be happy. Everyone in heaven has work they can do - a position to fill in the greater scheme of things and all souls evolve." (Arthur Yensen)

"In heaven there is an overall awareness of what is going to happen on earth six weeks, six months, or perhaps two years ahead. At times it is rather like being in an airplane looking down, and we get an overview or prevision of what is going to happen, due to our being able to see things in broader perspective." (Margaret Tweddell)

HELL

As with heaven, NDErs have witnessed numerous variations of hell realms. These hell realms are neither for judgment nor punishment, nor are they eternal. They are states of mind which acts as a "time out" condition for reflection, education and purification of negative thought patterns. We can also witness numerous manifestations of these hell realms right here on earth. You can see people rotting away in prison; alcoholics passed out on Skid Row; addicts out of their minds in crack houses; people killing each other out of hatred; unsatisfied people living in luxury; all kinds of hellish conditions involving unnecessary suffering. While hell realms can be seen on earth, they are merely a reflection of the inner hell within people. Hell realms in the spirit world are the perfect outward manifestation of the inner hellish condition within people. This is because when we die, we "step into" the inner spirit realm we have cultivated within us our entire life. And because time does not exist in the spirit realms, a person's stay in these realms can seem like an eternity or a second. People in these hellish spirit realms remain in this condition for however long best serves their spiritual development. The way out of these hellish realms is to have a willingness to see the light and seek love. Eventually, like prodigal sons, every suffering soul in these hellish realms will see the light and heaven.

Between the earth realm and the heavenly realms exists two hellish realms known as (1) the earthbound realm (which this article is about) and (2) the Void. Both of these realms can be considered hell because they are the two darker levels. This web page will focus only on the earthbound realm. The earthbound realm is a hellish dimension that overlaps the physical realm. It is a dimension where souls who are bound by some strong earthly fixation, may remain indefinitely until they are able to extract themselves from this fixation. After death, most souls expand very quickly through the dark hellish realms of the earthbound realm and the void, by means of the tunnel and on to higher realms.

The following are highlights concerning the earthbound hell which will be described. It is a state of mind where earthly, physical desires cannot be satisfied and is due to a lack of spiritual development. This hellish state of mind is the result of living a hellish life. The ways to escape from the earthbound realm will be discussed and the reasons why negativity must be removed in order to enter heaven. NDE examples of the earthbound realm, including traditional hell, fire and brimstone NDEs, will be presented. Religious descriptions of the earthbound realm and scriptures suggesting universal salvation will be provided here.

"Hell is a state of mind. When we die, we are bound by what we think." (Angie Fenimore)

"Hell is a psychological condition which represents the hellish inner thoughts and desires within some souls. In hell, souls become uninhibited and their hellish condition is fully manifested. No demons are there to inflict punishment. Each soul acts out their own anger and hatred by warring and tormenting others." (Emanuel Swedenborg)

"The hell of hells is knowing you were your own devil." (Arthur Yensen)

"It is your mind which creates hell." (Dr. Timothy Leary)

"Hell refers to levels of negative thought-forms that reside in close proximity to the earth realm. It is where we go to work out, or remain within, our hang-ups, addictions, fears, guilt, angers, rage, regrets, self-pity, arrogance, or whatever else blocks us from the power of our own light." (P.M.H. Atwater)

"Hell is a level of consciousness which can be experienced in or out of the body." (Arthur Yensen)

"Hell is a place where everyone retains the physical desires they were fixated on without a way to satisfy them. Hell is real hell for anyone who lives only to satisfy their selfish desires." (Arthur Yensen)

"One level of hell exists right here on earth where an earthly desire is craved but cannot be satisfied." (Dr. George Ritchie)

"Hell contains people who have been alcoholics or drug addicts, who find these cravings still with them after death. They stay near the earth to be near alcoholics or drug addicts who are still in the physical body, in order to participate vicariously in the sensations which alcohol and drugs give. They can be helped in the world beyond to clear their soul bodies of these cravings so that they, too, may go on and progress. However, this is a long and tedious process." (Margaret Tweddell)

There is no geographic hell. We build our hells right here in our own lives. (Harry Hone)

"The quality of life after death for a suicide is determined by their motive for killing themselves. Those who kill themselves in order to hurt someone or get revenge, or who kill themselves out of hatred for someone else, will haunt the living by being aware of every horrible consequence their suicide had on others. Those who, because of mental illness, confusion, or a terminal illness, take their own life, are allowed many opportunities from God to grow in love just as any other person would who had not committed suicide." (Dr. George Ritchie)

Earthbound souls linger around the living, usually to try to satisfy a physical desire. (Betty Bethards)

If an addiction isn't conquered before death, it could keep your soul earthbound. (Ruth Montgomery)

Your personality - your likes and dislikes, your hopes, your fears-are still attached to you, although in a more nebulous form that when you are on earth in a physical body. (Margaret Tweddell)

"Hell is a lack of wisdom and not moving forward to progress. Hell is not a place." (Cecil)

"Hell is a spiritual condition we create by being away from God until we choose to return to God. Hell is a spiritual condition that is totally devoid of love." (Sandra Rogers)

"Hell is the pain, anguish, hurt and anger that you have caused others or who suffered as a result of your actions/words to others. Hell is what you have created for yourself within your soul by turning your back on unconditional love, compassion and peace." (Tina)

"What people call hell is really a spiritual time-out condition in which souls reflect and work out the things that blocked them from the power of their own light." (P.M.H. Atwater)

"Concerning hell, heat is molecules in motion, while cold is their lack of motion. Likewise, love is a fast vibration of the soul, while hate is a slower vibration. Complete love would be God, while complete hate would be death, leaving the soul extinct." (Arthur Yensen)

"Heaven and hell are spiritual states of being. They are not static states but are states in which there can be growth and progress toward ultimate wholeness of being." (Margaret Tweddell)

"The difference between life on earth and life in the spirit is that your spirit world corresponds to your inner nature." (Nora Spurgin)

"As there are degrees of heaven or hell on earth, so there are degrees of heaven or hell in the spiritual world." (Margaret Tweddell)

"After death people gravitate into homogenous groups according to the rate of their soul's vibrations much like throwing a small pebble into a threshing machine. It goes into the box that fits its proper size and weight. After death, we are sorted by the high or low vibrations of our soul. Everyone goes where they fit in! High vibrations indicate love and spiritual development, while low vibrations indicate debasement and evil. All one has to do is to love so unselfishly that their soul-vibrations rise high enough to fit into heaven." (Arthur Yensen)

"An extreme neglect of spiritual matters on earth can result in an earthbound condition. This is the condition people often associate with ghosts." (Dr. Michael Newton)

"People who have an orientation of hate, for instance, find themselves unable to appreciate a realm of love and harmony. Therefore, they continue in their state of bitterness and are 'closed' to the glory which exists around them." (Margaret Tweddell)

"Those who have stunted their spiritual growth through an undeveloped or misdirected lifestyle, have led a purely self-centered life or have hurt other people, their spiritual environment will reflect something of these realities. A self-centered life on earth places one in an area of the spirit world with like-minded people who have yet to learn the value of unselfishness for the advancement of the soul." (Nora Spurgin)

"The spiritual state of being you have on earth is the spiritual state you take with you to the world beyond when you die. There is no sudden metamorphosis from an idle person into an active person, from a nonreligious person into a religious person, from a money-centered person into a God-centered person. This is not an automatic thing." (Margaret Tweddell)

"Environments distant from God are said to be dark, cold and inhospitable. Indeed, they reflect the spirits of those dwelling there." (Nora Spurgin)

"We create our own hell within us while we live on earth. After death, we step into this hell." (Kevin Williams)

"In the spirit world, everyone lives in the kind of a heaven or hell that they have prepared for themselves while on earth." (Arthur Yensen)

"People are in hell before they die. At death, we are gathered together with those who think as we do." (Angie Fenimore)

"The general rule of thumb is this: hellish life, hellish afterlife - heavenly life, heavenly afterlife. Death will not change a hellish life into a heavenly afterlife, nor does it change a heavenly life into a hellish afterlife." (Dr. Melvin Morse)

"Occasionally, the encounter with light is perceived as a reflection of the fires of hell." (IANDS FAQ)

"Physical desires can be carried over into the afterlife but physical desires cannot be satisfied there. This can create a hellish condition for those who have them." (Nora Spurgin)

"There is no condemnation in hell, only the outworking of our own misjudgments, mistakes, misalignments, or misappropriations." (P.M.H. Atwater)

"Those with too many negative thought patterns might flee the light of God after death because they are too ashamed or too afraid to have their inner thoughts and negative natures revealed to everyone." (Dr. George Ritchie)

"After his death, Jesus descended into the lower afterlife regions to 'unlock' the gates of hell. But souls still remaining there - for them - the gates are locked from the inside. Nevertheless, NDE evidence reveals Jesus continues to rescue souls from hell during a near-death experience." (Kevin Williams)

"I saw the reasons for all of my actions and understood why I did what I had done. There was a place for all of my positive and negative actions. There was no action that was necessarily wrong, but there were actions I took that did not enhance positive growth." (David Oakford)

"In hell, we have the opportunity to either revel in our folly or come to grips with the reality of consequences -- that every action has a reaction, what is inflicted on another can be returned in kind. This is not a punishment for our sins but a confrontation with any distortion of our sense of values and priorities." (P.M.H. Atwater)

"Just knowing the bad mistakes you made through your carelessness or your selfishness is a hell. You don't need a devil prodding you with a fork." (Margaret Tweddell)

"God does not condemn anyone to hell and there is no eternal damnation. We have the ability to condemn ourselves to the hell we create within ourselves." (Kevin Williams)

"The God of love suffers for those in darkness, ignorance and misery." (Nora Spurgin)

"Many people believe that those who don't give verbal assent to Jesus are cast headlong into eternal fire to burn forever. It should be common sense to anyone that a God of love would never treat people this way. As Jesus said, even an evil father knows how to give good things to children." (Kevin Williams)

While Benedict was in hell, he called out to the light and the light opened up and formed a tunnel that insulated him from all that fear and pain. (Mellen-Thomas Benedict)

"The way out of these hellish realms is to have a willingness to see the light and seek love for others and God." (Angie Fenimore)

To escape the darkness, you must cry out to God. Then the light will appear. (Rev. Howard Storm)

"From what may anyone be saved? Only from themselves! That is, their individual hell. They dig it with their own desires." (Edgar Cayce)

"The gates of hell are open. Those in hell will eventually join up, link hands, and walk out of hell together." (Mellen-Thomas Benedict)

"We stay in hell for however long best serves our development. We do not leave until we have changed our attitudes and perceptions." (P.M.H. Atwater)

"Souls in the hellish realms do not have the same powers to progress and achieve joy that others with more light in the higher afterlife realms have. Their progress is limited - a result of divine justice. However, these souls can choose to grow if they wish." (RaNelle Wallace)

"The living have auras of light surrounding their bodies. If the aura becomes distorted through alcohol or drugs, an earthbound soul can temporarily possess the body." (Dr. George Ritchie)

"There are no permanent sinners. Even the saddest example of humanity can become the greatest." (Harry Hone)

"Accept the greater power around you and let go of the earth and its desires." (Margaret Tweddell)

"Based on a soul's desire and willingness, those in hell are given an opportunity for an upward journey." (Nora Spurgin)

"To appreciate heaven well it is good for a man to have some fifteen minutes of hell." (Will Carleton)

"At this point, I could feel this group of beings eliminate or pull from me the negative energy of my life in the physical world and fill me with love beyond what I can describe." (Sherry Gideon)

"After death, if a soul has been too bad, they go to a realm of lower vibrations where their kind of thoughts can live. If they entered heaven, they would be annihilated by the Master-Vibration of God. This is because souls gravitate into groups according to the rate of their soul's vibrations. If the percent of discord in a soul is small, it can be eliminated by God; then the remaining good can live on in heaven. However, if the percentage of bad were too high, this couldn't be done, and the person would have to gravitate to a lower level and live with people of his own kind. Birds of a feather flock together."(Arthur Yensen)

"Since I had lived such a totally self-serving existence, I was in a hellish state of indescribable agony and sorrow. I was in shear agony. I still remember being on my knees while this blinding light broke and crushed my false-ego. This breaking process was extremely painful." (Daniel Rosenblit)

"Negative thoughts cannot be expressed in the heavenly realms - only positive ones." (Ned Dougherty)

"God is the Master-Vibration who neutralizes all negative thoughts so that you think only the good thoughts, such as love, freedom and happiness." (Arthur Yensen)

"God's love looks at all of us throughout the eyes of eternity. God's overriding desire is to purify the darkness of our souls, irrespective of the suffering God has to put us through to achieve that end. However, it will greatly minimize our suffering if we learn to accept instead of fighting against our situation in life." (Daniel Rosenblit)

"There are earthbound spirits of low vibrations, whom we may regard as devils because they annoy us through mental telepathy. These demons tune in on us through our low vibrations of hate, fear and greed. They can be tuned out with unselfish love, or if necessary be chased away by the stronger spirit of Jesus Christ." (Arthur Yensen)

"The only thing that burns in hell is the part of you that won't let go of your life: your memories, your attachments. They burn them all away, but they're not punishing you, they're freeing your soul." (Meister Eckhart)

"The purpose of religion is not so much to get us into heaven, or to keep us out of hell, but to put a little bit of heaven into us, and take the hell out of us." (E. Stanley Jones)

"What all people seek, what sustains them, is love, the light told me. What distorts people is a lack of love. The revelations coming from the light seemed to go on and on. Then I asked the light, "Does this mean that humankind will be saved?" Then, like a trumpet blast with a shower of spiraling lights, the Great Light spoke, saying, "Remember this and never forget; you save, redeem and heal yourself. You always have. You always will. You were created with the power to do so from before the beginning of the world. In that instant I realized even more. I realized that WE HAVE ALREADY BEEN SAVED, and we saved ourselves because we were designed to self-correct like the rest of God's universe." (Mellen-Thomas Benedict)

"Life is a cycle of improvements and humans are not perfect yet. Most people have this secret revealed to them when they die." (Dr. Frank Oski)

"All souls were created in the beginning and are finding their way back to God." (Edgar Cayce)

"We are immortal and indestructible. We have always been alive, we always will be, and there is no way in this world that we can ever be lost. It is impossible for anyone to fall into a crack in the universe somewhere and never be heard from again. We are utterly safe and we have always been forever and ever." (Jayne Smith)

"From the light we have come, and to the light we all shall return." (Josiane Antonette)

"It is God's love for us that sends us on our journey and it is our love for God that allows us to return to God's loving arms again." (David Goines)

"A central aspect of our eternal existence is continued spiritual growth through love and service. We can spend what seems like an eternity before incarnating in the flesh. During that period in the spirit world, soul growth can be attained there as well." (Nora Spurgin)

"It [reincarnation] is a universal process, and prevails not only in the human kingdom but also throughout the whole of nature. Whenever we find a living form, the consciousness of that form is also evolving, using temporarily for that purpose the physical form in order that it may gain physical experience. In each incarnation we have a different physical body, a different name, and may have different souls acting as parents, but these changes do not in the slightest imperil our individuality ... Reincarnation is not an endless process, and when we have learned the lessons taught in the World-School we return no more to physical incarnation unless we come back of our own accord to act as Teachers of humanity or as Helpers in the glorious plan of evolution." (Amber Wells)

"Without physical bodies, feelings of hate and fear are intensified as souls [in hell] vainly try to hide from their enemies. Their only hope is to reincarnate. Then unfortunately when they do, they may forget all about their torment in hell and again lead lives of greed and tyranny. This miserable cycle can continue forever unless they find salvation in one of their lifetimes. Such people really need a savior, since they are not able to help themselves. I'm sure Christ incarnated to help them because he said, 'I came not to call the righteous, but sinners to repentance.'" (Arthur Yensen)

SPIRIT GUIDES

Peg Abernathy (www.self-full-life.com) is a near-death experiencer who knows a lot about spirit guides. Her near-death experience and subsequent transformation is documented in her book The Self-Full Life: A True Story That Will Help Your Soul Remember where she deals extensively with spirit guides. According to Abernathy, long before we fell asleep and began the dream-play we now call our life, there was a meeting that took place between our Spiritual Essence and our chosen team of Angels and Guides. We came together within the All There Is, in order to full-fill our karmic destiny at the time deemed most appropriate. And it was decided that this life would transpire and that we would incarnate, act out our life-play and apply the lessons that we brought forth from previous lives. And as a young school child that bursts forth through the front door with the latest picture or lesson, we, at the completion of our incarnated existence, run through the Light with our newly acquired experiences and into the welcoming arms of these comrades of feelings and Love. We have awakened into the All There Is and we have completed our destiny of this life-lived.

Peg Abernathy was asked about whether we all have spirit guides? According to Peg Abernathy, "Yes, absolutely. And they are always with us, talking to us through our intuition, through our hearts, minds and feelings. And some people, blessed with the ability to quiet the mind and receive messages and wisdom within that silence, are able to communicate with these wondrous Beings who wait patiently for us to call out. We are always here. Never do we leave and the moment your thoughts turn to the Light, ours will be directed in that path as well. That is why we are here: to Guide you towards this Light, The Knowing of the Light. Our gentle Guidance of your Soul is just that, Guidance. It is you who make the ultimate choice. And that is the Power of Will. You must understand that we are no better than you, that we seek the same Light as you. If a person wishes to directly contact their Spirit Guides while in the physical body, it can be done. But it takes great determination and the ability to completely quiet the mind. We are always mentally chattering away, thinking and asking yet never taking the time to actually listen, to be utterly still in order to hear the answers. That is where the miracle lives, within the silent mind. That is where we will hear and sometimes see our team, our most ardent admirers of this dream we call our life. But if we can believe and ultimately remember all that we brought with us, and that these beautiful Spirits are just a breath away and within reach of our touch, then we Know, we Become, once again, a merging of Lighted energies and Love. We are home."

The following information was given to Peg Abernathy by a spirit guide during her NDE: "We see a future of hope, of reason and of acceptance for all people - time when expression of ideas, beliefs and experiences are encouraged freely and welcomed with unabandoned joy. We yearn for that Universal power of all things and we seek others of like-minds. We look for those struggling to understand and we reach out to them with an unconditional hand. Our Purpose, our reason for Being in this life experience is limited only by our minds and the boundaries within. The choices we make and the dreams we share, define our existence upon the earth and vulnerability is the realization that we all matter. Every one of our lives is simply a confirmation of our own intuition: delicate, sweet moments in time. And tenderly, we sing and rejoice in The All There Is." (Peg Abernathy)

The following are Christian Andreason's NDE insights on spirit guides.

What was your experience with a spirit guide like? Andreason's answer: "I saw an uncountable amount of wonderful places that were not of this world and many spiritual truths were Lovingly and generously revealed to me with mind-bending answers. Almost the whole time I was guided mostly by a being who appeared in the form of the most beautiful woman I have ever seen. Following us were three other guides who all appeared as men. All were robed with a beautiful glistening white, diamond-like material. I could also distinguish that they had Light coming from underneath their garments. I knew that this Light was their true bodies. The moment they came into my awareness, I recognized these beings as having been some of my closest friends that have been with me for all time. They were very kind to me and very caring about my feelings. There are no secrets in Heaven, so information that might have been considered embarrassing was treated with tremendous sensitivity. And even in moments where I might have cried knowing that someone knew my deepest darkest secrets, wonderful warm laughter was often exchanged between us instead. No matter any unpleasantness they may have known about me, I knew that I was eternally and unconditionally Loved! For many years, after my experience, I have continued to stay in contact with these dear ones through dreams and meditations. During my experience it was revealed to me that they had made many appearances to me during my life, particularly during difficult times in my childhood and adolescence, only I was not consciously aware of them or their presence at the time ... At first, I did not see God immediately. However, I did FEEL the presence of God everywhere! When I found myself in the Realm, initially I spoke with my very Loving guides, absorbed amazing information and took in the bigness of everything that was shown to me in God's Heaven..."

What goes on in the "Divine Realm?" Andreason's answer: "Lots of things! Individuals are laughing, relaxing and enjoying one another's company. Some are off working together in pairs (or larger), so that they might bring a new concept or idea, or accomplish a Divinely intended goal for the planet. Some are off to themselves reflecting in far away, peaceful places and learning how to work with and trust the power they hold within them. Others form close-knit groups and enjoy learning together as they are taught by various Loving, advanced teachers and guides of Spirit."

How many Angels do each of us have? Andreason's answer: "As many as we need. Some need one, but I understand that most have two or even three. These Angels mostly come in the form of guides. However, winged guardian Angels are never far away and always have a watchful eye on us to make sure nothing prevents us from accomplishing our Divine purpose."

Who are our guides and what are their roles in our lives? Andreason's answer: "Our guides are what I call our wingless Angels. They are our most cherished friends and supporters in Heaven. They never leave our side ... Never for a single second. In fact, what many do not know is that somewhere right here on earth, in our families or somewhere in a line of dear personal friends, there is always one who acts as a Heavenly go between for us and the Realm. Hence the verse, 'Angels walk among you unaware!'" (Christian Andreason)

The following is Diego Valencia's NDE insights on spirit guides: "The guides told me I was in the threshold of death. I wondered if the persons who were dying and leaving their bodies in that moment, knew where they were. The guides that accompanied me were kind, tactful and VERY COMPLIANT, but impenetrable when certain questions were asked, and when they did, they answered with only a smile. The communication was by telepathy and they knew instantly what I was thinking, but their answers were essential, concise and certain. My guides were very calmed, unadorned and with a tender sense of humor. It was then that the judgment began - only I was the one who judged me. Although they considered everything was evident, they allowed me to understand all the contradictions, actions, guilt and non-guilt which I was feeling from the events of my life. They comforted me with precise words and calmed me. When I felt within myself a violent dialogue, justifying or blaming myself, they made me understand that it was all within the game of evolution and that in the depth, the events of my life were transcendental. Then I had the sensation that I was still in a foggy place near earth. They told me I could take the decision to continue, but it was with a maximum risk for my physical body or life. Then, identifying myself with my Diego ego in the earthly realm, I accepted to continue since the guides were willing to accompany me. I worried because of the risk. Nevertheless I accepted discretely and humbly, although with the haughtiness of my earth identity that wanted to have the experience. At the same time my cosmic conscience allowed me to take the decision without panic. We then began to ascend at great speed without friction or effort, as when one is falling but instead ascending. I was in a state of reverberation - hearing a zooming sound and feeling a little dizzy as though in a car at great speed ... I had then a slight, but vital sensation of unrest and anguish, because I again understood I had traversed the threshold, so I asked my guides for an answer. They told me that the decision did not depend on them anymore because we found ourselves in realms that were not of their reach. The answer made me feel dazzled. I asked them if they could keep on accompanying me because I wanted to have a dialogue with someone, and they kindly accepted. I felt a nostalgic abandonment. I later had the sensation that they took my hand." (Diego Valencia)

The following is Karen Schaeffer's NDE insights on spirit guides: "I was feeling lighter all the time. But wait ... my son. I couldn't leave my son! Babies need their mommies. I needed to be his mommy. I couldn't let go. So much patience was shown to me - so much love. My guides explained that the feelings I was having were still a connection to my human side. Once my human-ness wore off, I would feel light as air, utter happiness, and extreme love ... At a time when I felt the closest to accepting my death, I experienced a resurge of sorrow and pain, longing for my son, for my life. I couldn't let go of my human life. My guides tried their hardest. They never gave up. They never became discouraged. It is unbelievable the amount of patience and love they exuded. Finally, my hysteria was calmed by a higher spirit who seemed to envelop me in love. My guides were instructed to allow me to return. Despite their pleas to allow them more time, they were told that at this point, my spirit would not rest. It was best to let me return, to settle my spirit, learn further lessons." (Karen Schaeffer)

The following is David Oakford's NDE insights on spirit guides: "I could see many spirits leave Gaia (earth) with guides and could see spirits returning to Gaia without guides. The being told me that some of these spirits were the ones that were doing the work with humans on Gaia. I could make out the type of spirits that were doing the work and the spirits that were coming to the great city to become replenished to eventually go back to Gaia to experience and further evolve." (David Oakford)

The following is May Eulitt's NDE insights on spirit guides: "The guides taught us that doctrine and creed and race meant nothing. No matter what we believed we were all children joined under one God, and that the only rule was God's true law - do unto others as you would have them do unto you. We should treat all people as if they were a part of our soul because they were. All living things in the universe were connected to one another. They said that soon humanity would mature enough to assume a higher place in the universal scheme of things, but until then we must learn acceptance and tolerance and love for each other. They said there would come a new age when people would not be able to endure seeing others homeless and hungry. We would realize that only by helping each other could we truly help ourselves." (May Eulitt)

The following is Betty Eadie's lesson from her spirit guides from book, "Embraced by the Light" about an important lesson she learned from her spirit guides during her NDE in her own words:

My friends (spirit guides) in the garden were full of love as they stood around me, and they realized that I didn't want to go back yet, that I wanted to see more. In their desire to please me, they showed me much more.

Coming to earth is much like selecting a college and choosing a course of study. We are all at various levels of spiritual development, and we have come here in the stations that best suit our spiritual needs. The minute we judge others for their faults or shortcomings, we are displaying a similar shortcoming in ourselves. We don't have the knowledge to judge people accurately here.

As if to illustrate this principle for me, the heavens scrolled back, and I saw the earth again. This time my vision focused on a street corner in a large city. There, I saw a man lying in a drunken stupor on the sidewalk near a building. One of my guides said, "What do you see?"

"Why, a drunken bum lying in his wallow," I said, not understanding why I had to see this.

My guides became excited. They said, "Now we will show you who he really is."

His spirit was revealed to me, and I saw a magnificent man, full of light. Love emanated from his being, and I understood that he was greatly admired in the heavens. This great being came to earth as a teacher to help a friend that he had spiritually bonded with.

His friend was a prominent attorney who had an office a few blocks away from this corner. Although the drunk now had no recollection of this agreement with his friend, his purpose was to be a reminder to him of the needs of others. I understood that the attorney was naturally compassionate, but seeing the drunk would spark him to do more for those who needed his means. I knew that they would see each other, and the attorney would recognize the spirit within the drunk - the man within the man - and be moved to do much good. They would never know their covenanted roles here, but their missions would be fulfilled nonetheless. The drunk had sacrificed his time on earth for the benefit of another. His development would continue and other things he might need for progression would be given him later.

I recollected that I, too, had met people who had seemed familiar to me. The first time I met them I felt an instant closeness, a recognition, but hadn't known why. Now I knew that they had been sent to my path for a reason. They had always been special to me.

My escorts spoke again, bringing me out of my thoughts, and said that because I lacked pure knowledge I should never judge another. Those who passed by the drunk on the corner could not see the noble spirit within, and so judged by outward appearances. I had been guilty of this kind of judgment, silently judging others based on their wealth or outward abilities. I saw now that I had been unjust, that I had no idea of what their lives were like, or, more importantly, what their spirits were like.

The thought also came to me, "For ye have the poor with you always, and whensoever ye will ye may do them good."

But even as this scripture came to me it bothered me. Why do we have the poor with us? Why couldn't the Lord provide everything? Why couldn't he just prompt the attorney to share his money with others? The guides broke into my thoughts again and said, "There are angels that walk among you, that you are unaware of."

I was puzzled. The guides then helped me to understand. We all have needs, not just the poor. And all of us have made commitments in the spirit world to help each other. But we are slow to keep our covenants made so long ago. So the Lord sends angels to prompt us, to help us be true to these obligations. He won't force us, but he can prompt us. We don't know who these beings are - they appear like anybody else - but they are with us more often that we know.

I didn't feel rebuked, but I knew I had clearly misunderstood - and underestimated - the Lord's help for us here. He will give us all the help he can without interfering in our personal agency and free will. We must be willing to help each other. We must be willing to see that the poor are as worthy of our esteem as the rich. We must be willing to accept all others, even those different from us. All are worthy of our love and kindness. We have no right to be intolerant or angry or "fed up". We have no right to look down at others or condemn them in our hearts. The only thing we can take with us from this life is the good that we have done to others. I saw that all of our goods deeds and kind words will come back to bless us a hundred fold after this life. Our strength will be found in our charity.

My escorts and I were silent a moment. The drunk was gone from my sight. My soul was filled with understanding and love. Oh, that I could help others as that drunk will help his friend. Oh, that I could be a blessing to others in my life. My soul reverberated with the final fact: Our strength will be found in our charity.

I was humbled by the knowledge pouring into me about humanity, about the heavenly worth of each soul. I hungered for more light and knowledge. (Betty Eadie)

The following are various NDE insights on spirit guides.

"The world is changing. Soon, everybody will be in direct communication with his or her angels and guides." (Donna Gatti)

"Spirit guides who talk through mediums are often in this dimension as well, bringing their enhanced knowledge to earth." (Spiritualism)

"Once we have fully evaluated our lives, we are debriefed in an orientation process. This is when we discuss the lifetime previously lived and reviewed in the scanning machine. We meet with guides who are trained orientators who discuss ways of amending for previous mistakes. We receive help if we were unprepared for our crossing over into the spirit realm." (Sylvia Browne)

"A dream may be of a physical, mental, or spiritual nature and may deal with all manner of psychic manifestations. These include telepathy, clairvoyance, prophetic visions, out of body traveling, remembrance of past lives, communication with beings in other realms including deceased friends and relatives, spirit guides, angels, Christ, and even the voice of God." (Edgar Cayce)

"The Native American chief White Thunder, during his visit to the world of spirits, was shown by his spirit guides 'various areas of the spirit world - some containing happy spirits and others peopled by unhappy evildoers.'" (Dr. Craig Lundahl)

"As in other realms we are not resident but transient in the Fourth Region, and we also take leave of this region occasionally to visit others. We never travel alone but are guided

144

and helped by spirit guides in our journeys. When visiting another realm we take on the form of that realm, or we could not exist fully within it." (Edgar Cayce)

The following are questions and answers from NDE expert Nora Spurgin's NDE research:

Question: Can spiritual growth take place on the other side? Answer: "Yes, it appears to be a law of the universe that growth is always possible. According to many accounts, the spiritual world has teachers and guides (those who have died, sometimes centuries before, who have the mission to guide newcomers who want to learn and grow in the spirit world). For children, teachers are provided to give them basic knowledge, and people in the position of parents provide them with essential love. Those who are lacking in emotional growth, or who have lived unloving, resentful, vengeful, or selfish lives will be given the opportunity to serve and help others in order that they may advance to higher realms. They may even come back to earth as spiritual helpers, like guardian angels, to influence people to avoid misdeeds and harmful lifestyles, and to overcome unloving attitudes. Those who have passed on often come back to their descendants to help and protect them. In so doing, spiritual growth takes place for both. Desire for such spiritual growth arises from a desire to be close to God. The spiritual world is a world where an ever-increasing unity with the love of God is the goal of one's growth."

Question: Do our prayers for the deceased help? Answer: "Praying for someone who has passed on will be a boost on the other side to enlist the help of spiritual guides for the new arrival. Indeed, living in the spirit world, spirit persons may be even more sensitive to the beneficial effects of prayer than they were on earth ... It is extremely important on passing into the spiritual world to look toward the light and accept orientation from spiritual guides. If a person dies ignorant of the spiritual world, an earth-bound state or spirit possession may result, severely hindering the growth of all involved. A prayer or call for help may be enough to move us through the tunnel and into the light described in NDEs. Most psychics who espouse reincarnation do not believe that one must immediately inhabit another body upon physical death. Long periods (centuries in physical time) are used for continued growth by entities who earn merit by temporarily visiting earth as spiritual guides and teachers."

Question: Are there demonic spirits and angels? Answer: "There is, therefore, evil and darkness in the spirit world. The darkness may be a result of ignorance and lack of understanding. Spiritual guides will enlighten willing souls and offer growth opportunities to lead the spirit into the light and warmth of higher realms. Some accounts inform us that ignorance of the need to seek growth may keep someone in a state of darkness for a long period of time." (Nora Spurgin)

The following is from Dr. Michael Newton's past-life regression research: "Those subverted by criminal abnormalities do undergo separation in the spirit world, and this happens at the time of their orientation with guides. They are not activated along the same travel routes as other souls and will go into seclusion upon reentering the spirit world. These souls don't appear to mix with other entities in the conventional manner for quite a while ... Once our souls advance into the intermediate ranges of development, group cluster activity is considerably reduced. This does not mean we return to the kind of isolation that occurs with novice souls. Souls evolving into the middle development level have less association with primary groups because they have acquired the maturity and experience

145

for operating more independently. These souls are also reducing the number of their incarnations. These souls are at last ready for more serious responsibilities. The relationship we have with our guides now changes from teacher-student to one of colleagues working together. Since our old guides have acquired new student groups, it is now our turn to develop teaching skills which will eventually qualify us for the responsibilities of being a guide to someone else. This is a significant stage for souls in their development because now they are given increased responsibilities for younger souls. The status of a guide is not given to us all at once, however. As with many other aspects of soul life, we are carefully tested. The intermediate levels are trial periods for potential teachers. Our mentors assign us a soul to look after, and then evaluate our leadership performance both in and out of physical incarnations. Only if this preliminary training is successful are we allowed to function even at the level of a junior guide. Not everyone is suited for teaching, but this does not keep us from becoming an advanced soul. Guides, like everyone else, have different abilities and talents, as well as shortcomings. By the time we reach the advanced level, our soul aptitudes are well known in the spirit world. We are given occupational duties commensurate with our abilities. Different avenues of approach to learning eventually bring all of us to the same end in acquiring spiritual wholeness. I believe that people on earth who possess souls which are both old and highly advanced are scarce. A person whose maturity is this high doesn't seek out a regression therapist to resolve life-plan conflicts. In most cases, they are here as incarnated guides. Having mastered the fundamental issues most of us wrestle with daily, the advanced soul is more interested in making small refinements toward specific tasks." (Dr. Michael Newton)

MUSIC

Once I, the author, attended a lecture by Dr. Stephen Halpern, the master of music and music physiology. He said something very interesting I will never forget. He said the entire human body is a receiver of sound vibrations. Our ears are not the only organ that is sensitive to sound vibrations. He stated how the chakras (the spiritual centers in the body) are greatly influenced by sound vibrations. For example, our sexual organs (the lowest chakra) are more sensitive to low rhythmic beats. Our heads (the highest chakra) are more sensitive to higher beat-less vibrations. This may explain why music with a low rhythmic beat is so popular among young people with raging sexual hormones. The low rhythmic beat played an important role in the tribal rituals of early human cultures around the world. Spiritual enlightenment occurs when you spiritually activate the body's chakras from the lowest to the highest using varying levels of vibration and music.

According to Dr. Joel Funk, a professor of psychology at Plymouth State College in New Hampshire, about 50% of near-death experiencers hear music during their NDE. They describe this music mostly as "music with a beautiful, floating sound." Dr. Funk played various kinds of music for 60 near-death experiencers and found that they identified New Age style synthesized music as nearest to what they had heard during their NDE. Dr. Funk comments, "Some people burst into tears when they recognize the music of their NDEs."

Steve Roach of Tucson, Arizona, had an NDE after a bike crash and heard "the most intensely beautiful music you could ever imagine" and decided "to dedicate my life to re-creating the exact same sound." The result is a record entitled "Structures from Silence."

146

Says Roach, "Many people contact me after hearing my recordings to tell me that they've heard the exact same music during their NDEs." If you would like to buy Steve Roach's music and other NDE music, visit Gilles Bedard's NDE and Music Page is a near-death experiencer and has done some excellent research into the music of the NDE.

The following is a summary of the insights concerning NDE music: The universe was created using the tools of music, harmony, and balance. Everything is kept in place by the all-pervading vibration of God. Near-death accounts provide many interesting descriptions of the music that is often heard in the spirit realms. Some of these descriptions are: transcendental, unearthly harmonic beauty, angelic, sublimely beautiful, exquisite harmonies, heavenly, a celestial choir of angels, a tone so sublimely perfect, joyous and beat-less melody, an orchestra of voices, the Music of the Spheres, hymns to God, mystical tones, harmonic perfection, music that transcends all thought, bells and wind chimes, celestial symphony, glorious tones and rhythms and melodies, complicated rhythms with unearthly tones, deeper and more profound than new age music, music that is experienced from within, and music that puts Bach to shame. In the spirit realm, gardens sing and colors can be heard. It is a realm where light and sound, color and geometrical patterns are all combined into a totality of harmonic perfection. This is music that is on a level that is beyond hearing. It comes from within the very core of your soul. It is like being on a universal wave length that envelops you totally. NDE music revelations show the great importance that music plays in the universe, in the spirit realms, our souls and God.

The following is Dr. Dianne Morrissey's musical aftereffect from her NDE. Dr. Dianne Morrissey was a clarinet player for a symphony and a self-proclaimed music snob. All she listened to was classical music and she would not tolerate being around anybody who didn't. At one time in her life, she had no idea of who even the Beatles were. That's how narrow her musical tastes were. This all changed, of course, when she had an NDE. Dianne's NDE changed her life so much that she can no longer listen to classical music. She states that the reason is because she can't stand to remember the music snob she once was and how she used to judge. Since then, Dianne has never picked up the clarinet again to the total disbelievement of her friends. Now, she sees the beauty in all music. Dianne gave up her limited life of classical music and now writes and teaches people how to have out-of-body experiences. (Kevin Williams)

The following are some examples of musical experiences in NDEs.

There exist some very interesting ideas concerning the music and sound heard during many NDEs. One experiencer, Gilles Bedard was so impressed by the music he heard in his NDE, that he devoted his life to recreating and researching the music he heard. Other experiencers, such as Steve Roach, have done the same. Mr. Roach has produced some very beautiful music that can only be described as transcendental.

"Based on my experience, I would say that people usually have a romanticized view of the music heard during near-death experiences. That's why most people think first of new age music, harp or soothing music. From the outside, it would seem like that, but the music experienced from within is deeper and more profound than that ... When I heard Structures from Silence from Steve Roach, I recognized the sound I heard on the Other Side." (Gilles Bedard)

"I heard what seemed like millions of little golden bells ringing, tinkling; they rang and rang. Many times since, I've heard those bells in the middle of the night. Next I heard humming and then a choir singing. The singing got louder and louder, and it was in a minor key. It was beautiful and in perfect harmony. I also heard stringed instruments." (Lorraine Tutmarc)

"Music surrounded me. It came from all directions. Its harmonic beauty unlike earthly vocal or instrumental sounds was totally undistorted. It flowed unobtrusively like a glassy river, quietly worshipful, excitingly edifying, and totally comforting. It provided a reassuring type of comfort much like a protective blanket that whispered peace and love. I had never sensed anything like it. Perhaps angelic would describe it. This music was sounding within my head, not from an eardrum. Obviously it was not airborne. Most unusual to me was the absence of any beat. Then I realized that without time this heavenly music could have no beat which is a measure of time! I was hearing harmonic perfection, undistorted by any interposed medium between me and its source, as heard mind-to-mind ... The music around me suddenly seemed louder. I rushed to a nearby tree and grasped its trunk to my ear: it was singing. I lifted my right elbow to my head; it too emitted the same joyous, beatless melody. Excitedly I stopped to pick some flowers, and found them already in my hand. They too were playing the tune." (Dr. Richard Eby)

"In the beginning, God desired to self-expression, and desired companionship. Therefore, the cosmos and souls were projected. The cosmos was built with music, arithmetic, and geometry; harmony, system, and balance. The building blocks were the life essence. It was a power sent out from God, which by changing the length of its wave and the rate of its vibration became a pattern of differing forms, substance, and movement. This created the law of diversity which supplied endless designs for the pattern. God played on this law of diversity as a person plays on a piano, producing melodies and arranging them in a symphony. Each design carried within it the plan of its evolution, which was to be accomplished by change. This corresponds to the sound of a note struck on a piano. The sounds of several notes unite to make a chord; chords in turn become phrases; phrases become melodies; melodies intermingle and move back and forth, across and between and around each other, to make a symphony. The music ends as it began, leaving emptiness, but between the beginning and the finish there has been glorious beauty and a great experience." (Edgar Cayce)

"And then I heard the MUSIC. It was a tone so sublimely perfect that remembering it still brings me to tears. I knew then, and know now, that I was hearing the symphony of angels, the song of the universe, what some have called the Music of the Spheres. All thoughts melted in its melody and everything else ceased to be of any importance. I closed my eyes and began to dance, moving to the resonant vibration that coursed through my essence. The melody seemed to issue from a single point and was composed of one verse, a song whose mystical tone my entire being knew and sang. I bathed in its melody as utter joy filled my being, and as the sound washed over my spirit, I felt all confusion purged from my consciousness ... I was once more in my magical gown, moving alone in harmony with the MUSIC. In that moment I chose to merge with that self and began to dance. Each step drew me closer to the Light ... The MUSIC, the celestial symphony, continued to fill the air with a psalm of Oneness, played on unseen instruments of peace. (Lynnclaire Dennis)

"Just as the colors of the rainbow show the effects of the different vibrations of light, and the melodies on the piano show the effect of the different notes, so, too, does the entire universe contain various octaves, or rates of vibration. These universal harmonics comprise the different levels of existence." (Jerry Gross)

"This time we were audience to a choir of angels singing. Angels were totally outside my reality at the time, yet somehow I knew these beautiful beings to be angelic. They sang the most lovely and extraordinary music I had ever heard. They were identical, each equally beautiful." (Dr. Allan Kellehear)

"Traveling through the tunnel, normal cities and towns can be seen on the sides of the tunnel. As you travel further, you become conscious of sounds, at first indistinct rumblings, then music, laughter, and singing of birds. There is more and more light, the colors become very beautiful, and there is the sound of wonderful music. The houses are left behind; ahead there is only a blending of sound and color." (Edgar Cayce)

"And the whole garden was singing. The flowers, grass, trees, and other plants filled this place with glorious tones and rhythms and melodies; yet I didn't hear the music itself. I could feel it somehow on a level beyond my hearing. As my grandmother and I stopped a moment to marvel at the magnificent scene, I said to myself, "Everything here seems to be singing," which was woefully inadequate to describe what I felt. We simply don't have language that adequately communicates the beauty of that world." (RaNelle Wallace)

"I could see all the energy that this solar system generates, and it is an incredible light show! I could hear the Music of the Spheres. Our solar system, as do all celestial bodies, generates a unique matrix of light, sound and vibratory energies. Advanced civilizations from other star systems can spot life as we know it in the universe by the vibratory or energy matrix imprint. It is child's play. The earth's Wonder Child (human beings) make an abundance of sound right now, like children playing in the backyard of the universe." (Mellen-Thomas Benedict)

Vicki Umipeg also began to hear sublimely beautiful and exquisitely harmonious music akin to the sound of wind chimes. With scarcely a noticeable transition, she then discovered she had been sucked head first into a tube and felt that she was being pulled up into it. The enclosure itself was dark, Vicki said, yet she was aware that she was moving toward light. As she reached the opening of the tube, the music that she had heard earlier seemed to be transformed into hymns and she then "rolled out" to find herself lying on grass. (Vicki Umipeg)

"And so I followed Him into other buildings of this domain of thought. We entered a studio where music of a complexity I couldn't begin to follow was being composed and performed. There were complicated rhythms, tones not on a scale I knew. 'Why,' I found myself thinking. 'Bach is only the beginning!'" (Dr. George Ritchie)

"The stars began to change shapes before my eyes. They began to dance and deliberately draw themselves into intricate designs and colors which I had never seen before. They moved and swayed to a kind of rhythm or music with a quality and beauty I had never heard and yet ... remembered. A melody that humans could not possibly have composed, yet was so totally familiar and in complete harmony with the very core of my being. As if it were the rhythm of my existence, the reason for my being. The extravagance of imagery and coloration pulsed in splendid unison with the magnificent ensemble. I felt completely at peace, tranquilized by the vision and the melodic drone. I could have stayed in this place for eternity with this pulse of love and beauty beating throughout my soul. The love poured into me from all corners of the universe." (Virginia Rivers)

149

"As we walked toward it, I heard voices. They were melodious, harmonious, blending in chorus and I heard the word, 'Jesus.' There were more than four parts to their harmony. I not only heard the singing and felt the singing but I joined the singing. I have always had a girl's body, but a low boy's voice. Suddenly I realized I was singing the way I had always wanted to ... in high, clear and sweet tones. After a while the music softened. Then the unseen voices picked up a new chorus. The voices not only burst forth in more than four parts, but they were in different languages. I was awed by the richness and perfect blending of the words - and I could understand them! I do not know why this was possible except that I was part of a universal experience. The words sung in all the different languages were understandable, but I don't know how or why. We all seemed to be on some universal wave length. I thought at the time, "I will never forget the melody and these words. But later I could only recall two: Jesus and redeemed." (Betty Malz)

Dr. Diane Komp, a pediatric oncologist at Yale, was transformed by witnessing children's' NDEs, such as that of an 8-year-old with cancer envisioning a school bus driven by Jesus, a 7-year-old leukemia patient hearing a chorus of angels before passing away. "I was an atheist, and it changed my view of spiritual matters," recalls Komp. "Call it a conversion. I came away convinced that these are real spiritual experiences." (Dr. Diane Komp)

"Turning back to the interior of the temple, I saw that creative activities were taking place in different areas. There were a number of individuals sitting at easels painting, and I saw one man playing a flutelike instrument that emitted the sweetest of sounds. Farther on, dancers moved with ethereal grace, performing with a lightness impossible to the physical human form. As I watched in utter delight, I became aware that the musical background for this visual feast came from what I would call a celestial choir - an orchestra of voices creating heavenly music for the dance. This Music of the Spheres was indeed singing the praises of the Creator." (Jan Price)

"Permeating the colors and patterns was sound, countless octaves of sound. It was as though the colors could be heard. It reminded me of bagpipes. Filling the entire region were the droning sounds: octave upon octave of invigorating, vitalizing sound. It was very subtle, practically imperceptible but immense. It seemed to reach to infinity. Superimposed on this vast life-giving hum, was the melody, which was created by the individual sound of every living thing. Light and sound, color and geometrical patterns were all combined into a totality of harmonic perfection." (John Star)

"When we first arrived in the Seventh Region we were certain that we had reached our eternal home. So in tune were we with it that there was not even a hint of internal conflict. We could not conceive of any higher order of life than here, from where we were certain the Music of the Spheres originated. Gradually we learn that there are higher realms of life, and we are in yet another stage of growth." (Harvey Green)

"I am still utterly amazed at what I find here. Utterly amazed! There is love and there is harmony. There is music that transcends all thought. Then I became conscious of different sounds of bells ringing and music. I realized that I had been hearing these bells and music while I was out in space. In the midst of this sound I became aware of the fact that at the present time I may see and I may observe, but my consciousness will have to expand further before I may know how all of this takes place, and why." (Margaret Tweddell)

"At the time I felt the presence of that extreme love I could also hear beautiful music. I'm not sure if it was instrumental music, but somehow I think it was more massed voices giving that sound. But there were no words - it was more just a resonance of sound." (Janet)

"Everything began to become peaceful and a type of music without sound played that enveloped me totally - through every cell." (Kurt Hilden)

"Facing all the splendor made me acutely aware of my lowly condition. My response was, 'No, you've made a mistake, put me back.' And he [Jesus] said: 'We don't make mistakes. You belong.' Then he called out in a musical tone to the luminous entities who surrounded the great center. Several came and circled around us." (Rev. Howard Storm)

"Just when I thought to speak, to question, the being spoke to me. It's voice was as a chorus of voices, not male not female, not loud not soft, not deep but perfect and all encompassing." (Lou Famoso)

"In the bardo of becoming, as well as many other kinds of visions, the mental body will see visions and signs of different realms. A small percentage of those who have survived a near-death experience report visions of inner worlds, paradises, and cities of light with transcendental music." (Lingza Chokyi)

"I also heard music different music. It was usually like classical music; I like classical music. It wasn't exactly the music I've heard, but it was along that line. It made me relaxed. The fears went away when I listened to it. Again, the feeling of hope, that there's something better somewhere else (He then became aware of a voice). I think [it was] a woman's voice, but I didn't recognize the voice. I just remember that it was a soothing voice. I kind of remember that with the grayness her voice kind of calling, my moving toward it." (Dr. Kenneth Ring)

"Everything in the spirit world is kept in place by an all pervading Master-Vibration (God), which prevents aging. That's why things don't get dirty, or wear out, and why everything looks so bright and new. This is why heaven is eternal. Our thoughts in heaven are vibrations which are controlled by the Master-Vibration. It neutralizes all negative thoughts and lets you think only the good thoughts, such as love, freedom and happiness. After death people gravitate into homogenous groups according to the rate of their soul's vibrations much like throwing a small pebble into a threshing machine, it would go into the box because of its proper size and weight. We are sorted by the high or low vibrations of our soul. Everyone goes where they fit in! High vibrations indicate love and spiritual development, while low vibrations indicate debasement and evil. All one has to do is to love so unselfishly that their soul-vibrations rise high enough to fit into heaven." (Arthur Yensen)

"Out-of-body realms are usually areas of intense experience where the dominant reality is that of light, sound, vibration, motion or emotion. For example, the soul may sense a powerful vibration or sound that causes them to be caught up in that energy. Sometimes these sounds or vibrations propel them at a great speed through a tunnel. They may experience the feeling of inner sounds or vibrations but not the experience of movement and acceleration. Often, such experiences involve hearing spiritual music or sounds, and can be quite ecstatic. These inner sounds along with inner lights can sometimes act as a means of transition between waking experience and some formed inner world. Sounds which occur during conscious transitions out of the body are usually very powerful, and may result in the obliteration of the body image. Some of the sounds which occur are of a spiritual or mystical nature rather than transitional sounds that carry the traveler to a different place. These "higher" spiritual sounds are of a heavenly nature and are ecstatic beyond description. Some sample sounds one may encounter are the sounds of a speeding train, a loud buzzing, a flute, or the sounds of nature like the roar of a waterfall. These sounds or vibrations are of such intensity that they seem to pass right through the body, overpowering the other senses." (Robert Monroe)

TIME

What is time? Is it the movement of the sun across the sky? Is it a ratio of numbers on a clock that represents change from one state to another? Albert Einstein's Theory of Relativity proved that time is subjective to a person's own relative position. Einstein's theory even allows for time travel which is an aspect to many reported near-death experiences. The following is a brief introduction of all the insights concerning time from near-death experiencers profiled on this website.

After death when we enter the spirit realm, it feels as though we were there just a moment ago. Our time on earth seems like only a brief instance. Time in the spirit realm does not exist. By getting rid of the illusion of time from our minds, we have the power to expand our consciousness. We will realize that we are already living in timelessness right now. This means a person can remain in heaven for eternity if they desire before deciding whether to return for another earth life. In the spirit realm, if we desire, we can travel instantaneously from the beginning of earth history to the end. We have the power to grow forever. We are powerful spiritual beings.

The following are examples of time as experienced by those having NDEs.

"The fact of a pre-earth life crystallized in my mind, and I saw that death was actually a "rebirth" into a greater life ... that stretched forward and backward through time." (Betty Eadie)

"Time's measurement on the physical plane is based on the vibration rate of cesium atoms, which was approved by international agreement in 1964. On the Other Side, time is simply the sequence of activity recorded in consciousness. And since our awareness is on a higher frequency in that world, progression (what we see happening) is greatly accelerated. In some situations it would seem to be at the speed of light. In 'Return from Tomorrow,' George Ritchie, M.D., writes about his life review during a near-death experience: 'There were other scenes, hundreds, thousands, all illuminated by that searing Light, in an existence where time seemed to have ceased. It would have taken weeks of ordinary time even to glance at so many events, and yet I had no sense of minutes passing.' The specified lengths of time that we on Earth call seconds, minutes, hours, days, and so forth do not apply over there. The Bible's definition of God's time (the plane of heaven) is that one thousand years equals one day - a remarkable extension of third-dimensional time. I was out of my body for close to four minutes. If we agree with the Bible equation, that would be about three years on the higher plane. That seems like an awfully long time for my particular experience; maybe I just didn't adjust to 'heavenly time' the way others have. For example, in the book Intra Muros by NDE experiencer Rebecca Ruter Springer says: 'Days lengthened into weeks, and weeks into months, and these in turn crept into years, and the duties and joys of heaven grew clearer and dearer with each passing hour." (Jan Price)

"It does not matter that we leave family and friends behind because time becomes irrelevant. It is certain that once we enter the spirit realm, it will be just a blink of the eye before they join us." (Mac Wright)

"Before we're born, we have to take an oath that we will pretend time and space are real so we can come here and advance our spirit. If you don't promise, you can't be born." (Jeanie Dicus)

"Space and time are illusions that hold us to the physical realm; in the spirit realm, all is present simultaneously." (Beverly Brodsky)

"Time did not make any sense. Time did not seem to apply. It seemed irrelevant. It was unattached to anything, the way I was. Time is only relevant when it is relative to the normal orderly sequential aspects of life. So I was there for a moment or for eternity. I cannot say but it felt like a very long time to me." (Grace Bubulka)

"During an NDE, you can't tell if you were in that light for a minute of a day or a hundred years." (Jayne Smith)

"Earthly time has no meaning in the spirit realm. There is no concept of before or after. Everything - past, present, future - exists simultaneously." (Kimberly Clark Sharp)

"From the onset of this rather superconscious state of the darkness of the tunnel, there was something that was totally missing, and that was what we call time. There's no such thing as time in heaven! As I thought of and formulated a desire or a question, it would already have been recognized, acknowledged, and therefore answered. And the dialogue that took place, took place in no time. It didn't require a fifteen-minute duration in time; it simply happened." (Thomas Sawyer)

Albert Einstein's theory of relativity allows for the possibility of time travel. During an NDE, some people have reported traveling back in time and some have reported traveling into the future. The following from NDE references to time travel.

Don Brubaker's Time Travel NDE: Christ said to Don Brubaker, "Don, do you want to stay or go back?"

"I want to go back," I answered immediately, knowing I made the right choice.

Jesus smiled. "You have chosen well. Go. I am with you," Jesus said gently.

Everything changes again, as if someone has turned a page in a book. I see myself in the midst of a huge crowd. It's not a modern crowd. They are dressed in the clothes of Bible times. I look down at myself. "So am I.with you," Jesus says gently. The crowd seems to be jeering at me. Why? Then I see more: I help a man, someone who has been brutally whipped and abused. The crowd is upset because I am offering assistance. But the beaten man has eyes that burn with love and compassion. How could anyone want to hurt this man? I lift the man off of the dusty road to his feet. The man turns, and from somewhere he lifts a huge wooden cross to his back. The man begins moving toward a hill. The hill is called Golgotha. With each new moment, I realize more and more clearly what I am seeing. These people are going to crucify Christ. I follow, stunned, I watch in horror as Jesus is nailed to the cross, the spikes pounded through his wrists and the sensitive insteps of his feet. I watch helpless as the cross is propped up and dropped into position with an ugly thud. I cover my face with my hands. If only others could see what I've seen. The world would get on its knees ... The world would be at peace. (Don Brubaker)

"Everything in this experience merged together, so it is difficult for me to put an exact sequence to events. Time as I had known it came to a halt; past, present, and future were somehow fused together for me in the timeless unity of life ... I could be anywhere instantly, really there ... I felt it necessary to learn about the Bible and philosophy. You want, you receive. Think and it comes to you. So I participated, I went back and lived in the minds of Jesus and his disciples. I heard their conversations, experienced eating, passing wine, smells, tastes - yet I had no body. I was pure consciousness. If I didn't understand what was happening, an explanation would come. But no teacher spoke. I explored the Roman Empire, Babylon, the times of Noah and Abraham. Any era you can name, I went there." (Dr. George Rodonaia)

The light replied, "Let us go back in time, as far back as possible, and tell me how far back we should go". I was thinking for some time. Eventually I blurted out, "Stone Age?" I did not have much time to think about all this, because, all of a sudden, I saw human beings back on earth. I was looking down on a group of people, men and women, who were dressed in furs, sitting around campfire. (Guenter Wagner)

"The box opened to reveal what appeared to be a tiny television picture of a world event that was yet to happen. As I watched, I felt myself drawn right into the picture, where I was able to live the event. This happened twelve times, and twelve times I stood in the midst of many events that would shake the world in the future." (Dannion Brinkley)

The following are more NDE references to time.

When traveling through the tunnel during an NDE, one is traveling through the various afterlife realms. One of these realms is a realm of houses, walls, trees, etc., but everything is motionless. As you travel further up the tunnel, you can see more light and movement in what appear to be normal cities and towns. (Edgar Cayce)

Cayce didn't mention it, but the motionless realm he saw, I believe, is the physical realm. If it is, then it shows how time stands still in the physical realm when entering the spirit realm.)

"An expansion of consciousness can be achieved through meditation. With this expansion comes the realization that we are in eternity now." (Edgar Cayce)

"There is no time and space in the spiritual world. If one is in the highest realms, love reigns. And where there is love, there is happiness. Where there is happiness, there is no awareness of time. Therefore, there is no time as we know it there. In the lower realms, because people are very unhappy, time seems to drag forever. There is space, but it is a reflection of the qualities of the people who live there. Where love reigns, there is no distance between people." (Nora Spurgin)

"The occupants in outer darkness are there for various lengths of time. It is peculiar to discuss length of residence by a measure which does not exist in that dimension. For most of us it is very difficult to relate to a timeless condition, so the use of finite terms helps us to better understand. Some residents feel they have been in outer darkness for weeks or months, others for eons. No doubt all are correct in their assessment of length of time spent in this realm. In a reality of pain and torment, even a moment can seem like an eternity and there is no way to judge length of stay until after one has long departed. Some souls have occupied outer darkness for what we would measure as hundreds, even thousands of years. But it is more likely that most stay for a considerably shorter period. It is not possible for souls to be forever confined to outer darkness, since in such a case there would be no hope of redemption." (Harvey Green)

"In the void during an NDE, there is a profound stillness, beyond all silence. You can see or perceive FOREVER, beyond Infinity, in pre-creation, before the Big Bang, in the Eye of Creation. It is like toughing the Face of God and being at one with Absolute Life and Consciousness. You can experience all of creation generating itself. It is without beginning and without end. You realize the Big Bang is only one of an infinite number of Big Bangs creating Universes endlessly and simultaneously. The only images that even come close in human terms would be those created by supercomputers using fractal geometry equations. You learn that you are an immortal being and a part of a natural living system that recycles itself endlessly." (Mellen-Thomas Benedict)

"Time and space exists only in the physical realm. When you leave the physical realm, you leave such constraints. Existence there is never ending and ongoing, forever and ever eternal. The only true movement is without the distortion of time and space. It is expansion and contraction, as if the existence that exists were capable of breathing. What appears as a progression, a time-line of starts and stops and ever-changing variations, is but an overleaf, an illusion, that helps us to focus on whatever realm we currently inhabit so that we will accomplish what we set out to do (or at least have an opportunity to), and not be distracted by The Truth that under-girds reality. Using radio as an analogy, dying to this physical realm and entering a spirit realm is comparable to having lived all your life at a certain radio frequency when all of a sudden someone or something comes along and flips the dial. That flip shifts you to different frequency. The original frequency where you once existed is still there. It did not change. Everything is still just the same as it was. Only you changed, only you speeded up to allow entry into the next radio frequency on the dial. You then fit into your particular spot on the dial by your speed of vibration. You cannot coexist forever where you do not belong. (P.M.H. Atwater)

"When you die, you enter eternity. It feels like you were always there, and you will always be there. You realize that existence on earth is only just a brief instant." (Dr. Kenneth Ring)

"After death, you can literally travel at the speed of light and see all of the people on earth simultaneously in one moment. You can see people in all manner of activity instantaneously. You can see people praying in mosques and temples, synagogues, and churches. You can see people individually expressing their own silent prayers. You can see indigenous tribes in all different parts of the world drumming and chanting. You can see God sending multitudes of angels to earth to assist in answering all of the countless, millions of prayers being offered up at that single moment." (Dr. Liz Dale)

"When you die, everything stops and you enter eternity. It is like finally getting to the nanosecond, where time stops. Like a watch, our body stops at that time. Yet our spirit and consciousness continue to live on in a dimension beyond sequential time. We go beyond nanoseconds into a space-time measurement we cannot know here on earth. It is the eternal now where past, present, and future are all merged into one. Eternity is the present, the now that never ends." (Dr. Gerard Landry)

"After death, you can go through the end of time all the way back through the beginning of time, then back into the present time where you started. It lasted forever, and was over in an instant. It is a paradox." (Dee Rohe)

155

"After death, you can view one afterlife realm as if it was first grade. People stay there until they were ready to go to the next afterlife realm. This is the eternal progression, from one realm to the next." (Cecil)

"The sense of timelessness after death makes you feel unaware of how long things last, but it can feel like a long time - maybe days or maybe weeks." (Rev. Howard Storm)

"Everything in the spirit realm is kept in place by an all pervading Master-Vibration which prevents aging. Things don't get dirty or wear out. Everything looks so bright and new. You can then understand how heaven is eternal." (Arthur Yensen)

"In the spirit realm, travel takes no time at all. Any experience can seem like eons. But that same experience also seems like seconds." (Dr. George Ritchie)

"In the spirit realm, It can take eons of time as we understand it before some people go into the light. It depends on the person. You're in control. You hold the reins. Those who've come through those darker levels have said that they've had to face themselves and realize that if they don't shape up, in other words, learn more about themselves, they're not getting anywhere." (George Anderson)

"Space and time are illusions that hold us to this physical realm. In the spirit realm, all is present simultaneously." (Beverly Brodsky)

"After death, each person shapes their own eternity to correspond with their real inner nature. Some are taught by their friends about the state of eternal life." (Emanuel Swedenborg)

"One experience in the spirit realm can feel like forever. Time no longer seems to apply and seems irrelevant. Time is only relevant when it is relative to the normal orderly sequential aspects of life. The experience can feel like a moment and an eternity. You realize that you are eternal and indestructible. You realize that you have always been, that you always will be, and there was no way you could ever be lost. It is impossible to fall into a crack in the universe somewhere and never be heard from again. You are utterly safe and always have been forever and ever." (Jayne Smith)

"Life is about having experiences forever and ever and ever. As we bring this awareness permanently into our consciousness, our connection with God will be there and not somewhere in our unconscious. We will be consciously aware of who we are all the time." (Jayne Smith)

"The experience lasted for hours or eons and now it seems that eons passed in only moments." (Virginia Rivers)

"We wandered in this beautiful place for what seemed an eternity." (Karen Schaeffer)

"The experience was a few seconds, but it seemed like an eternity." (Rev. Kenneth Hagin)

"In the spirit realm, time and space becomes nothing more than attenuated wisps of human invention. Both were webs of light created in my consciousness." (Lynnclaire Dennis)

"The human spirit is eternal and we are not alone in the cosmic scheme of things." (Brad Steiger)

"In the spirit realm, people don't talk about time. They talk about opportunity. People don't think about time because it is not measured off in days and nights and months and years." (Margaret Tweddell)

"Our souls are immortal and eternal." (Sandra Rogers)

"Many events of eternity can pass through you. You can bathe in them and become them. They can be infused into your soul." (RaNelle Wallace)

"We are intricately connected to all that exists throughout eternity." (Jan Price)

"On the other side, one event follows another just like on earth. But looking at it another way, time on the other side doesn't pass at all because there is not enough change to make the passage of time evident. From another viewpoint, time in the afterlife stands still because it is always now. The past and future are of equal length because there never was a beginning and never can be an end. This flexibility of time on the other side can be compared to the earth experience when a person is enjoying themselves and time just seems to fly by. But another person having the same experience but who is absolutely miserable, time can seem to last forever. As Einstein discovered, time is a factor that is relative to a person's own experience." (Kevin Williams)

"I glanced at my wrist to note the time, since there was no sun in the sky. My wrist had no watch on it, nor was there any telltale evidence of a watchband ... A strange sense of timelessness gripped me. It was simply awesome! ... We exist here in that timelessness, the eternity of God, the kind of life that does not perish! It is our gift of love, eternal life!" (Dr. Richard Eby)

"There is an overall awareness of the earth's future as it will be in six weeks, six months, or perhaps two years ahead. It is like being in an airplane looking down, and you can get a prevision of what is going to happen, due to being able to see things in broader perspective. However, there is not a complete vision of the entire future of earth. But there are souls in the spirit realm who, through much tribulation and service, have been permitted to see the earth's future in a more extended way." (Margaret Tweddell)

"Time is not linear. Energy moves in a continuum and if we would consider the past as a time passed we would release pain from the body. We get stuck because we stay in the past, instead of realizing that we have passed!" (Lynnclaire Dennis)

The following is John Star's extraordinary NDE concerning time: One day, without any warning, John Star found himself face to face with the fact that life in this world is terminal. He was swimming in Lake Michigan about half a mile offshore when he got in trouble. He was swimming free style, like he had done at swimming competitions, when he turned his head to breathe and inhaled water from an oncoming wave. His lungs were full of water when he wondered if he could swim half a mile at top speed without breathing. He tried. What resulted was an extraordinary near-death experience and a miraculous return to life. Here is the account of his near-death experience in his own words.

"I had only gone a few yards when my head began to buzz and I felt dizzy. A few yards more and I heard a loud snap. Suddenly the world was calm and clear. I could see the shoreline, still in the distance and noticed the sun shining overhead. It seemed brighter than usual. When I looked down I got the surprise of my life. There was my body, still swimming toward shore, moving as straight and smooth as a motor boat. I watched for a while, indifferent to the plight of my body. I was far more concerned with trying to figure out where I was.

"I noticed a light coming from somewhere behind me. It was a peculiar light. It had feeling. When I turned to see where this light was coming from, it would remain behind me. Somehow though, I managed to get turned around so I could look right into the light.

"The light was delicious. I soaked it up like a dry sponge soaks up water. I felt like I had been sealed up in a vacuum packed jar for as long as I could remember. Now the jar was opened and the pressure was gone. I could breathe again. I could feel energy flowing into me, loosening and softening parts of my being that I did not even know I had. My whole being thrilled with well-being and joy: a feeling that I had known before, though I could not remember where or when.

"Time itself seemed to be softening. For as long as I could remember, the minutes, days and years of my life seemed to be fixed, like the markings on a steel ruler. Now, the measuring stick of time was becoming soft and flexible. It would stretch and shrink, like a rubber band. I could return to events of my past, examining them with greater clarity and detail than when they had originally happened, lingering there for what seemed like hours. But then, when I would return to where I was, it seemed like no time at all had gone by. Back and forth I went. Deep into episodes of my personal history, and then back into the light.

"Time could also be contracted, I found. Centuries would condense into seconds. Millenniums would shrink into moments. The entire civilization that I was part of passed by in the blink of an eye.

"'Look at that,' I marveled. 'The whole civilization is no more permanent and no more important that a patch of wild flowers! It's so simple from here, and so beautiful. Whether it is a patch of wild flowers or a mighty civilization, the process is the same. It is only life, trying out different shapes and then returning from where it came.'

"I was being pulled into the light. Or was it that the world and the life that I knew was receding, the life that I had come to assume was the only life there is. All of my certainties and all of my doubts, all of my pride and all of my guilt, all of my pleasures and all of my fears, were all fading away. All that remained was the light and the awesome feeling of well-being that the light contained. It felt like I was waking up, like I had been in a deep sleep, dreaming an intense and detailed dream when somebody came into the room and turned on the lights. Now I was waking up and the dream was fading away.

"As my sleepy eyes slowly became adjusted to the brilliant radiance, I could make out shapes in the light. There were people there! People that I knew and loved. The place was completely familiar, as though I had been there just a few moments before.

"'Did you have a nice rest?' one of my friends asked.

"My other friends broke out into roaring laughter. They were making a joke. They all knew what a grueling ordeal such ventures into the material world can be. They had all made such ventures themselves, many times before. I joined in the laughter. How good it felt to laugh so freely. How strange, to be so open, and yet it was all so familiar. I was totally alive again - an aliveness that was beyond beginning and ending - an aliveness that was eternal.

"The world that I had entered was now as solid and real as the world that I had left behind, but the light was still visible. It was a living light. It had vitality and feeling. It was focused in every living thing just as the sun can be focused to a point with a magnifying glass. There were colors, too, not only the colors that I had known on Earth but many octaves of color. Surrounding all my friends and every other living thing was color, arranged in intricate geometrical patterns, each pattern unique, every pattern original. Permeating the colors and patterns was sound, countless octaves of sound. It was as though the colors could be heard. It reminded me of bagpipes. Filling the entire region were the droning sounds. Octave upon octave of invigorating, vitalizing sound. It was very subtle, practically imperceptible but immense. It seemed to reach to infinity. Superimposed on this vast life-giving hum was the melody, which was created by the individual sound of every living thing. Light and sound, color and geometrical patterns were all combined into a totality of harmonic perfection.

"It seemed like years had gone by. There was no way to tell, though, whether it had been minutes, hours or years. Where I was now, be-ing was the only reality. Be-ing, which was inseparable from the moment, inseparable from the eternal NOW, inseparable from the life that was in all other beings. Even though this place was as solid and real as the world I left behind, time and space was not an obstacle.

"To an animal, a closed door is an insurmountable obstacle. They do not have the faculties necessary to overcome such a barrier. In the world that I had left behind, time and space were just such an insurmountable obstacle. I did not have the faculties necessary to overcome such a barrier. Now I was free, like an animal that had learned how to work a doorknob. I could go in and out of worlds without getting stuck. I could stay inside as long as I wanted. I could become acquainted with people that lived there and get to know their particular customs and their curious opinions, conclusions and beliefs. Then I could leave that world and return to a world without end - a place where there were no opinions, conclusions, or beliefs. It was a place where there was only be-ing, a place of awesome beauty and joy, a place of total harmonic perfection.

"Images of my former life began to flicker in my mind. Fleeting images at first, but now they were growing stronger and clearer. Visions of people who were dear to me that I had left behind. Visions of things I wanted to see and things I had wanted to do. From somewhere deep within my being, a powerful voice welled up:

"You have seen enough of eternity. It's not time yet for you to stay. Return now to the Land of Shadows where the mortal creatures play and be a puff of dust in the wind without being blown away."

Whooooshshsssss, whoooshshssss.

"I raised my head to see what was making that sound. It was tiny wavelets breaking along the edge of a mirror-still lake, rattling the small pebbles that lined the shore. I was lying in the sand on the shore of Lake Michigan, just a few inches from the water. I felt good, like I just had the best rest that I had ever had."

REINCARNATION

Reincarnation is considered by some to be the greatest "unknown" scientific discovery of modern times. In the last chapter of Dr. Ian Stevenson's book entitled Twenty Cases Suggestive of Reincarnation (1967), he provides exhaustive scientific reasoning which concludes that reincarnation is the only viable explanation that fits the facts of his study. He considers every possible alternative explanation for his twenty cases of young children who were spontaneously able to describe a previous lifetime as soon as they learned to talk. He was able to rule out alternative explanations using one or more of his cases. Later research also bolstered his findings in favor of the reality of reincarnation. His study is also reproducible for any skeptic who doubts the validity of his study to repeat it for themselves. I believe it is only a matter of time before these findings are realized by the scientific community to be one of the great scientific discoveries of all time.

Many people would be very surprised at the tremendous amount of references to reincarnation in the Bible. The most compelling references in the Bible comes from the teachings of Jesus concerning John the Baptist and his former life as Elijah the prophet

The following are NDE insights showing that reincarnation is not an eternal process.

"One of the purposes of the life review is to make an informed choice between remaining in spirit and returning to flesh. Should we choose to merge completely with the light of God, we will never again be able to choose, on our own decision, to return to physical life. The decision to merge in the light is the best decision." (Thomas Sawyer)

"We are to live on earth in such a way that we will not need to return to earth after death." (Cecil)

"In time, we who are trapped in the cycle of birth and rebirth can once again come to know our original state and purpose, and regain our celestial birthright as a companion to God. In time we can again come to realize that the conditions in our current life is the result of our free actions and choices from past lives." (Edgar Cayce)

"If a person dies and merges completely into the light, another reincarnation is improbable. However, it is more usual for people to have earthly attachments and not merge completely with the light. Such souls may have characteristics of their personality, which they do not want merged with the light." (Thomas Sawyer)

"The law of karma demands that we meet every bit of our karmic debts. However, an even greater law exists, the law of forgiveness. If we wrong someone and that person forgives us, when the day comes that we approach God, we realize our memories which are incompatible with God, but forgiveness removes the barrier of separation. The law is so precise (what one gives one receives; no exceptions) that if we begin forgiving others, we begin to receive forgiveness upon ourselves. Unless, of course, we refuse to forgive ourselves." (Edgar Cayce)

"Our attraction to worldly desires can hinder the free expression of our souls and only when they are no longer a hindrance can our earth incarnations be finished. The free expression of our souls happens when our wills become compatible with the thoughts of God. At this time, our conscious spiritual identity with God will merge with our soul consciousness (subconscious mind). This is when the soul merges with the light of God. The return of the soul is the return of the thought that God imagined and is becoming aware of being a part of all God and everything." (Edgar Cayce)

"Some souls desire to return again and again to the physical state without spending enough time in spirit to evaluate and plan their next incarnation in the flesh. Any habit-forming pleasure, and they are endless, traps them into the cycle of rebirth over and over, until their appetites are finally put aside while they are in the flesh. The lust for money, lust for power, lust for sex, and other habits such as an unnatural craving for alcohol, drugs, tobacco, or any habit they are unable to break loose from, can keep souls earthbound. Some are so overly fond of the bodies they left behind that they are hardly able to wait for an opportunity to reincarnate and set to work indulging their new bodies. These souls will not be able to advance spiritually until they learn to give less thought to appetites of the flesh." (Ruth Montgomery)

The following is the author's theory of the mechanics of reincarnation using an analogy.

The purpose of reincarnation is education - particularly, learning the eternal lessons of love. Using the analogy of a school, my theory of reincarnation is described below. I describe stages of reincarnation and with each stage I use a "school analogy" to help clarify it. I consider this description of the mechanics of reincarnations as "the curriculum for the world-school we are currently enrolled in and the academic degree we are trying to graduate with":

(1) We are born into this world with the mission to learn lessons of love for the purpose of becoming forever at-one with everyone and everything (God). ANALOGY: We begin a new grade in school with the goal of graduating and receiving a degree.

(2) During our lives, we are subjected to severe hardships for the purpose of soul growth. ANALOGY: During the school year, we must subject ourselves to difficult homework in order to learn.

(3) After death we have a life review to decide if we have earned the right to advance to a higher heavenly position. If we have earned that right, we can assume that position at any opportunity we desire. In the meanwhile, we can spend an eternity with family and friends then reincarnate to lower realms to help others progress if we desire. ANALOGY: When the school year is over, we then find out if we have earned the right to enroll in the next grade or whether we must repeat the grade. Either way, we then spend a long summer vacation at home on with family and friends before beginning another school year.

(4) Some people have made such tremendous mistakes in life that, after death, they set themselves back some degree from progressing and need to re-experience a lower afterlife realm before reincarnating for another earth life. ANALOGY: Some students flunk out so badly that they have to spend some time in detention and be sent back a grade.

(5) Because our ultimate goal is to be forever at-one with all things at a conscious level (the divine consciousness), we inherently desire more soul growth until we attain this goal. This goal is attained by leaving the realm we currently reside in (Death is the way people leave the physical realm - other realms have other ways.) and entering another realm we have earned the right to enter for the purpose of further soul growth. Analogy: Because our ultimate goal is to graduate, get a degree, and become co-partners in the God R Us Corporation, we leave home to go to school to earn our degree. Based on whether we have passed the grade from the previous school year, we enroll into a higher grade in school or return to the same grade from the previous year.

(6) People in the lower realms will be given opportunities to reincarnate to higher realms, including the physical realm, as many times as it takes for them to learn the lessons necessary to earn and advance to a higher position. ANALOGY: Students who flunked out of school the previous year will be allowed to repeat the grade until they pass it.

(7) It will take a lot of love and effort, but eventually everyone will be reunited - the Godhood will be restored as it was in the very beginning - a good time will be had by all -

perhaps another Big Bang will happen. But until everyone attains at-one-ment, we will enter and leave realms for our own soul growth and to help others in their own soul journey to God. ANALOGY: It will take a lot of studying and hard work, but eventually all students will graduate, get their degree, and join the firm. But after we graduate, if we choose first to become a teacher before accepting our position as a permanent co-partner in the firm, we choose to help other students (perhaps our loved ones) graduate as well. (Kevin Williams)

The following are factors influencing reincarnation.

According to Amber Wells' NDE reincarnation research the factors influencing reincarnation are: (1) Individual choice (free will); (2) Karmic patterns or ties to other souls; (3) Learning or enlightenment

"Life itself is a series of learnings. The lessons are universal, the two most important being truth and forgiveness." (Amber Wells' NDE research)

"The chief purpose of reincarnation is education. To this end we are born again and again on earth, not because of any external pressure, but because we, as souls, desire to grow." (Amber Wells' NDE research)

"It (reincarnation) is a universal process, and prevails not only in the human kingdom but also throughout the whole of nature. Whenever we find a living form, the consciousness of that form is also evolving, using temporarily for that purpose the physical form in order that it may gain physical experience. In each incarnation we have a different physical body, a different name, and may have different souls acting as parents, but these changes do not in the slightest imperil our individuality ... Reincarnation is not an endless process, and when we have learned the lessons taught in the World-School we return no more to physical incarnation unless we come back of our own accord to act as Teachers of humanity or as Helpers in the glorious plan of evolution." (Amber Wells' NDE research)

"The spirit needs to embody itself in matter to experience it and learn. There are karmic patterns to learn lessons and to work spirit in matter." (Amber Wells' NDE research)

"The only way to bypass bad karma is to develop so much unselfish love that paying for bad karma will serve no purpose - much like a college student challenging a course he already knows." (Arthur Yensen)

"If we do enough good works we will eventually run out of bad karma and only good things will happen to us, and vice versa. The goal of karma is to force us to learn life's lessons whether we want to or not." (Arthur Yensen)

"If we do not wish to reincarnate to the physical state to learn our lessons, there are schools in the spirit were we can learn them. However, learning our lessons in the physical state is the fastest way to learn them." (David Oakford)

"We have lived and died many times. The reason we don't remember our former lives is because our vast soul memories are not transferred to our baby brains at birth. All we know in this life is what we have learned, most of which is a partial memory of things we learned in past lifetimes. At the beginning of each lifetime, we are cleared of all past prejudices, learning blocks and wrong teachings, and are ready for a fresh start - just like a new term in school - and, like school, when we have learned enough of life's lessons, we graduate and don't have to come back to this earth anymore, except as volunteers to teach stragglers." (Edgar Cayce)

"All of our karma has to be met. And yet, no one is given more than it can bear to carry. We are given the time we need to turn away from selfish ways and return home like the prodigal son. Reincarnation is not a way to avoid responsibility. It is a way to allow us enough time to correct our mistakes." (Edgar Cayce)

"After death, when we are ready, we can choose to view our past lives for the purpose of instruction. (Betty Bethards)

Life is a cycle of improvements and humans are not perfect yet. Most people have this secret revealed to them when they die. (Dr. Frank Oski)

"At some point, our desire to advance will lead us to reincarnate. Our guides help us decide an incarnation that will help to achieve our goals. After a period of farewell with family and friends, we can meet with a great spiritual teacher (such as Jesus, Buddha, etc.) to give us strength. After this, we descend into the womb to be born again. We leave paradise not just for our own advancement, but to bring paradise to earth and God will light our path throughout our time on earth and bring us safely home afterward." (Sylvia Browne)

Reincarnation is karma. Reincarnation and karma together explains divine justice and why some people are born into favorable conditions or are born into unfavorable conditions. Personality traits are also carried over from past lives.

(1) Whatever we think, that thought makes an impression on the Universal Consciousness. Nothing is lost or done in secret. Everything is done within the Universal Consciousness, and the Whole is affected by it (as well as all others within the Whole). Reactions to past thoughts and actions become our destiny and karma. Our destiny is simply the rebounding effects of previous choices remembered by the soul. (Edgar Cayce)

(2) "A man acts according to the desires to which he clings. After death he goes to the next world bearing in his mind the subtle impressions of his deeds; and, after reaping there the harvest of those deeds, he returns again to this world of action. Thus he who has desire continues subject to rebirth. He who lacks discrimination, whose mind is unsteady and whose heart is impure, never reaches the goal, but is born again and again. But he who has discrimination, whose mind is steady and whose heart is pure, reaches the goal and, having reached it, is born no more." (Upanishads)

The NDE and religious evidence shows that some people reincarnate from hell realms.

"Hell is a spiritual condition that some people are allowed to experience whose goal is to purge aspects of their personality so that they can participate once again in the cycle of reincarnation." (Hindu NDEr)

"Without physical bodies, feelings of hate and fear are intensified as souls [in hell] vainly try to hide from their enemies. Their only hope is to reincarnate. Then unfortunately when they do, they may forget all about their torment in hell and again lead lives of greed and tyranny. This miserable cycle can continue forever unless they find salvation in one of their lifetimes. Such people really need a savior, since they are not able to help themselves. I'm sure Christ incarnated to help them because he said, 'I came not to call the righteous, but sinners to repentance.'" (Arthur Yensen)

"After death, people who accrued severe negative karma will enter a hellish realm for a short period. After they have reflected upon their actions, they will be allowed to reincarnate." (Sylvia Browne)

CHAPTER 4: NDES AND RELIGION

"If anyone asserts the fabulous preexistence of souls, and shall assert the monstrous restoration which follows from it, let him be anathema [excommunicated]." - Decrees of the Fifth General Council of the Church

Many Christian critics argue the NDE, and specifically the "being of light," is "of the devil." They argue the light deceives people and turns people away from traditional interpretations of the Bible. They say the NDE is false because everyone experiences a heaven and no hell, although this is not actually the case with NDEs. Such critics believe a God of infinite love and mercy would create people in order to torture them forever in the fire of hell. Because non-Christians are seen to go to heaven in NDEs, they reason this proves the NDE to be deceptive and contrary to the Bible.

This kind of criticism doesn't apply solely to NDEs either. Many critics outright reject all supernatural phenomenon and claim the NDE comes from "demons" and "false prophets." The rest of this book will be devoted to proving these arguments wrong.

It is true the NDE is a threat to particular brands of Christianity. It is a threat to the archaic concept of a "God of wrath" as described in the Old Testament, who is human-like, wrathful, jealous, hateful, egocentric and murderous. Such false concepts of God are mostly the result of elevating the Bible above common sense. Often, it is the result of claiming a particular interpretation of the Bible to be the only valid interpretation. The NDE reveals God to be of infinite love and mercy beyond human comprehension - the same God suggested by Jesus in the New Testament. To attribute wrath, jealousy, hatefulness and such to God, as many Old Testament verses (as well as many in the New Testament) do, is a big mistake.

My main purpose here is not to discredit the Bible, but to prove the God of the NDE is the God of Christianity, using the Bible itself. Since all Christians believe the Bible to be the highest court of appeal for all disagreements, I will appeal to the Bible to prove my case. At this juncture, I would like to point out the NDE reveals God is not limited to one religion. The God revealed in the NDE is the God of everyone, not just a chosen few or particular religious denomination. Even the Bible agrees with this statement: "Is God the God of Jews only? Is he not the God of Gentiles too?" (Romans 3:29)

With that in mind, here is a list of what I will prove:

1. NDEs are not unscriptural
2. NDEs are not of the devil
3. NDEs and the Bible affirm God is unconditional love
4. NDEs and the Bible affirm universal salvation
5. NDEs and the Bible affirm reincarnation

1. NDES ARE NOT UNSCRIPTURAL

Some Bible verses can be interpreted as denying even the possibility of returning from death. Here are a couple of them:

"A person is destined to die once, and after that to face judgment." (Hebrews 9:27)

"..[At death we are] like water spilled on the ground, which cannot be recovered, so we must die." (2 Samuel 14:14)

Some Christians, who hold the belief that everyone sleeps in their graves until Judgment Day, use the following Bible verse to support that belief: "For the living know that they will die, but the dead know nothing; they have no further reward, and even the memory of them is forgotten." (Ecclesiastes 9:5)

The following counter-argument reveals the false interpretation of these verses. We know even from other Bible verses that some people have died more than once. Lazarus died not once, but twice (John 11:43-44). The same is true for everyone resurrected from the dead with the exception, of course, of Jesus Christ (Mark 5:21-42; Luke 7:11-15). Some were resurrected at the time of Christ's death (Matthew 27:52). The apostles resurrected people from the dead (Acts 20:9-12). The Old Testament talks of several people who came back to life from the dead (1 Kings 17:17-24; 2 Kings 4:34; 2 Kings 13:21). All of these resurrected people had to die a second time. The prophet Elijah, Enoch and Melchezedek did not even die at all according to the Bible. For these reasons, no Bible verses can be interpreted to mean people cannot be revived from death. Such a false interpretation also contradicts the testimony of millions of people who had an NDE.

Before we continue, I would like to share a specific Bible verse refuting the notion of people sleeping in their graves until Judgment Day: "...as long as we are at home in the body we are away from the Lord." (2 Corinthians 5:6-8).

The logical conclusion to this statement is that when we are "away from the body" we are "at home with the Lord." Biblically speaking, this means to die is to be present with the Lord. No sleeping in the graves is mentioned here. This verse can also be used to make the claim that everyone who was brought back from the dead has seen the Lord.

Another Bible argument used by critics against reviving from death is the parable of the rich man and Lazarus. In the parable, Lazarus dies and is carried by angels to "Abraham's side." An unrepentant rich man likewise dies, but is sent to hell. In hell, the rich man is "in torment" and sees Lazarus with Abraham. The rich man implores Abraham to send Lazarus to comfort him with some water. Abraham's reply is: "... between us and you a great chasm has been fixed, so that those who want to go from here to you cannot, nor can anyone cross over from there to us." (Luke 16:19-31)

Critics who say the dead cannot leave their location in the afterlife often use this parable to prove their point. But this interpretation cannot be true. The verses previously discussed provide one reason. Another reason is related in an incident in the Old Testament where Saul has a medium conjure up the spirit of the prophet Samuel (1 Samuel 28:7-25). Since this verse actually documents a spirit being summoned up from the land of the dead, we can be safe in saying that the gulf between life and death can be crossed. The story of the rich man and Lazarus is a parable. Parables are symbolic and should not to be taken literally. Parables usually have a spiritual interpretation behind the literal symbols.

Another argument critics use against the NDE is the claim by experiencers that they have actually seen God. They quote verses such as these:

"... you cannot see my [God's] face, for no one may see me and live." (Exodus 33:20)

"No one has ever seen God, but God the One and Only, who is at the Father's side, has made him known." (John 1:18)

The rebuttal against this false interpretation is the following Bible verse written by the Apostle Paul: "I know a person in Christ who fourteen years ago was caught up the third heaven. Whether it was in the body or out of the body I do not know -- God knows. And I know that this person -- whether in the body or apart from the body I do not know, but God knows -- was caught up to paradise. He heard inexpressible things, things that people are not permitted to tell." (2 Corinthians 12:2-4)

This verse obviously describes an NDE where someone is taken to heaven and returns. All the evidence for it being an NDE is there: the out-of-body experience, the reference to more than one heaven and hearing inexpressible things. This is no different than what experiencers describe today. Also, many bible scholars believe Paul is actually referring to his own experience. In context, this above verse has to do with "rival preachers" boasting about their own knowledge, in which Paul compares himself to them. Paul does a lot of boasting himself in that particular chapter, but then goes on to describe the experience of a person whom "he knows." His description of the out-of-body experience sounds as if it truly is a personal experience. This becomes even more apparent in light of this Bible verse saying Paul was stoned and left for dead: "They stoned Paul and dragged him outside the city, thinking he was dead. But after the disciples had gathered around him, he got up and went back into the city." (Acts 14:19-20)

Another Bible verse supporting the NDE comes from the Old Testament concerning Jacob's Stairway or Ladder. In it, Jacob has a dream where he sees the "gate to heaven:" "He [Jacob] had a dream in which he saw a stairway resting on the earth, with its top reaching to heaven, and the angels of God were ascending and descending on it. There above it stood the Lord, and he said: 'I am the Lord, the God of your father Abraham...' When Jacob awoke from his sleep, he thought, 'Surely the Lord is in this place, and I was not aware of it.' He was afraid and said, 'How awesome is this place! This is none other than the house of God; this is the gate of heaven'." (Genesis 28:12)

Jacob's Ladder is an excellent description of the "tunnel" or "passageway" people having NDEs see and travel through. Experiencers often see angels in this passageway as well. This passageway extends to heaven and at the end of it is God.

A fundamentalist may argue that Jacob was not near death when he received this vision. But a person does not need to be dead to have an NDE. Researchers have recorded people having them during extreme gravitational forces, extreme stress, meditation, psychedelic drugs or situations where consciousness is altered.

Another Biblical account describes an experience where a person sees God and heaven. Stephen, the first Christian martyr, is stoned to death after having what appears to be an NDE: "But Stephen, full of the Holy Spirit, looked up to heaven and saw the glory of God, and Jesus standing at the right hand of God. 'Look,' he said, 'I see heaven open and the Son of Man standing at the right hand of God.'" (Acts 7:54-56)

For this, Stephen was stoned to death, because it was believed to be blasphemy. Stephen's description of heaven opening up and seeing God is a good description of the initial stage of an NDE.

There are also Gnostic writings such as the "Apocalypse of Paul," described earlier in this book and documents Paul's trip to heaven. There is also the apocalypse of John described in the Book of Revelation.

Another argument supporting the NDE is a particular event in the gospels where Jesus is transformed into a "being of light" similar to the "being of light" found in the NDE: "After six days Jesus took with him Peter, James and John the brother of James, and led them up a high mountain by themselves. There he was transfigured before them. His face shone like the sun, and his clothes became as white as the light. Just then there appeared before them Moses and Elijah, talking with Jesus." (Matthew 17:2-3)

From all that has been discussed thus far, it should be clear that people are able to go to heaven, see God and return to earth. Since the Bible itself describes people seeing God and heaven, then this shows the NDE does not conflict with scripture. We can now say for certain that any interpretation of the Bible that states God has never been seen or can be seen, contradicts all the verses saying God has been seen.

There are certain facts concerning the NDE supported by the Bible. The following are the most important ones I am aware of.

A. Your entire life will be reviewed after death -- every word, thought and deed.

"But I tell you that men will have to give account on the day of judgment for every careless word they have spoken. For by your words you will be acquitted, and by your words you will be condemned." (Matthew 12:36-37)

"For the word of God is living and active. Sharper than any double-edged sword, it penetrates even to dividing soul and spirit, joints and marrow; it judges the thoughts and attitudes of the heart. Nothing in all creation is hidden from God's sight. Everything is uncovered and laid bare before the eyes of him to whom we must give account." (Hebrews 4:12-13)

"Everyone who does evil hates the light, and will not come into the light for fear that his deeds will be exposed. But whoever lives by the truth comes into the light, so that it may be seen plainly that what he has done has been done through God." (John 3:20-21)

B. After death, you are your own judge. Neither God nor Jesus judges anyone.

"Moreover, the Father judges no one, but has entrusted all judgment to the Son." (John 5:22)

"I [Jesus] pass judgment on no one." (John 8:15)

"As for the person who hears my words but does not keep them, I do not judge him. For I did not come to judge the world, but to save it. There is a judge for the one who rejects me and does not accept my words, that very word which I spoke will condemn him at the last day." (John 12:47-48)

While the above Bible verses show that God and Jesus judges no one, there are verses suggesting God's judgment is actually our own conscience judging us: "Indeed, when Gentiles, who do not have the law, do by nature things required by the law, they are a law for themselves, even though they do not have the law, since they show that the requirements of the law are written on their hearts, their consciences also bearing witness, and their thoughts now accusing, now even defending them. This will take place on the day when God will judge men's secrets through Jesus Christ, as my gospel declares." (Romans 2:14-16)

Another Bible verse reveals how we ourselves are judges: "Do you not know that the saints will judge the world? And if you are to judge the world, are you not competent to judge trivial cases? Do you not know we will judge angels?" (1 Corinthians 6:2-3)

The angels we judge may in reality be ourselves.

C. Communication in the afterlife is by direct thought transfer. There are no secrets in the afterlife.

"Nothing in all creation is hidden from God's sight. Everything is uncovered and laid bare before the eyes of him to whom we must give account." (Hebrews 4:13)

"Everyone who does evil hates the light, and will not come into the light for fear that his deeds will be exposed. But whoever lives by the truth comes into the light, so that it may be seen plainly that what he has done has been done through God." (John 3:20-21)

"But if an unbeliever or someone who does not understand comes in while everybody is prophesying, he will be convinced by all that he is a sinner and will be judged by all, and the secrets of his heart will be laid bare. So he will fall down and worship God, exclaiming, 'God is really among you!'" (1 Corinthians 14:24-25)

"Knowing their thoughts, Jesus said, 'Why do you entertain evil thoughts in your hearts?'" (Matthew 9:4)

"For who has known the mind of the Lord that he may instruct him? But we have the mind of Christ." (1 Corinthians 2:16)

"All the believers were one in heart and mind." (Acts 4:32)

D. Hell is having your faults revealed to everyone. Heaven is having your goodness revealed to everyone.

"This is the verdict: Light has come into the world, but men loved darkness instead of light because their deeds were evil. Everyone who does evil hates the light, and will not come into the light for fear that his deeds will be exposed. But whoever lives by the truth comes into the light, so that it may be seen plainly that what he has done has been done through God." (John 3:19-21)

This verse also shows how people send themselves to the darkness of hell to escape from having their inner nature exposed to everyone in the light of God. It also suggests that living in the light brings such an overwhelming experience that some people cannot endure it. Such is the case of Jayne Smith, whose NDE is profiled in this book. John, in the Book of Revelation, has such an experience as well: "When I saw him, I fell at his feet as though dead. Then he placed his right hand on me and said: "Do not be afraid. I am the First and the Last." (Revelation 1:17-18)

E. There are many dimensions to the afterlife and earth is one of them.

"In my Father's house are many mansions [abodes]; if it were not so, I would have told you. I am going there to prepare a place for you." (John 14:2)

"I know a person in Christ who fourteen years ago was caught up to the third heaven... And I know that this person ... was caught up to paradise." (2 Corinthians 12:2-4)

Heaven begins here on earth within us and is carried with us at death: "... the kingdom of God is within you." (Luke 17:20-21)

2. NDES ARE NOT OF THE DEVIL

The following are rebuttals against the arguments of a well-known Christian seminary professor and critic of the NDE. In his book, the professor discounts all NDEs not conforming to his narrow interpretation of the Bible as being the work of the devil.

The professor asks: Who is this being of light appearing in NDEs?

My answer is: There are many beings of light appearing in NDEs. The Bible declares God is light (1 John 1:5). People in the higher spirit realms emanate this light which is God. The being of light can be literally anyone: Jesus, Buddha, the Hindu god of death, an angel or even a deceased loved one. It usually depends on the person's religious bias and cultural background. The NDE reveals God's light is manifested within many beings in the spirit realm.

The professor argues: It is claimed the being of light is Jesus Christ. This seems to be wrong because this being says and does things contrary to the Jesus in the Bible. Because Jesus never changes (Hebrews 13:8), it would be impossible for this to be the same Jesus. I believe many of the people having NDEs encounter a counterfeit Jesus.

My rebuttal is: The being of light in the NDE cannot be counterfeit because this being passes the test given by Jesus. It is the test to determine whether the spirit is of God or not: "Do not believe every spirit, but test the spirits to see whether they are of God..." (1 John 4:1)

Jesus Himself gives us the test. According to the gospels, religious leaders accused Jesus of performing miracles by the power of Satan. This is the same accusation the professor brings against the being of light in the NDE. This accusation is made even though both Jesus and the being of light bear incredible love, joy, peace and all the fruits of the Holy Spirit.

Jesus reply to this accusation is: "Every kingdom divided against itself will be ruined, and every city or household divided against itself will not stand. If Satan drives out Satan, he is divided against himself. How then can his kingdom stand? And if I drive out demons by Beelzebub, by whom do your people drive them out? So then, they will be your judges.

But if I drive out demons by the Spirit of God, then the kingdom of God has come upon you... Make a tree good and its fruit will be good, or make a tree bad and its fruit will be bad, for a tree is recognized by its fruit." (Matthew 12:24-37)

Anyone familiar with the NDE knows the being of light gives an astonishing amount of goodness, holiness, love, joy, peace and such. Jesus made it very clear that a bad tree cannot bear good fruit, nor can a good tree bear bad fruit.

Some critics use the Bible verse below to discredit the being of light: "Satan himself masquerades as an angel of light." (2 Corinthians 11:14)

Notice the verse states Satan can only "masquerade" as an angel of light. The verse does not say he actually is an angel of light. It only refers to Satan's ability to deceive people into believing he is an angel of light. But we cannot be deceived if we use the test given by Jesus. Using this test we can ask: Is there good fruit involved with the being of light? If so, then it must be of God. Is there no good fruit involved? If there isn't, then the being of light must be of Satan. It is obvious to anyone who is familiar with the being of light that the test actually confirms the being to be of God. In my NDE research, an experience of astonishing love from the being of light or the NDE in general, is the most common characteristic appearing in fifty NDEs. Since God is light, there is no light in darkness. Neither is darkness found in light. Satan is no angel of light. The being of light has a tremendous amount of light. Light can only come only from God. Satan is neither an angel of light nor an angel of love.

There are very serious consequences of attributing things of God to Satan. When Jesus was accused of performing miracles by the power of Satan and before he gave the test, he said: "And so I tell you, every sin and blasphemy will be forgiven men, but the blasphemy against the Spirit will not be forgiven. Anyone who speaks a word against the Son of Man will be forgiven, but anyone who speaks against the Holy Spirit will not be forgiven, either in this age or in the age to come." (Matthew 12:31-32)

Jesus makes very clear the grave consequences of attributing to Satan the works of the Holy Spirit. Like the professor, many critics are quick to declare the being of light in the NDE to be of Satan, not realizing they may be dangerously close to blaspheming the Holy Spirit, something Jesus said cannot be forgiven.

The idea that the being of light in NDEs is sinister or "of the devil" ignores common sense. Dr. Raymond Moody, considered by many the father of the NDE, responded to this kind of criticism in his latest book, The Last Laugh.

"Fervent critics see nothing amiss in preaching to Aunt Florene, bereft and kindly and fragile though she may be, that it was not really the spirit of Uncle Hamperd who visited her last week to comfort her and to tell her where he put those important papers. No, it was actually a malignant demon disguised as uncle Hamperd, there to lure her into Hell, so she had better go home and read the Bible. The doctrine that the Devil can disguise himself as Christ must be particularly troubling to fundamentalist authorities as they consider the possibilities of pediatric near-death experiences. Does God permit Satan to fool dying kids by masquerading as Jesus? Or is God powerless to prevent that kind of satanic deception? If so, common decency dictates that funda-Christian NDExperts urgently prepare clear, precise instructions that will enable desperately ill, dying preschoolers to distinguish a satanophanic Jesus from the real, true funda-Christian one. And would God allow the Devil to sneak up on a dying toddler by appearing as Santa Claus or Pat Robertson, Jerry Falwell or the Easter Bunny?" (69)

To demonstrate how foolish the professor's arguments are, here is a direct quote from professor's own book on how the being of light is a counterfeit Jesus: "Even if the loving, brilliantly illuminated being you meet during a near-death experience introduces Himself as Jesus, and looks just like him from the paintings, don't believe him for a minute! You've got to put him to the professor's ideological test first. Jesus has to pass the professor's Bible exam, before he can even be him!" (70)

Such statements are completely absurd. The professor errs because he limits Jesus to his own narrow interpretation of the Bible. Any NDE bearing the fruit of the Holy Spirit passes Christ's test and must not be said to be "of the devil." It would be blasphemous to do so. Perhaps this explains why the NDE described in 2 Corinthians 12:2-4 states these are inexpressible things which people were not permitted to talk about in those days. These matters may have simply been too high for first century Christians to understand (and some twentieth century professors, as well). We must test the spirit of the NDE -- not using the test of the professor, but rather the test from Jesus. In doing so, you will find the NDE to bear much fruit of the Holy Spirit.

The professor argues: The being of light of the NDE teaches such things as death is good and is not to be feared.

My rebuttal is: This is not true. The NDE shows that if a person is not prepared for death, their experience after death is not very good and should be greatly feared. A case in point is Howard Storm and his NDE. Howard lived the life of an atheist and treated people very badly. He was not prepared for death when he died because he ends up in "hell" when he does. The result of death is that some people go to "hell." Hellish NDE make up a large number of reported NDEs. It is false to claim the being of light teaches death to be good and should not be feared. In fact, the NDE proves otherwise.

The professor argues: The being of light of the NDE teaches sin is not a problem. In fact, the being of light often responds to human sin and shortcomings with humor.

My rebuttal is: This is not true. The NDE shows that if a person lives a sinful life, their experience will be a big problem for them after death. The fact is that Jesus appears in NDEs to be very sad about the sin of humanity. Dr. George Ritchie and his NDE is a case in point. During his NDE, Dr. Ritchie notices how sad Jesus is for those in hell. To say otherwise is to display ignorance about NDEs.

The professor argues: The being of light of the NDE teaches there is no hell to worry about.

My rebuttal is: This is not true. Dr. George Ritchie's NDE and Howard Storm's NDE are perfect examples of the reality of hell.

The professor argues: The being of light of the NDE teaches all people are welcome to heaven, regardless of whether or not they are a Christian.

My rebuttal is: This is not true. The NDE shows that some people go to hell. Although it is God's will for everyone to go to heaven (1 Timothy 2:3-4 and 2 Peter 3:9) many people do not. The NDE also shows that faith in Christ alone does not guarantee anyone a ticket to heaven. Scripture supports this as well:

"Not everyone who says to me, 'Lord, Lord,' will enter the kingdom of heaven, but only he who does the will of my Father who is in heaven. Many will say to me on that day, 'Lord, Lord, did we not prophesy in your name, and in your name drive out demons and perform many miracles?' Then I will tell them plainly, 'I never knew you. Away from me, you evildoers!'" (Matthew 7:21-23)

The professor argues: The being of light of the NDE teaches all religions are valid.

My rebuttal is: This is not true. The NDE shows a person's religious beliefs (or lack thereof) can make the difference in determining how close to God and therefore whether they have a "heavenly" NDE or a "hellish" NDE. For example, after Howard Storm was rescued from hell during his NDE, he had this exchange with Jesus:

I asked them, for example, which was the best religion. I was looking for an answer, which was like: "Presbyterians." I figured these guys were all Christians. The answer I got was: "The best religion is the religion that brings you closest to God." [71]

This information shows that the goal of religion is to bring a person closer to God. It is also implied that some religions bring you closer to God than others. Although a person's religious beliefs (or lack thereof) can influence the quality of their afterlife experience, a person's religious affiliation or church membership itself does not seem to matter much to Jesus. Jesus did not come preaching some new religion. Jesus preached love. The NDE reveals it is love, not religion, creating spiritual growth and saving us from a hell of our own making. It is clear from the gospel accounts alone, that Jesus is not concerned about a person's religious status. Jesus told the religious leaders who killed him that the prostitutes were going to enter heaven before they did (Matthew 21:31). It is clear from the NDE, the Bible and common sense that religion is a cultural institution. Love, however, is universal and not limited to a particular culture. According to the Sermon on the Mount, love is the greatest "religion" there is. Love is also what many of the great world religions is all about. However, not everyone practices this "religion" of love.

The professor argues: In view of the fact that these ideas go against what the Jesus of the Bible taught, we have reason to conclude that the Jesus of the NDE is in fact a lying spirit.

My rebuttal is: This is not true. The Jesus of the NDE does not go against what the Bible teaches. They may go against the professor's narrow interpretation of what Jesus said, but they do not go against what Jesus said. The professor has not tested the spirits properly. He is making the same mistake of the Pharisees by testing the spirits using one's own narrow interpretation of scripture. The correct test is to judge by their fruit. If no fruit of the Holy Spirit is present, then it is safe to assume it is not of God. Jesus bore much fruit of the Holy Spirit yet was condemned by the religious leaders because he did not fit into their interpretation of scripture. Had they properly tested the spirits and judged Jesus on the basis of his fruit, he probably would not have been crucified. In the same way, if the professor would test the Jesus of the NDE based on his fruit, he would not be accusing him of being a lying spirit.

The professor argues: The Jesus of the NDE is happy to mimic Jesus if the end result is that he can lead people away from the true Jesus of the Bible.

My rebuttal is: The Jesus of the NDE bears fruit of the Holy Spirit. Remember, Jesus of the Bible had this to say about testing the spirits: "Make a tree good and its fruit will be good, or make a tree bad and its fruit will be bad, for a tree is recognized by its fruit." (Matthew 12:24-37) And: "A good tree cannot bear bad fruit, and a bad tree cannot bear good fruit." (Matthew 7:18)

Even the professor must admit the Jesus of the NDE does bear the fruit of love. But since the professor is testing the spirits using his own narrow interpretation of scripture and not testing by the fruit, it is he who is leading people astray.

The professor argues: Many people who have had NDEs come away from the experience with a lesser view of the Bible. One person even concluded "the Lord isn't interested in theology," and another said God "didn't care about church doctrine at all." The Jesus of the Bible, however, is certainly interested in correct doctrine.

My rebuttal is: Such generalities concerning experiencers who have a lesser view of the Bible is completely bogus. Common sense tells one that generalities such as this cannot be true. One cannot make a correlation between having an NDE and having a lower view of the Bible. Notice the professor does not cite the NDEs that lead him to this conclusion. Nevertheless, the person the professor mentions who concluded, "the Lord isn't interested in theology" is Howard Storm. It is a true statement to say that God is not interested in theology. Here is the complete account of what Howard Storm said: "I asked, for example, "What about the Bible?" They responded: "What about it?" I asked if it was true, and they said it was. Asking them why it was that when I tried to read it, all I saw were contradictions, they took me back to my life's review again, something that I had overlooked. They showed me, for the few times I had opened the Bible, that I had read it with the idea of finding contradictions and problems. I was trying to prove to myself that it wasn't worth reading. I observed to them that the Bible wasn't clear to me. It didn't make sense. They told me that it contained spiritual truth, and that I had to read it spiritually in order to understand it. It should be read prayerfully. My friends informed me that it was not like other books. They also told me, and I later found out this was true, that when you read it prayerfully, it talks to you. It reveals itself to you. And you don't have to work at it anymore." [At the end of his experience, Howard Storm says:] "I try not to impose my Christianity on other people. If people have God-like characteristics, a feeling of compassion and living that out, then it's ok. I respond more to behavior than philosophy. God really doesn't care a fig about theology." (20)

If one reads Howard Storm's and Dr. George Ritchie's NDEs, one will see why God does not care about theology or "how many angels can dance on the head of a pin." Nevertheless, the NDE does reveal a great concern for the commands of God. Love is the command of God (Romans 13:10, John 15:12). However, concerning theology, rules taught by men, it is clear that Christ Himself doesn't care about it:

"You hypocrites! Isaiah was right when he prophesied about you: 'These people honor me with their lips, but their hearts are far from me. They worship me in vain; their teachings are but rules taught by men.'" (Matthew 15:7-9)

"'They worship me in vain; their teachings are but rules taught by men. You have let go of the commands of God and are holding on to the traditions of men.' And he said to them: 'You have a fine way of setting aside the commands of God in order to observe your own traditions! For Moses said, 'Honor your father and your mother,' and, 'Anyone who curses his father or mother must be put to death.' But you say that if a man says to his father or mother: 'Whatever help you might otherwise have received from me is Corban' (that is, a gift devoted to God), then you no longer let him do anything for his father or mother. Thus you nullify the word of God by your tradition that you have handed down. And you do many things like that." (Mark 7:7-13)

Paul has this to say about rules taught by men: "Since you died with Christ to the basic principles of this world, why, as though you still belonged to it, do you submit to its rules: 'Do not handle! Do not taste! Do not touch!' These are all destined to perish with use, because they are based on human commands and teachings. Such regulations indeed have an appearance of wisdom, with their self-imposed worship, their false humility and their harsh treatment of the body, but they lack any value in restraining sensual indulgence." (Colossians 2:20-23)

The professor argues: The Jesus of the Bible is certainly interested in correct doctrine. John 8:31-32 supports this: "To the Jews who had believed in him, Jesus said, 'If you hold to my teachings, you are really my disciples. Then you will know the truth, and the truth will set you free.'" (John 8:31-32)

My rebuttal is: The teachings of Christ are not theology. Jesus taught unconditional love, not theology. Jesus taught that love is the sign of a true disciple of Christ: "All men will know that you are my disciples if you love one another." (John 13:35).

Jesus did not say, "All men will know that you are my disciples if you hold the teachings of the Church" or "hold the teachings of the Bible" or "hold the teachings of Christian theology" or even "hold the teachings of the Christian religion." It is clear Jesus taught love as the way to eternal life (Luke 10:25-28), not theology.

Many critics are completely ignorant about the NDE. Many refuse to find out for themselves and test the spirits for themselves. Instead, ignorant things are said about the NDE because these things were not judged by their fruit.

The professor argues: Other people affiliated with non-Christian religions claim the being of light to be Buddha or Krishna or some other religious figure. Certainly this should raise "red flags" in a Christian's mind.

My rebuttal is: The only thing this proves is that there are many beings of light appearing in NDEs. God is light. Many beings can manifest this light regardless of their religious affiliation or church membership. Jesus Himself had this to say about beings of light: "You are the light of the world. A city on a hill cannot be hidden. Neither do people light a lamp and put it under a bowl. Instead they put it on its stand, and it gives light to everyone in the house. In the same way, let your light shine before men, that they may see your good deeds and praise your Father in heaven." (Matthew 5:14-16)

The professor sounds as if he is either a religious bigot or religiously intolerant. Jesus certainly taught religious tolerance. Jesus was a Jew who was killed by religiously intolerant people.

The professor argues: The Jesus of the NDE is Satan trying to keep people away from the Jesus of the Bible.

My rebuttal is: This is not true. The professor seeks to keep people away from the Jesus of the NDE. Jesus' gospel of unconditional love was too dangerous for the political structure of the religious establishment in his day. Jesus' message of unconditional love found in NDEs is too dangerous for the political structure of today's religious establishment. Ignorance prevented the religious establishment from accepting the message of Christ then; ignorance is preventing the religious establishment in general from accepting the message of Christ in NDEs now.

3. NDES AND THE BIBLE AFFIRM GOD IS UNCONDITIONAL LOVE

The greatest Biblical support for the NDE comes from all the New Testament verses concerning love. Like the teachings of Jesus, the NDE reveals the critical importance of love in all facets of life and death. The NDE compliments Jesus' teachings of unconditional love and forgiveness. Here are those verses supporting the unconditional love of God and how this love is the way to heaven: "On one occasion an expert in the law stood up to test Jesus. 'Teacher,' he asked, 'What must I do to inherit eternal life?' 'What is written in the law?' he (Christ) replied. 'How do you read it?' he answered: 'Love the Lord your God with all your heart and with all your soul and with all your strength and with all your mind, and, love your neighbor as yourself.' 'You have answered correctly,' Jesus replied, 'Do this and you will live.' (Luke 10:25-28)

It cannot get any clearer than this. The verse above clearly shows love is the way to eternal life. The reason is because God is love. "Everyone who loves has been born of God and knows God." (1 John 4:7)

Everyone, no matter what their religious affiliation, who loves, knows God, "because God is love" (1 John 4:8). If our God is love, then love and God are one and the same. This means that as certain as (X = Y) and (Y = X), God is love, and love is God.

"And now these three remain: faith, hope and love. But the greatest of these is love." (1 Corinthians 13:13) This verse shows love to be greater even than religious faith.

"If I have the gift of prophecy and can fathom all mysteries and all knowledge, and if I have a faith that can move mountains, but have not love, I am nothing." (1 Corinthians 13:2) This verse clearly refutes the false idea held by many that salvation is by faith in Jesus alone.

"If I give all I possess to the poor and surrender my body to the flames, but have not love, I gain nothing." (1 Corinthians 13:3)

"If I speak in the tongues of humans and of angels, but have not love, I am only a resounding gong or a clanging cymbal." (1 Corinthians 13:1)

"Above all, love each other deeply, because love covers over a multitude of sins." (1 Peter 4:8) Love covers sins because God is love.

"It (love) keeps no record of wrongs." (1 Corinthians 13:5) Since God is love, the logical conclusion is that God keeps no record of wrongs. This agrees with what has been said thus far.

"Therefore love is the fulfillment of the law." (Romans 13:10) This means the law of God is love.

"The only thing that counts is faith expressing itself through love." (Galatians 5:6)

"He (God) is before all things, and in him all things hold together." (Colossians 1:17) This is an interesting verse because it suggests God is the power holding all things together, the power of the atom. God, who is love, is the power holding the universe together.

"Love is patient, love is kind. It does not envy, it does not boast, it is not proud. It is not rude, it is not self-seeking, it is not easily angered, it keeps no record of wrongs. Love does not delight in evil but rejoices with the truth. It always protects, always trusts, always hopes, always perseveres. Love never fails." (1 Corinthians 13:4-8) Since God is love, the verse is an excellent description of God.

"God is love. Whoever lives in love lives in God, and God in him." (1 John 4:16) This verse is another way of saying God is love and love is God.

"Whoever does not love does not know God, because God is love." (1 John 4:8) Love is the sign of whether or not one knows God. No love, no God. Know love, know God.

"For anyone who does not love his brother, whom he has seen, cannot love God, whom he has not seen." (1 John 4:20) In other words, if you don't love others, you don't love God.

"We know that we have passed from death to life, because we love our brothers. Anyone who does not love remains in death." (1 John 3:14) This is another verse suggesting love is the way to eternal life.

"By this [love] all humans will know that you are my disciples, if you love one another." (John 13:35) Love is the sign of a true disciple of Jesus. If love for others is not present, then it is a sign the person is not a disciple of Christ.

"And this is love: that we walk in obedience to his commands. As you have heard from the beginning, his command is that you walk in love." (2 John 1:6) This verse tells us to love Jesus means to walk in love.

"In the same way, faith by itself, if it is not accompanied by action, is dead." (James 2:17) Religious faith alone does not create spiritual growth or save us from a hell of our own making.

"We love because he (God) first loved us." (1 John 4:19) One might conclude from this verse that our salvation is based on love.

"For God so loved the world..." (John 3:16) Love is the gospel for the whole world. Love held Jesus to the cross, not nails. The gospel is all about love; and God is love.

"Jesus answered them, 'I am the way and the truth and the life. No one comes to the Father except through me.'" (John 14:6) If the Spirit of Jesus is love, then this makes perfect sense. Jesus was no egocentric person. No one can come to God except through love, the Spirit of Christ, which is God. Jesus came to show the way to heaven. The way to heaven is love. Jesus and his Spirit of Love is the way to heaven.

"They (people going to hell) perish because they refused to love the truth and so be saved." (2 Thessalonians 2:10) The truth is God and God is love. The Kingdom of God is within (Luke 17:20-21). If one does not have love, then one does not have heaven within and he or she is already living in hell on earth. Love, being God, is our salvation from a hell within us of our own making.

"My son, do not make light of the Lord's discipline, and do not lose heart when he rebukes you, because the Lord disciplines those he loves, and he punishes everyone he accepts as a son." (Hebrews 12:5) Even God's so-called "wrath" is a sign of his love. Since God loves the whole world, it would be safe to say God disciplines everyone. Love is certainly a taskmaster.

"The fear of the Lord is the beginning of wisdom..." (Psalm 111:10) "But perfect love drives out fear, because fear has to do with punishment. The one who fears is not made perfect in love." (1 John 4:18) The one who fears God is only beginning to be wise. Advanced wisdom comes when fear is replaced with love. The preacher who likes to preach fear instead of love in order to gain converts is not being very wise.

"For I am convinced that neither death nor life, neither angels nor demons, neither the present nor the future, nor any powers, neither height nor depth, nor anything else in all creation, will be able to separate us from the love of God that is in Christ Jesus our Lord." (Romans 8:39) This verse shows the strength of the power of love being God.

"And I pray that you, being rooted and established in love, may have power, together with all the saints, to grasp how wide and long and high and deep is the love of Christ, and to know this love that surpasses knowledge - that you may be filled to the measure of all the fullness of God." (Ephesians 3:19) Faith implies the possibility of doubt. Knowledge implies certainty. Love is greater than both of them.

All the verses above describe the unconditional love that is God. This agrees totally with what is revealed in NDEs. People having NDEs realize the importance of love, which is true inner spirituality, as opposed to religion, which is an outward cultural affiliation. God loves the world unconditionally and this means everyone. This is the identical message of the NDE.

Many Christians make the mistake of believing we get to heaven by worshiping Jesus. The NDE reveals we get to heaven, not by worshiping Jesus, but by emulating Jesus by living a life of unconditional love for everyone. The NDE also reveals the true relationship between Christ and God. Jesus often appears in NDEs shining a tremendous amount of light. The reason for this is that Jesus has a tremendous amount of love for others. The NDE and the Bible agree that light is God and those who love others the most will shine more of this light that is God. This is because the light of God is love - a love beyond any human comprehension according to experiencers.

4. NDES AND THE BIBLE AFFIRM UNIVERSAL SALVATION

Universal salvation is the concept that everyone will eventually attain salvation and go to heaven. This is a foreign concept to most Christians today, although it was not to many early Christians. Many Christians today cannot accept the NDE because it generally affirms universal salvation. While it is true universal salvation is generally affirmed in NDEs, it is not true this means everyone enters heaven immediately upon death. It is well documented in NDEs people going to a hell upon death. However, NDEs show hell to be a temporary spiritual condition, much like Catholic purgatory, not eternal damnation.

The NDES of Dr. George Ritchie and Howard Storm are among the best NDEs I have read that proves this point. Howard Storm is rescued from hell the moment he asks God for help. This demonstrates even the hardened sinner can be rescued from hell as long as they turn to God for help. Common sense tells you this is the case with a God of infinite love and mercy.

Many experiencers, such as Howard Storm, went to hell and were able to escape from it. Some experiencers have witnessed other people escape from hell. These people verify hell not to be a place of literal flames but a spiritual condition of separation from everything pleasant such as love, joy and peace. Those experiencers who have escaped from hell know first-hand there is a way out for those who are repentant. Such NDEs are convincing evidence that hell is not a place of eternal punishment, but a temporary spiritual condition of purification for the purpose of attaining heaven. The NDE suggests hell to be a kind of spiritual time-out where people reflect on their spiritual condition.

Another convincing argument for universal salvation comes from the nature of Christ's death itself. If it is true as Christians claim that Christ died for the wrongs of the whole world, and if Christ has forgiven the whole world of their wrongs, then the logical conclusion is that the world stands redeemed, forgiven, justified and saved. If this is true, the NDE reveals people are still going to hell despite being redeemed. But this may merely be demonstrating the concept of God not forcing anyone to heaven or hell. A person may be forgiven and redeemed, but there is no assurance of God forcing the person to heaven. If all wrongs have been forgiven, then why are people seen in hell during NDEs? They can't be in hell to pay for their own wrongs because according to Christian doctrine, Christ paid for them all. In other words, if Christ paid for all sins, how can God require anyone to pay for them also? The only logical conclusion is that hell is not a place for punishment, but of correction. This is exactly what the NDE reveals about the nature of hell.

Christians in general affirm Jesus provided universal redemption by paying for the wrongs of every human being. Universal redemption implies universal salvation and here is the scriptural evidence supporting it: "When he has done this [God putting everything under Christ's feet], then the Son himself will be made subject to him who put everything under him, so that God may be ALL in ALL." (1 Corinthians 15:28) This verse suggests God will someday be in all.

"This is good, and pleases God our Savior, who wants ALL men to be saved and to come to a knowledge of the truth." (1 Timothy 2:3-4) There is no doubt about it; God wills the salvation of everyone.

"I know that you [God] can do all things; NO PLAN of yours can be thwarted." (Job 42:2) This verse suggests the will of God cannot be thwarted. If God wills everyone to go to heaven and nobody can thwart the will of God, then the logical conclusion is everyone will eventually go to heaven.

"He [God] is patient with you, not wanting ANYONE to perish, but everyone to come to repentance." (2 Peter 3:9) God does not will anyone to perish in hell; therefore, everyone will eventually go to heaven. There is no escaping this logic.

"But I, when I am lifted up from the earth, will draw ALL men to myself." (John 12:32) This verse shows everyone coming to God.

"For as in Adam all die, so in Christ ALL will be made alive." (1 Corinthians 15:22) If everyone is made alive in God, then everyone is on the road to heaven.

"For God so loved THE WORLD..." (John 3:16) God's love extends to every member of the human race.

"He [Christ] is the atoning sacrifice for our sins, and not only for ours but also for the sins of the whole world." (1 John 2:2) If Christ paid for the sins of the world, the logical conclusion is the whole world has been redeemed.

These above verses show God providing salvation for everyone. The NDE, the Bible and common sense tells us it is futile to go against God's will. One experiencer, Arthur Yensen, gave some insight in the nature of God when asked if he believed in the Devil. His reply was: "No, but if there is one, he would have to be an insane angel who was crazy enough to fight with God, which would be as futile as for us to try to stop the sunrise." [72]

His NDE revealed to him a God so powerful, it would be crazy to think you can stop God.

"He [God] does as he pleases with the powers of heaven and the peoples of the earth. No one can hold back his hand or say to him: 'What have you done?'" (Daniel 4:35) If God wills everyone saved and it is impossible to go against the will of God and God has provided a plan of salvation for him or her, then the only logical conclusion is everyone will be saved.

Some Christians have the view of God being willing but unable to save everyone. Is God not able to do as God wills? Isn't it a dishonor to view God in such a helpless way?

"It [salvation] does not, therefore, depend on man's desire or effort, but on God's mercy." (Romans 9:16) This verse flat out says salvation is determined by the will of God. Since we have already proven God wills all to be saved, then we can conclude from this all will be saved.

Now the question is this: Has God, before the beginning of time, predestined a multitude of his children to be tortured forever in hell? Isn't it dishonoring to God to believe so? Didn't God provide for the salvation of those in hell also? Is God's plan of salvation so weak it cannot save those it was intended to save? The only logical and reasonable answer is this: Yes, God provided for the salvation of those in hell. No, those in hell are not tortured forever. Yes, God provides a way of escape from hell.

"And God is faithful; he will not let you be tempted beyond what you can bear. But when you are tempted, he will also provide a way out so that you can stand up under it." (1 Corinthians 10:13) This verse applies to temptation, but it could equally apply to hell.

"To him who is able to keep you from falling and to present you before his glorious presence without fault and with great joy..." (Jude 1:24) This verse also applies to temptation, but could equally apply to God having the ability to save people in hell.

"And he [the man whose faith is weak] will stand, for the Lord is able to make him stand." (Romans 14:2-4) This verse applies to God keeping someone from falling away completely, but could equally apply to God keeping people from falling away forever.

It is difficult for any honest Christian to conceive of a God of infinite love and mercy who would permit even one soul to be tortured forever in hell. Common sense tells us that a few minutes in hell may be enough for even the hardest of sinners to change their mind and repent. What kind of God creates a person knowing they will ultimately end up tortured forever in hell? Common sense tells us it would be best for God to not even have brought such a person into existence. If even an evil father will treats his children better than this, how much more so God?

"Which of you, if his son asks for bread, will give him a stone? Or if he asks for a fish, will give him a snake? If you, then, though you are evil, know how to give good gifts to your children, how much more will your Father in heaven give good gifts to those who ask him!" (Matthew 7:9-11)

While it is true scriptures describe hell as a place existing forever, NDEs show a person's citizenship there does not. The scripture above suggests God's arm of mercy extends even to those in hell. We will now examine more scriptural evidence. Scripture will be used to support the following points:

A. There is forgiveness in hell for wrongs committed in life.
B. "Fire" is a metaphor used to describe the purification of people in hell.
C. Once a person has been purified by the "fire," they can escape.
D. "Eternal" is a word used to describe the nature of hell, not the length of incarceration.
E. "Fire" is a metaphor used to describe the purification of people on earth.
F. "Fire" is a metaphor also used to describe God and manifestations of God.
G. "Light" is a metaphor similar to "fire," used to describe God.

H. "Light" is a metaphor also used to describe spiritual knowledge. "Darkness" is spiritual ignorance.

I. "Darkness" is a metaphor also used to describe hell.

J. Darkness" is a metaphor also used to describe the world.

K. Suffering is necessary to attain spiritual perfection in this world and in hell.

Certain conclusions will be drawn from the points listed above. God considers wrongs committed in this world forgiven in this world as God considers them forgiven in heaven and hell. This world and hell are places of purification. This purification is by "fire" and "light," metaphors for spiritual knowledge and God. People in this world and in hell live in "darkness," a metaphor for spiritual ignorance. The world and hell are places of suffering whose purpose is to bring about spiritual perfection through the abandonment spiritual ignorance.

Now let's examine each point one by one.

A. There is forgiveness in hell for wrongs committed in life.

"And whosoever shall speak a word against the Son of man, it shall be forgiven him: but he that shall speak against the Holy Spirit, it shall not be forgiven him, neither in this world, nor in the world to come." (Matthew 12:32). It is one thing to be forgiven for an offense in one world, and it is a different thing to be forgiven for the same offense in a different world -- meaning life after death. This verse only makes sense if the possibility of wrongs being forgiven after death is true. In other words, if all wrongs committed in this world could not be forgiven in the world to come, then why single out a particular wrong by saying it cannot be forgiven in the world to come? This would only make sense if sins other than speaking against the Holy Spirit were forgivable in the world to come.

Here's another scripture verse suggesting a way of redemption after death: "For Christ died for sins once for all, the righteous for the unrighteous, to bring you to God. He was put to death in the body but made alive by the Spirit, through whom also he went and preached to the spirits in prison who disobeyed long ago when God waited patiently in the days of Noah while the ark was being built." (1 Peter 3:18-20)

This verse refers to the people who have already died and which Christ set free from hell. In an apocryphal book of the Old Testament, it states: "For if he were not expecting that those who had fallen would rise again, it would have been superfluous and foolish to pray for the dead." (2 Maccabees 12:43-46)

At the time of the Maccabees the leaders of the people of God had no hesitation in asserting the efficacy of prayers offered for the dead, in order that those who had departed this life might find pardon for their sins and the hope of eternal resurrection. This verse suggests praying makes possible the redemption of those who have died unredeemed.

The apocryphal book of Maccabees was a part of Biblical canon until Martin Luther removed it during the beginning of the Protestant Reformation. It may be argued Maccabees is not a part of the Bible. However, even Paul, in the Book of Jude, quotes from a book not found in the Bible today. It is called the Book of Enoch; a book considered part of scripture in Jesus day: "Enoch, the seventh from Adam, prophesied about these men: 'See, the Lord is coming with thousands upon thousands of his holy ones to judge everyone, and to convict all the ungodly of all the ungodly acts they have done in the ungodly way, and of all the harsh words ungodly sinners have spoken against him.'" (Jude 1:14,15)

B. "Fire" is a metaphor used to describe the purification of people in hell.

The early Church developed the concept of purgatory based on particular passages of the Bible. The early Church taught that some sins are purged away by a purifying fire after death. St. Augustine argued: "Some sinners are not forgiven either in this world or in the next, would not be truly said unless there were other [sinners] who, though not forgiven in this world, are forgiven in the world to come." [73] This same interpretation was believed by Gregory the Great [74]; St. Bede [75]; St. Bernard [76] and other eminent Church writers.

Origen taught that purgatory is the true manifestation of "hell." He believed if people depart this life with lighter faults, they are condemned to fire, which burns away the lighter materials, preparing their souls for the kingdom of God, where nothing defiled may enter. He states: "For if on the foundation of Christ you have built not only gold and silver and precious stones; but also wood and hay and stubble, what do you expect when the soul shall be separated from the body? Would you enter into heaven with your wood and hay and stubble and thus defile the kingdom of God; or on account of these hindrances would you remain without and receive no reward for your gold and silver and precious stones? Neither is this just. It remains then that you be committed to the fire which will burn the light materials; for our God to those who can comprehend heavenly things is called a cleansing fire. But this fire consumes not the creature, but what the creature himself has built, wood, and hay and stubble. It is manifest that the fire destroys the wood of our transgressions and then returns to us the reward of our great works." [77]

Origen based this statement on 1 Corinthians 3:11-15 reprinted below.

C. Once a person has been purified by the "fire," they can escape.

"For no one can lay any foundation other than the one already laid, which is Jesus Christ. If any man builds on this foundation using gold, silver, costly stones, wood, hay or straw, his work will be shown for what it is, because the Day will bring it to light. It will be revealed with fire, and the fire will test the quality of each man's work. If what he has built survives, he will receive his reward. If it is burned up, he will suffer loss; he himself will be saved, but only as one escaping through the flames." (1 Corinthians 3:11-15) This verse describes a process of purification and a way to escape it.

"But anyone who says, 'You fool!' will be in danger of the fire of hell. Therefore, if you are offering your gift at the altar and there remember that your brother has something against you, leave your gift there in front of the altar. First go and be reconciled to your brother; then come and offer your gift. Settle matters quickly with your adversary who is taking you to court. Do it while you are still with him on the way, or he may hand you over to the judge, and the judge may hand you over to the officer, and you may be thrown into prison. I tell you the truth, you will not get out until you have paid the last penny." (Matthew 5:22-26) This verse has Jesus equating hell to a prison that allows prisoners to get out.

"Prison" was used as a metaphor for hell in a verse we have already discussed. Here it is again: "He [Jesus] was put to death in the body but made alive by the Spirit, through whom also he went and preached to the spirits in prison who disobeyed long ago when God waited patiently in the days of Noah while the ark was being built." (1 Peter 3:18-20)

Here is another scriptural reference to hell as a prison: "For if God did not spare angels when they sinned, but sent them to hell, putting them into gloomy dungeons to be held for judgment." (2 Peter 2:4)

D. "Eternal" is a word used to describe the nature of hell, not the length of incarceration.

The Bible talks of the unquenchable fire and eternal punishment of hell, where people are in torment, but not consumed: "The ax is already at the root of the trees, and every tree that does not produce good fruit will be cut down and thrown into the fire. I [John the Baptist] baptize you with water for repentance. But after me will come one who is more powerful than I, whose sandals I am not fit to carry. He will baptize you with the Holy Spirit and with fire. His winnowing fork is in his hand, and he will clear his threshing floor, gathering his wheat into the barn and burning up the chaff with unquenchable fire." (Matthew 3:10-12)

"If your hand causes you to sin, cut it off. It is better for you to enter life maimed than with two hands to go into hell, where the fire never goes out... And if your eye causes you to sin, pluck it out. It is better for you to enter the kingdom of God with one eye than to have two eyes and be thrown into hell, where 'their worm does not die, and the fire is not quenched.' Everyone will be salted with fire." (Mark 9:43-49)

"Then he will say to those on his left, 'Depart from me, you who are cursed, into the eternal fire prepared for the devil and his angels. For I was hungry and you gave me nothing to eat, I was thirsty and you gave me nothing to drink, I was a stranger and you did not invite me in, I needed clothes and you did not clothe me, I was sick and in prison and you did not look after me.' They also will answer, 'Lord, when did we see you hungry or thirsty or a stranger or needing clothes or sick or in prison, and did not help you?' He will reply, 'I tell you the truth, whatever you did not do for one of the least of these, you did not do for me.' Then they will go away to eternal punishment, but the righteous to eternal life." (Matthew 25:41-46) This description of hell agrees with what experiencers have experienced. Don Brubaker experienced these flames of hell first hand. This is what he experienced:

"There was a low murmuring all around me, as if I was in the midst of a huge group of grumbling people. Before me, suddenly, stood a huge black door. The air began to glow and shimmer with oppressive heat. I watched as the door opened upon a vast, flaming oven. I felt myself drawn like a magnet into the center of the flames -- although I was terrified to go in. There were hundreds of others already there, roasting to death, but not dead. Once I was inside, the door slammed shut behind me. The worst, dreadest feelings sloshed around inside me, like so much poison. 'Is this actually what hell is?' I asked aloud. I passed my hands through blue-tipped flames. The fire itself was cold, and it did not hurt me. From nowhere, a thought flashed through my mind: Death, where is thy sting? God, even in the midst of this holocaust, was truly in control of everything. I began to laugh, and the others laughed with me. Our laughter bounced off the walls of the oven and echoed over the roar of the flames. And instantly, as if someone had flipped the channel selector, I was alone again in darkness. [78] Don Brubaker's experience shows the flames of hell are not painful and are escapable.

E. "Fire" is a metaphor used to describe the purification of people on earth.

The Bible talks of people on earth being purified, refined and baptized by fire. These are all referring to the process of purification.

"These have come so that your faith -- of greater worth than gold, which perishes even though refined by fire -- may be proved genuine and may result in praise, glory and honor when Jesus Christ is revealed." (1 Peter 1:7)

"I counsel you to buy from me gold refined in the fire, so you can become rich; and white clothes to wear, so you can cover your shameful nakedness; and salve to put on your eyes, so you can see. Those whom I love I rebuke and discipline." (Revelation 3:18-19)

"But who can endure the day of his coming? Who can stand when he appears? For he will be like a refiner's fire or a launderer's soap. He will sit as a refiner and purifier of silver; he will purify the Levites and refine them like gold and silver." (Malachi 3:2-3)

"He will cleanse the bloodstains from Jerusalem by a spirit of judgment and a spirit of fire." (Isaiah 4:4)

"I baptize you with water for repentance. But after me will come one who is more powerful than I, whose sandals I am not fit to carry. He will baptize you with the Holy Spirit and with fire." (Matthew 3:11)

F. "Fire" is a metaphor also used to describe God and manifestations of God.

The verses below describe God and manifestations of God through the metaphor of fire. These verses also use the metaphor of fire as a reference to the purifying power of God.

"Our God is a consuming fire." (Hebrews 12:29)

"Do not put out the Spirit's fire." (1 Thessalonians 5:19)

"They saw what seemed to be tongues of fire that separated and came to rest on each of them. All of them were filled with the Holy Spirit and began to speak in other tongues as the Spirit enabled them." (Acts 2:3-4)

"In speaking of the angels he says, 'He makes his angels winds, his servants flames of fire.'" (Hebrews 1:7)

"This will happen when the Lord Jesus is revealed from heaven in blazing fire with his powerful angels." (2 Thessalonians 1:7)

"I [Jesus] have come to bring fire on the earth, and how I wish it were already kindled!" (Luke 12:49)

G. "Light" is a metaphor, similar to "fire," used to describe God.

The verses below use the metaphor of light to describe God and God's purifying power.

"This is the message we have heard from him and declare to you: God is light; in him there is no darkness at all." (I John 1:5)

"For no one can lay any foundation other than the one already laid, which is Jesus Christ. If any man builds on this foundation using gold, silver, costly stones, wood, hay or straw, his work will be shown for what it is, because the Day will bring it to light. It will be revealed with fire, and the fire will test the quality of each man's work. If what he has built survives, he will receive his reward. If it is burned up, he will suffer loss; he himself will be saved, but only as one escaping through the flames." (1 Corinthians 3:11-15)

"There he was transfigured before them. His face shone like the sun, and his clothes became as white as the light." (Matthew 17:2)

"When Jesus spoke again to the people, he said, 'I am the light of the world. Whoever follows me will never walk in darkness, but will have the light of life.'" (John 8:12)

One can see the scriptures using the metaphors light and fire interchangeably to describe God and God's manifestations.

H. "Light" is a metaphor also used to describe spiritual knowledge. "Darkness" is spiritual ignorance.

"For God, who said, 'Let light shine out of darkness,' made his light shine in our hearts to give us the light of the knowledge of the glory of God in the face of Christ." (2 Corinthians 4:6)

"If you are convinced that you are a guide for the blind, a light for those who are in the dark, an instructor of the foolish, a teacher of infants, because you have in the law the embodiment of knowledge and truth -- you, then, who teach others, do you not teach yourself? You who preach against stealing, do you steal?" (Romans 2:19-21)

"Then Jesus told them, 'You are going to have the light just a little while longer. Walk while you have the light, before darkness overtakes you. The man who walks in the dark does not know where he is going.'" (John 12:35)

"But whoever hates his brother is in the darkness and walks around in the darkness; he does not know where he is going, because the darkness has blinded him." (1 John 2:11)

"No one lights a lamp and puts it in a place where it will be hidden, or under a bowl. Instead he puts it on its stand, so that those who come in may see the light. Your eye is the lamp of your body. When your eyes are good, your whole body also is full of light. But when they are bad, your body also is full of darkness. See to it, then, that the light within you is not darkness. Therefore, if your whole body is full of light, and no part of it dark, it will be completely lighted, as when the light of a lamp shines on you." (Luke 11:33-36)

These verses show the spiritual condition of hell to be darkness, the lack of the knowledge of God. This spiritual condition begins as a spiritual condition on earth and is realized at death.

I. "Darkness" is a metaphor also used to describe hell.

The verses below describe how the metaphor of darkness is used to describe hell.

"And the angels who did not keep their positions of authority but abandoned their own home -- these he has kept in darkness, bound with everlasting chains for judgment on the great Day." (Jude 1:6)

"These men are blemishes at your love feasts, eating with you without the slightest qualm -- shepherds who feed only themselves. They are clouds without rain, blown along by the wind; autumn trees, without fruit and uprooted-- twice dead. They are wild waves of the sea, foaming up their shame; wandering stars, for whom blackest darkness has been reserved forever." (Jude 1:12-13)

"But the subjects of the kingdom will be thrown outside, into the darkness, where there will be weeping and gnashing of teeth." (Matthew 8:12)

"These men are springs without water and mists driven by a storm. Blackest darkness is reserved for them." (2 Peter 2:17)

From these verses, one can conclude that hell is darkness, a metaphor for ignorance of God.

J. "Darkness" is a metaphor also used to describe the world.

Similar to hell, the world is a place of darkness, spiritual ignorance. The following verses point this out.

"Land of Zebulun and land of Naphtali, the way to the sea, along the Jordan, Galilee of the Gentiles -- the people living in darkness have seen a great light; on those living in the land of the shadow of death a light has dawned." (Matthew 4:15-16)

"For our struggle is not against flesh and blood, but against the rulers, against the authorities, against the powers of this dark world and against the spiritual forces of evil in the heavenly realms." (Ephesians 6:12)

"For he has rescued us from the dominion of darkness and brought us into the kingdom of the Son he loves." (Colossians 1:13)

"This is the verdict: Light has come into the world, but men loved darkness instead of light because their deeds were evil. Everyone who does evil hates the light, and will not come into the light for fear that his deeds will be exposed. But whoever lives by the truth comes into the light, so that it may be seen plainly that what he has done has been done through God." (John 3:19-21)

This world and hell have something in common. Both are filled with the darkness of spiritual ignorance.

K. Suffering is necessary to attain spiritual perfection in this world and in hell.

The scriptures are clear on how suffering in this world leads toward spiritual perfection. The scriptures show God giving us suffering in order to create character and perseverance, and to cause us to rely more on him and not in our own strength (or weakness). Suffering should never be viewed as a curse from God, but rather a blessing in disguise. The same should be viewed of the suffering in hell. It is God's will for us to suffer in this world and in hell in order to bring about spiritual perfection. The following scriptures prove it:

"In bringing many sons to glory, it was fitting that God, for whom and through whom everything exists, should make the author [Jesus] of their salvation perfect through suffering." (Hebrews 2:10)

"Yet it was the Lord's will to crush him [Jesus] and cause him to suffer." (Isaiah 53:10)

"For it has been granted to you on behalf of Christ not only to believe on him, but also to suffer for him." (Philippians 1:29)

"For this you were called, because Christ suffered for you, leaving you an example, that you follow in his steps." (1 Peter 2:21)

"To keep from becoming conceited because of these surpassingly great revelations, there was given me a thorn in my flesh, a messenger of Satan, to torment me. Three times I pleaded with the Lord to take it away from me. But he said to me, 'My grace is sufficient for you,' for my power is made perfect in weakness, so that Christ's power may rest on me. That is why, for Christ's sake, I delight in weaknesses, in insults, in hardships, in persecutions, in difficulties. For when I am weak, then I am strong." (2 Corinthians 12:7-10)

"We rejoice in our sufferings, because we know that suffering produces perseverance." (Romans 5:3)

"Brothers, as an example of patience in the face of suffering, take the prophets who spoke in the name of the Lord. As you know, we consider blessed those who have persevered. You have heard of Job's perseverance and have seen what the Lord finally brought about. The Lord is full of compassion and mercy." (James 5:10-11)

"As he [Jesus] went along, he saw a man blind from birth. His disciples asked him, 'Rabbi, who sinned, this man or his parents, that he was born blind?' 'Neither this man nor his parents sinned,' said Jesus, 'but this happened so that the work of God may be displayed in his life.'" (John 9:1-3)

"For just as the sufferings of Christ flow over into our lives, so also through Christ our comfort overflows. If we are distressed, it is for your comfort and salvation, if we are comforted, it is for your comfort, which produces in you patient endurance of the same sufferings we suffer. And our hope for you is firm, because we know that just as you share in our sufferings, so also you share in our comfort... But this happened that we might not rely on ourselves but on God, who raises the dead." (2 Corinthians 1:5, 9)

"These (sufferings) have come so that your faith -- of greater worth than gold, which perishes even though refined by fire -- may be proved genuine and may result in praise, glory and honor..." (1 Peter 1:7)

"Blessed are the poor in spirit, for theirs is the Kingdom of heaven. Blessed are those who mourn, for they will be comforted ... Blessed are those who are persecuted because of righteousness, for theirs is the Kingdom of heaven." (Matthew 5:3-4; 10)

We can conclude from the verses above that the reason for suffering in this world is for purposes of purification and education. It is a small step to attribute the same reasons to the sufferings in hell. Using this attribution, it is easy to conclude that universal salvation is the goal and the reason for the suffering in hell and in this world.

It should be noted at this point that the concept of purgatory did not originate with the early Church. It came directly from Jewish sources as discussed in the Torah, the Talmud and other Jewish texts. In these texts, hell is called "Gehinnom" (in Yiddish, "Gehenna") and it is a place of intense punishment and cleansing. This place is also known as "She'ol" and other names. Gehinnom takes its name from the Valley of Hennom, where pagans once sacrificed children.

One line of Jewish thought argues that after death the soul has to be purified before it can go on the rest of its journey. The amount of time needed for purification depends on how the soul dealt with life. One Jewish tradition mentions a soul needing a maximum of 11 months for purification, which is why, when a parent dies, the kaddish (memorial prayer) is recited for 11 months. [20]

From all that has been presented thus far from the Bible, from NDEs, from extra-Biblical references, from Jewish tradition, from early Christian tradition, and from common sense, one can conclude the following: God has a plan to save everyone in hell and eventually everyone will go to heaven. Can man continue forever to defy his Creator? Common sense tells us the answer is no. Common sense tells us a God of infinite in love and mercy would be willing and able to save those in hell. Any other view is dishonoring to God.

5. NDES AND THE BIBLE AFFIRM REINCARNATION

"Him who overcomes I will make a pillar in the temple of my God. Never again will he leave it." – Jesus Christ, Book of Revelation 3:12

Reincarnation often shows up in NDEs. In Jeanie Dicus' NDE, Jesus asks her if she wants to reincarnate. In Sandra Rogers' NDE, Jesus asks her the same question. Reincarnation is the reason some Christians reject the NDE altogether, because they reject the concept of reincarnation. But to ask if there are any verses concerning reincarnation in the Bible is like asking if there any stars in the sky. The answer is yes; it is filled with them.

The first-century Jewish historian Flavius Josephus stated that the Pharisees, the Jewish sect that founded rabbinical Judaism to whom Paul once belonged, believed in reincarnation. He writes that the Pharisees believed the souls of evil men are punished after death. The souls of good men are "removed into other bodies..." and they will "have power to revive and live again." [80]

The Sadducees, the other prominent Jewish sect in Palestine, did not emphasize life after death and, according to the Bible, "...say there is no resurrection." (Matthew 22:23). From what has just been discussed, it should be clear what Matthew really means is that the Sadducees "say there is no reincarnation."

There are many Bible verses concerning reincarnation and in this section we will examine some of them. One episode in particular from the healing miracles of Jesus seems to point to reincarnation: "And as he was passing by, he saw a man blind from birth. And his disciples asked him, 'Rabbi, who has sinned, this man or his parents, that he should be born blind?' Jesus answered, 'Neither has this man sinned, nor his parents, but the works of God were to be made manifest in him.'" (John 9:1)

The disciples ask the Lord if the man himself could have committed the sin causing him to be born blind. Given the fact the man has been blind from birth, we are confronted with an unusual question. When could the man have committed such sins as to make him blind at birth? The only conceivable answer is in some past life. The question assumes people can commit sins prior to birth, suggesting a prior life. It should also be noted Jesus says nothing to dispel or correct the assumption. This verse provides irrefutable proof for the doctrine of human preexistence.

The episode in which Jesus identifies John the Baptist as Elijah is also very suggestive of reincarnation.

"For all the prophets and the law have prophesied until John. And if you are willing to receive it, he is Elijah who was to come." (Matthew 11:13-14)

"And the disciples asked him, saying, 'Why then do the scribes say that Elijah must come first?' But he answered them and said, 'Elijah indeed is to come and will restore all things. But I say to you that Elijah has come already, and they did not know him, but did to him whatever they wished. So also shall the Son of Man suffer at their hand.' Then the disciples understood that he had spoken of John the Baptist." (Matthew 17:10-13) This verse is a clear statement of reincarnation.

The first great father of the early Church was Origen, the first person since Paul to develop a system of theology around the teachings of Jesus. Origen was also a believer in reincarnation. He taught that human preexistence can be found in both the Old and New Testaments. It was only in later times, after his death, that Origen's teachings were suppressed. Despite the counter reaction that eventually to led to the declaration that Origen's doctrine of preexistence was heresy, modern Christian scholarship acknowledges preexistence as one of the foundational elements of Christian theology.

As for the John is Elijah episode, there is little doubt for its reason. Because Jesus identified the Baptist as Elijah, Jesus identified himself as the Christ. The gospels mention particular signs preceding the coming of the Christ.

"Behold I will send you Elijah the prophet, before the coming of the great and dreadful day of the Lord." (Malachi 4:5)

This is one of the messianic promises found in the Bible. According to Malachi, one of the signs the Messiah has come is that he will be preceded by the appearance of Elijah the prophet.

These "John is Elijah" passages demonstrate absolute proof of reincarnation. The Old Testament prophesied that Elijah himself (not someone "like" him or someone "similar" to him, but Elijah himself) would return before the advent of the Christ. Jesus declared that John the Baptist was Elijah when he stated, "Elijah has come."

Now, based on these passages alone, either one of two things must be true:

(A) John the Baptist was Elijah himself, meaning Elijah reincarnated. If this is true, then reincarnation must once again belong in Christian theology, and the concept of resurrection must be radically revised, or...

(B) John the Baptist was not Elijah himself, meaning Elijah himself had not returned.

If (B) is true, then either one of two things is true:

(1) Malachi's prophecy about Elijah coming before the Christ failed to happen (which would mean prophecy is fallible), or...

(2) Jesus was not the Christ.

It comes down to the question, what do you want to believe? Either one of these three statements must be true:

1. Reincarnation is true, or
2. Jesus was not the Christ, or

3. Bible prophecies are not reliable.

As surely as one plus one equals two, one of the above must be true. Either way, the verse in which Jesus says that John was Elijah is overt and direct: "But I tell you, Elijah has come." (Mark 9:13)

The following verse is used to refute this "John is Elijah" connection. The Bible tells us John the Baptist possessed: "... the spirit and power of Elijah." (Luke 1:17)

Critics of the NDE who refute reincarnation say John the Baptist merely came in the same ministry as Elijah. But, that is not what the verse says. The verse gives a perfect description of reincarnation: the spirit and power. Reincarnation is the reincarnation of the spirit -- not the body, mind or ministry. This verse explicitly reveals John the Baptist as possessing the spirit and power that was Elijah.

John the Baptist carried the living spirit of Elijah, not his physical memory. Because of this, John did not have the memories of Elijah. This explains why John the Baptist denied being Elijah: "They asked him, 'Then who are you? Are you Elijah?' He said, 'I am not.' 'Are you the Prophet?' He answered, 'No.' Finally they said, 'Who are you? Give us an answer to take back to those who sent us. What do you say about yourself?'

John replied in the words of Isaiah the prophet, 'I am the voice of one calling in the desert, "Make straight the way for the Lord."' Now some Pharisees who had been sent questioned him, 'Why then do you baptize if you are not the Christ, nor Elijah, nor the Prophet?' 'I baptize with water,' John replied, 'but among you stands one you do not know. He is the one who comes after me, the thongs of whose sandals I am not worthy to untie.'" (John 1:21-27)

Jesus, however, knew better and said so in the plainest words possible: "This is the one... there has not risen anyone greater than John the Baptist... And if you are willing to accept it, he is the Elijah who was to come. He who has ears, let him hear." (Matthew 11:11-15).

Jesus said that John was Elijah, and John said he wasn't. Which of the two is to be believed: Jesus or John? The answer should be very clear.

Also, notice that those questioning John were expecting a reincarnation. The question itself, whether John was Elijah, suggests those questioning John believed in reincarnation. But, like most people, the Baptist was not aware of being a reincarnation. However, this fact alone doesn't mean he was not, especially when Jesus said he was.

The Bible also reveals other appearances of Elijah the Prophet. In the Book of Revelation, there is a prophecy concerning the days leading up to the Second Coming of Christ. Two prophets are predicted to appear working the same miracles as those of Elijah and Moses: "And I will give power to my two witnesses, and they will prophesy for 1,260 days, clothed in sackcloth. These are the two olive trees and the two lampstands that stand before the Lord of the earth. If anyone tries to harm them, fire comes from their mouths and devours their enemies. This is how anyone who wants to harm them must die. These men have power to shut up the sky so that it will not rain during the time they are prophesying; and they have power to turn the waters into blood and to strike the earth with every kind of plague as often as they want." (Revelation 11:3-6)

While the above verse does not specifically identify the two prophets as Elijah and Moses, the description of these two prophets suggests it is them. If Elijah is to appear immediately before the Second Coming of Christ, the only realistic way for him to do so is through reincarnation.

The Bible describes a strong connection between Elijah, Moses and Jesus. Since Jesus already identified Elijah as appearing during Jesus first coming, it is not hard to conclude that Elijah will appear again at the Second Coming of Jesus. The Malachi prophecy we have already discussed concerning Jesus' first coming, may also apply to the Second Coming: "Behold I will send you Elijah the prophet, before the coming of the great and dreadful day of the Lord." (Malachi 4:5)

After the death of John the Baptist, Elijah appeared again along with Moses at the Mount of Transfiguration: "After six days Jesus took with him Peter, James and John the brother of James, and led them up a high mountain by themselves. There he was transfigured before them. His face shone like the sun, and his clothes became as white as the light. Just then there appeared before them Moses and Elijah, talking with Jesus. Peter said to Jesus, 'Lord, it is good for us to be here. If you wish, I will put up three shelters -- one for you, one for Moses and one for Elijah.' While he was still speaking, a bright cloud enveloped them, and a voice from the cloud said, 'This is my Son, whom I love; with him I am well pleased. Listen to him!' When the disciples heard this, they fell face down to the ground, terrified. But Jesus came and touched them. 'Get up,' he said. 'Don't be afraid.' When they looked up, they saw no one except Jesus. As they were coming down the mountain, Jesus instructed them, 'Don't tell anyone what you have seen, until the Son of Man has been raised from the dead.' The disciples asked him, 'Why then do the teachers of the law say that Elijah must come first?' Jesus replied, 'To be sure, Elijah comes and will restore all things. But I tell you, Elijah has already come, and they did not recognize him, but have done to him everything they wished. In the same way the Son of Man is going to suffer at their hands.' Then the disciples understood that he was talking to them about John the Baptist." (Matthew 17:1-13)

In very explicit language, Jesus identifies Elijah, who appeared with him at the Mount of Transfiguration, as John the Baptist. Even his disciples understood what Jesus meant.

Due to the declaration of reincarnation as heresy by church officials, centuries after the death of Jesus, reincarnation is now an enemy doctrine to Christianity. However, reincarnation was certainly not an enemy doctrine to the people of Israel around the time of Jesus. It was certainly not an enemy doctrine to Jesus himself. Israel in those days was a geographic crossroads receiving a large flow of foreign travelers and ideas. Reincarnation was a familiar belief in Asia and the Middle East in the first century.

Throughout the history of Israel, there has been a belief that their prophets are sometimes reborn. The Israelites of the first century wondered if Jesus was the reincarnation of some prophet: "When Jesus came to the region of Caesarea Philippi, he asked his disciples, 'Who do people say the Son of Man is?' They replied, 'Some say John the Baptist; others say Elijah; and still others, Jeremiah or one of the prophets.'" (Matthew 16:13-14) It is apparent, the Israelites of the first century assumed Jesus had been openly promoting reincarnation when he claimed John the Baptist was the reincarnation of Elijah. When confronted with these rumors of Israelites believing in reincarnation, Jesus does not refute nor deny the doctrine. Instead, he spoke in support of it.

Another verse suggestive of reincarnation can be found when Jesus declares the following to the believers in the Church of Philadelphia: "Him who overcomes I will make a pillar in the temple of my God. Never again will he leave it." (Revelation 3:12) This verse has Jesus declaring people prior inhabitants of the temple of God. As soon as the person overcomes "the world," the person becomes a permanent inhabitant of this temple and never again has to leave it. The flip side to this is that after death those who do not overcome must leave this temple of God and return to the world

The following verse is also suggestive of reincarnation: "She gave birth to a son, a male child, who will rule all the nations with an iron scepter. And her child was snatched up to God and to his throne." (Revelation 12:5) This verse describes the birth of a child who is taken to heaven after his birth. The interesting aspect is that this child is to rule all the nations with an iron scepter. Because the child was taken to heaven after birth, reincarnation is the only way the child could return to the world to grow up to "rule all nations." Although Revelations is mostly symbolic and is often quite abstract, this verse implies the ability to incarnate more than once.

In the Sermon on the Mount, Jesus states the following: "Blessed are the meek, for they will inherit the earth." (Matthew 5:5) Such a statement makes sense only in light of reincarnation. It begs the question, "When does the meek inherit the earth?" Common sense tells us the meek do not inherit the earth in their lifetime. It is the strong that rules the earth. It is the law of survival of the fittest. This inheritance of the earth by the meek must come about through the means of another incarnation, a reincarnation, of the meek into the strong.

The following is another verse suggestive of reincarnation: "No one who has left home or brothers or sisters or mother or father or wife or children or land for me and the gospel will fail to receive a hundred times as much in this present age -- homes, brothers, sisters, mothers, children and fields... and in the age to come, eternal life." (Mark 10:29-30) It is difficult to imagine how such a promise could be fulfilled apart from reincarnation. In one lifetime, one can only have a single set of parents. Common sense tells us that the disciples, who left their homes and families to follow Jesus, never received compensation a hundred times. It is evident, Jesus was making a promise to the disciples that only reincarnation could fulfill.

The following verse is a clear statement of reincarnation: "All these people were still living by faith when they died. They did not receive the things promised; they only saw them and welcomed them from a distance. And they admitted that they were aliens and strangers on earth. People who say such things show that they are looking for a country of their own. If they had been thinking of the country they had left, they would have had opportunity to return. Instead, they were longing for a better country -- a heavenly one. Therefore God is not ashamed to be called their God, for he has prepared a city for them." (Hebrews 11:13-16) This verse describes people who could have had an opportunity to return to earth after death. This could only have come about through reincarnation.

There are also verses, such as the following, supporting discarnate preexistence: "He chose us in him before the foundation of the world, that we should be holy and without blemish in his sight and love." (Ephesians 1:4) This verse reveals God chose people before the world existed and before they could have physically been born. This suggests the people in question must have existed somewhere, even if only in the Mind of God. Such an existence does not rule out the preexistence of souls. After all, there may be no difference between a soul and a thought in the Mind of God.

Another verse suggestive of preexistence is the following: "Yet, before the twins were born or had done anything good or bad - in order that God's purpose in election might stand: not by works but by him who calls - she was told, 'The older will serve the younger.' Just as it is written: 'Jacob I loved, but Esau I hated.'" (Romans 9:11-13) This verse suggests that God loved Jacob and hated Esau before they were even born. Again, even if it were merely in the Mind of God, it would still be preexistence. Preexistence is a necessary doctrine associated with reincarnation.

Another verse suggestive of preexistence is the following: "'I tell you the truth," Jesus answered, "'before Abraham was born, I am!'" (John 8:58) Here, Jesus is shown telling his enemies he existed before Abraham was born. This would be impossible unless the preexistence of Jesus was true. If Jesus preexisted, it is a short step to assume we have all preexisted.

There are other verses suggestive of reincarnation. In the gospels, Jesus gives information about his return and who will be there to witness it. Several times, Jesus mentions that some of the people around him will be alive when he returns. One example is in the book of Matthew when Jesus gave the signs preceding his Second Coming. After revealing the signs, Jesus states: "I tell you the truth, this generation will certainly not pass away until all these things have happened." (Matthew 24:34). The generation of people around Jesus who heard him give this prophecy, died without seeing these signs. This verse makes more sense if it refers to these people being reincarnated immediately before his Second Coming.

Another verse suggestive of reincarnation is the following: "Truly I say to you, there are some of those who are standing here who will not taste death until they see the Son of Man coming in his kingdom." (Matthew 16:24-28). What does it mean to "taste death" until Jesus comes? The description of a person having to "taste death" until Jesus comes is a good description of reincarnation until Jesus comes.

There are several verses suggesting Jesus may have had past lives and had several incarnations in the flesh. Paul wrote of Adam as being: "... a pattern of the one who was to come [Jesus]" (Romans 5:14).

Paul also draws a parallel between Adam and Christ: "The first Adam became a living being; the last Adam [Jesus] became a life-giving spirit." (1 Corinthians 15:45). Christ is described as the last Adam, the man who, through obedience, reverses the outcome of the disobedience of the first Adam: "Therefore, just as sin entered the world through one man, and death through sin, and in this way death came to all men, because all sinned -- for before the law was given, sin was in the world. But sin is not taken into account when there is no law. Nevertheless, death reigned from the time of Adam to the time of Moses, even over those who did not sin by breaking a command, as did Adam, who was a pattern of the one to come. But the gift is not like the trespass. For if the many died by the trespass of the one man, how much more did God's grace and the gift that came by the grace of the one man, Jesus Christ, overflow to the many! Again, the gift of God is not like the result of the one man's sin: The judgment followed one sin and brought condemnation, but the gift followed many trespasses and brought justification. For if, by the trespass of the one man, death reigned through that one man, how much more will those who receive God's abundant provision of grace and of the gift of righteousness reign in life through the one man, Jesus Christ. Consequently, just as the result of one trespass was condemnation for all

193

men, so also the result of one act of righteousness was justification that brings life for all men. For just as through the disobedience of the one man the many were made sinners, so also through the obedience of the one man the many will be made righteous. The law was added so that the trespass might increase. But where sin increased, grace increased all the more, so that, just as sin reigned in death, so also grace might reign through righteousness to bring eternal life through Jesus Christ our Lord." (Romans 5:12-21)

These verses show the work of Adam being undone by the work of Jesus, a good description of how divine justice is meted out in the Bible. The only person who could satisfy divine justice in reversing what Adam did would have to be Adam himself or a reincarnation of Adam. Paul's description of this person as Jesus could satisfy divine justice only because Jesus indeed was a reincarnation of Adam.

That Jesus had many incarnations is not a new belief. The early Christian group known as the Ebionites taught that the Holy Spirit had first incarnated as Adam and later reincarnated as Jesus. Other Jewish Christian groups such as the Elkasaites and Nazarites also held this belief. The Clementine Homilies, an early Christian document, also taught many incarnations of Jesus. [81]

The Zohar, a book having much authority with Kabbalistic Jews, states: "So it is that when a man is about to depart from life, Adam, the first man, appears to him and asks him why and in what state he leaves the world. He says: 'Woe to thee that through thee I have to die.' To which Adam replies: 'My son, I transgressed one commandment and was punished for so doing; see how many commandments of your Master, negative and positive, you have transgressed.'" [82] What is interesting in this verse from the Zohar is that Adam appears to the dying person at death. In a great number of Jewish and Christian NDEs, it is Jesus who appears. Could this be merely a coincidence?

Another possible incarnation of Jesus is the Old Testament figure known as Melchizedek, the High Priest and King of Salem, who: "... without father or mother, without genealogy, without beginning of days or end of life, like the Son of God he remains a priest forever." (Hebrews 7:3).

It is clear from the book of Hebrews that Melchizedek was not an ordinary man, assuming he even was a man. The description of Melchizedek sounds uncannily similar to Jesus. The book of Hebrews even declares Jesus to be a: "... priest forever, in the order of Melchizedek." (Hebrews 7:17).

The verses above may be suggesting Melchizedek is an incarnation of Jesus.

There are several verses highly suggestive of the mechanics of reincarnation. Before his arrest, Jesus stated: "All who take the sword will perish by the sword." (Matthew 26:52)

Common sense tells us not all people who live by the sword will die by the sword. This statement can only be true if meant in the context of a future life. If in this life one lives by the sword, he or she will most certainly die by the sword, if not in the same lifetime, then in a future lifetime. This concept is identical to the ancient concept of "karma," a tenet of reincarnation that is the foundation of reality mostly in the East. Below are more Biblical references to karma:

"Do not be deceived: God cannot be mocked. A person reaps what he sows." (Galatians 6:7)

"Life for life, eye for eye, tooth for tooth, hand for hand, foot for foot, burn for burn, wound for wound, bruise for bruise." (Exodus 21:24-25)

"In anger his master turned him over to the jailers until he should pay back all he owed. This is how my heavenly Father will treat each of you unless you forgive your brother from your heart." (Matthew 18: 34-35)

"If any one slays with the sword, with the sword must he be slain." (Revelation 13:10)

"Settle matters quickly with your adversary who is taking you to court. Do it while you are still with him on the way, or he may hand you over to the judge, and the judge may hand you over to the officer, and you may be thrown into prison. I tell you the truth, you will not get out until you have paid the last penny." (Matthew 5:25-26)

The above passages can be seen to be at least suggestive of reincarnation.

In James 3:6, some translations (such as the American Standard Version) mention "the wheel of nature," which seems to resemble the cycle of endless reincarnation taught by the eastern religions. However, in this context the verse refers to controlling speech in order not to sin: "And the tongue is a fire: the world of iniquity among our members is the tongue, which defileth the whole body, and setteth on fire the wheel of nature, and is set on fire by hell." (James 3:6, ASV)

Nowhere in the Bible is reincarnation denied or refuted. Job asks: "If a person dies will he live again?" (Job 14:14) But he receives no answer.

Another Old Testament verse states: "Generations come and generations go, but the earth remains forever. The sun rises and the sun sets, and hurries back to where it rises. The wind blows to the south and turns to the north; round and round it goes, ever returning on its course. All streams flow into the sea, yet the sea is never full. To the place the streams come from, there they return again... What has been will be again, what has been done will be done again; there is nothing new under the sun." (Ecclesiastes 1:4-9)

The Jewish Kabbalists interpreted this verse to mean a generation dies and subsequently returns through reincarnation.

The following verse is often used to refute reincarnation: "... man is destined to die once, and after that to face judgment..." (Hebrews 9:27) This verse is often said to mean that people live and die only once, then face judgment. But if this is true, this verse not only applies to reincarnation, but to the modern concept of resurrection. In fact, this verse refutes resurrection, not reincarnation. As mentioned earlier in this book, the Bible describes many people being resurrected, all of whom, with the exception of Jesus, died more than one time. Other people, such as Enoch, did not even die at all.

The above verse does not refute reincarnation at all, because when a person dies and is reincarnated, it is not the same body reincarnating and eventually dying. The verse implies a one body/one death reality, which agrees with reincarnation and disagrees with the modern definition of resurrection. This definition is that after the physical body dies and faces judgment, the physical body will be raised from the grave someday to face possible death again (such as the so-called "second death" spoken of in Revelation 2:11) and judgment.

Resurrection assumes the same body rises. Reincarnation assumes a different body rises. So Hebrews 9:27 does not refute reincarnation at all, but does refute the modern concept of resurrection.

There is evidence that early Christians believed in reincarnation. Ancient Gnostic writings were discovered in 1945 revealing more information about the concept of reincarnation. The Orthodox Church ultimately destroyed the Gnostics for being heretics.

They and their writings were destroyed. The discovery in 1945 yielded writings including some long lost gospels, some of which were written earlier than the known gospels of Matthew, Mark, Luke and John. The Gnostic Christians claimed to possess the correct definition of "resurrection" -- based on Jesus' secret teachings, handed down to them by the apostles.

The existence of a secret tradition can be found in the New Testament:

"He [Jesus] told them, 'The secret of the kingdom of God has been given to you. But to those on the outside everything is said in parables so that, they may be ever seeing but never perceiving, and ever hearing but never understanding; otherwise they might turn and be forgiven!'" (Mark 4:11-12)

"No, we speak of God's secret wisdom, a wisdom that has been hidden and that God destined for our glory before time began." (1 Corinthians 2:7)

"So then, men ought to regard us as servants of Christ and as those entrusted with the secret things of God." (1 Corinthians 4:1)

The Secret Gospel of Mark, one of the Gnostic books discovered, describes Jesus performing secret initiation rituals. Before the discovery of this secret gospel, our only knowledge of it came from a letter written by Church Father Clement of Alexandria (150 AD - 211 AD). Clement quotes from this secret gospel and refers to it as "a more spiritual gospel for the use of those who were being perfected."

Clement also states: "It even yet is most carefully guarded [by the church at Alexandria], being read only to those who are being initiated into the great mysteries." [83]

Clement mentions elsewhere that Jesus revealed a secret teaching to those who were "capable of receiving it and being molded by it." Clement indicated he possessed the secret teaching handed down from the apostles. [84]

The Gnostics were harsh critics of the Church who accused the Church of watering down the gospel in order to popularize it for the masses. The Orthodox Church stressed salvation by faith alone. The Gnostics stressed "gnosis," which in Greek means knowledge. The Gnostic's secret knowledge emphasized spiritual rebirth rather than physical resurrection. Many Gnostics believed reincarnation to be the true interpretation of resurrection. To many Gnostics, physical resurrection (i.e. reincarnation) occurred to those who did not attain a spiritual resurrection (i.e. becoming born again of the Spirit) through knowledge of the secret teachings.

The New Testament talks about of gnosis (knowledge):

"Now to each one the manifestation of the Spirit is given for the common good. To one there is given through the Spirit the message of wisdom, to another the message of knowledge by means of the same Spirit, to another faith by the same Spirit, to another gifts of healing by that one Spirit, to another miraculous powers, to another prophecy, to another distinguishing between spirits, to speaking in different kinds of tongues, and to still another the interpretation of tongues." (1 Corinthians 12:7-10)

"For this reason, since the day we heard about you, we have not stopped praying for you and asking God to fill you with the knowledge of his will through all spiritual wisdom and understanding." (Colossians 1:9)

The verses below are some the secret teachings of Jesus from the Gnostic gospels affirming reincarnation and the secret knowledge:

"Watch and pray that you may not be born in the flesh, but that you may leave the bitter bondage of this life." (Book of Thomas the Contender 9:5)

"When you see your likeness, you are happy. But when you see your images that came into being before and that neither die nor become visible, how much you will bear!" (Gospel of Thomas, saying 84)

In the Book of Thomas the Contender, Jesus tells the disciple Thomas that after death, those people who were once believers but have remained attached to things of "transitory beauty," will be consumed "in their concern about life" and will be "brought back to the visible realm."

In the Secret Book of John, written by 185 AD at the latest, reincarnation is placed at the center of the discussion concerning the salvation of souls. The following is the Secret Book of John's perspective on reincarnation: Everyone has drunk from the water of forgetfulness and lives in a state of ignorance. Some people are able to overcome ignorance by having the life-giving Spirit descend upon them. These souls "will be saved and will become perfect," that is, escape the rebirth. John asks Jesus what will happen to those who do not attain salvation. They are hurled down "into forgetfulness" and thrown into "prison," the Gnostic symbol for a new body. (Secret Book of John 14:15, 17) Jesus says the only way for these souls to escape is to acquire knowledge after coming from forgetfulness. A soul can accomplish this by finding a teacher who can lead the soul in the right direction:

"This soul needs to follow another soul in whom the Spirit of life dwells, because she is saved through the Spirit. Then she will never be thrust into flesh again." (Secret Book of John 14:20)

Another Gnostic book, the Pistis Sophia, outlines a system of punishment and rewards that includes reincarnation. The book explains the differences in one's fate as a result of past-life actions. A "man who curses" will be given a body that is continually "troubled in heart." A "man who slanders" will be given an "oppressed" body. A thief will be given a "lame, crooked and blind body." A "proud" and "scornful" man will be given "a lame and ugly body" that "everyone continually despises." (Pistis Sophia 144, 146) From this, we can see how this earth, as well as hell, is a place of education through suffering.

According to the Pistis Sophia, some souls experience hell as a place of shadows and torture. However, after these souls pass through hell, they return to earth for further experiences. Only a relatively few extremely evil souls are not permitted to reincarnate. These souls are cast into "outer darkness" until a time when they are "destroyed and dissolved." (Pistis Sophia 145)

Several Gnostic books combine the ideas of reincarnation and union with God. The Apocalypse of Paul, which has previously been discussed, describes the reincarnation of a soul who was not ready to ascent into heaven. The Apocalypse of Paul demonstrates how both reincarnation and ascension into heaven fit into the theology of the Gnostics.

As Paul passes through the fourth heaven, he witnesses a soul being punished for murder. This soul is brought "out of the land of the dead" (Earth) by angels where three witnesses charge the soul with murder. The soul looks sorrowfully down and is cast down into a body that has been prepared for it. (Apocalypse of Paul 20:9-10; 21:16-18) The book describes Paul's journey through the heavens, which is also symbolic for the Gnostic process of union with God.

The Pistis Sophia combines the ideas of reincarnation and divine union in a verse beginning with the question: What happens to "a man who has committed no sin, but done good persistently, but has not found the mysteries?" The Pistis Sophia reveals such a soul will receive "a cup filled with thoughts and wisdom," allowing the soul to remember its divine origin and pursue the "mysteries of the light" until it finds them and is able to "inherit the light forever." (Pistis Sophia 145) To "inherit the light forever" is a Gnostic term for union with God.

For the Gnostics, resurrection meant not only rebirth of the physical body (i.e. reincarnation), but also rebirth of the soul (i.e. spiritual regeneration). Gnostics believed that people who experience the rebirth of the soul are able to experience eternal life or union with God, while on earth. After death, such people escape physical resurrection (i.e. reincarnation). People who don't experience the resurrection (i.e. rebirth of the soul, spiritual regeneration) and union with God while on earth will have to be physically resurrected (i.e. reincarnated). Jesus states the following in the Gnostic Gospels: "People who say they will first die and then arise are mistaken. If they do not first receive resurrection while they are alive, once they have died they will receive nothing." (Gospel of Philip 73:1-4)

In several verses, Paul states that resurrection involves a spirit body. Such a definition corresponds with spiritual resurrection:

"It [the dead body] is sown a natural body, it is raised a spiritual body. If there is a natural body, there is also a spiritual body." (1 Corinthians 15:44)

"I declare to you, brothers, that flesh and blood cannot inherit the kingdom of God, nor does the perishable inherit the imperishable." (1 Corinthians 15:50)

"When you were dead in your sins and in the uncircumcision of your sinful nature, God made you alive with Christ." (Colossians 2:13)

The Gnostics claimed their terminology could be found throughout the New Testament. For example, the author of Ephesians uses the words "awake," "sleep" and "dead" in a Gnostic sense: "But everything exposed by the light becomes visible, for it is light that makes everything visible. This is why it is said: 'Wake up, O sleeper, rise from the dead, and Christ will shine on you.'" (Ephesians 5:13-14)

Some of the New Testament words translated from Greek as "resurrection" can also mean to awake or rise. Therefore, argued the Gnostics, when Paul states that people can participate in the resurrection, he is really saying their souls can be awakened to God's Spirit.

In some verses, Paul describes the resurrection as not being a future event, but rather a past or present event: "Or don't you know that all of us who were baptized into Christ Jesus were baptized into his death? We were therefore buried with him through baptism into death in order that, just as Christ was raised from the dead through the glory of the Father, we too may live a new life. If we have been united with him like this in his death, we will certainly also be united with him in his resurrection. For we know that our old self was crucified with him so that the body of sin might be done away with, that we should no longer be slaves to sin -- because anyone who has died has been freed from sin. Now if we died with Christ, we believe that we will also live with him. For we know that since Christ was raised from the dead, he cannot die again; death no longer has mastery over him. The death he died, he died to sin once for all; but the life he lives, he lives to God. In the same way, count yourselves dead to sin but alive to God in Christ Jesus." (Romans 6:3-11)

Colossians also describes the resurrection as a present-day event: "Since, then, you have been raised with Christ, set your hearts on things above, where Christ is seated at the right hand of God." (Colossians 3:1) And: "Do not lie to each other, since you have taken off your old self with its practices and have put on the new self, which is being renewed in knowledge in the image of its Creator." (Colossians 3:9-10)

In the verse above, taking off your old self to put on the new self is a Gnostic term for the resurrection, also described as a present-life event.

The Gnostic writings reveal a clear and strong vision of the resurrection as a past and present event. Below is a verse in the Gospel of Thomas destroying the idea of the resurrection being a future event: "His followers said to him, 'When will the rest for the dead take place, and when will the new world come?' He said to them, 'What you look for has come, but you do not know it.'" (Gospel of Thomas, saying 51) In this verse, Jesus says the resurrection and the kingdom are already here, but people don't realize it yet.

Jesus explained the concept of resurrection before raising Lazarus from the dead: "Jesus said to her, 'Your brother will rise again.' Martha answered, 'I know he will rise again in the resurrection at the last day.' Jesus said to her, 'I am the resurrection and the life. He who believes in me will live, even though he dies; and whoever lives and believes in me will never die. Do you believe this?'" (John 11:23-26) In this verse, Jesus tells Martha her brother Lazarus will "rise again." Martha mistakenly thinks Jesus means Lazarus will come out of his grave at Judgment Day. Jesus corrects her by stating that those who believe in him will live, even though they die. Jesus is referring here to spiritual rebirth.

Next, Jesus states that, after death, those who have been spiritually reborn will never die (i.e. reincarnate and die again). The flip side to this is that those who die without spiritual rebirth will have to die again (i.e. reincarnate). By raising Lazarus from death, Jesus seems to be demonstrating that one does not wait until Judgment Day for Jesus to raise him or her.

Jesus flatly tells Nicodemus: "I tell you a truth, no one can see the kingdom of God unless he is born again." (John 3:3)

Nicodemus misunderstands what Jesus means by "born again:" "How can a person be born when he is old? Surely he cannot enter a second time into his mother's womb to be born!" (John 3:4)

In response, Jesus states: "I tell you the truth, no one can enter the kingdom of God unless he is born of water and the Spirit. Flesh gives birth to flesh, but the Spirit gives birth to spirit." (John 3:5-6) In context of this verse, Jesus is referring to physical and spiritual resurrection. Jesus describes physical resurrection as being born again of water. Spiritual resurrection is being born again of the Spirit. They are two similar, yet different processes.

One could make the case that this verse shows Jesus teaching salvation to Nicodemus as being the process of physical rebirth followed by spiritual rebirth.

In the Apocryphal book, Wisdom of Solomon, recognized as canonical by the Catholic Church, is the following verse: "...I was given a sound body to live in because I was already good." (Wisdom of Solomon 8:19-20) This verse raises the following question: How is it possible to get a body after you have already been good, unless reincarnation is true?

Flavius Josephus records that the Essenes of the Dead Sea Scrolls lived "the same kind of life" as the followers of Pythagoras, the Greek philosopher who taught reincarnation. According to Josephus, the Essenes believed the soul is immortal and preexistent. These are necessary tenets for belief in reincarnation.[85]

One particular Dead Sea Scroll entitled "The Last Jubilee" mentions reincarnation. This scroll is about the "last days" during which time it says, a "Melchizedek redivivus" (reincarnate) will appear and destroy Belial (Satan) and lead the children of God to eternal forgiveness. Below are parts of this message from this scroll. Parts of this message are unreadable. The unreadable parts will be denoted by this symbol (...). Here is the message: "When, therefore, the scriptures speaks of a day of atonement ... What is meant, ... is that ... by a day on which all the children of light and all who have cast their lot with the cause of righteousness will achieve forgiveness of their sins, whereas the wicked will reap their desserts and be brought to an end. There is a further reference to this final judgment in the continuation of the verse from the Psalter ... the allusion is to Belial and the spirits of his ilk -- that is to ... defy God's statutes in order to perfect justice ... King ... Melchizedek ... will execute upon them God's avenging judgment, and ... deliver the just from the hands of Belial and all those spirits of his ilk. With all the angels of righteousness at his aid, he will blast the council of Belial to destruction ... the eminence in question being the destination of all who are indeed children of God ... It will be from Belial ... that men will turn away in rebellion, and there will be a reestablishment of the reign of righteousness, perversity being confounded by the judgments of God. This is what scripture implies in the words, 'Who says to Zion, your God has not claimed his Kingdom!' The term Zion there denoting the total congregation of the 'sons of righteousness' that is, those who maintain the covenant and turn away from the popular trend, and your God signifying the King of Righteousness, alias "Melchizedek Redivivus," who will destroy Belial. Our text speaks also of sounding a loud trumpet blast throughout the land on the tenth day of the seventh month. As applied to the last days, this refers to the fanfare which will then be sounded before the Messianic King." [86]

As was mentioned earlier, Melchizedek was the High Priest described in the Bible who sounds remarkably like an incarnation of Jesus. It was also mentioned how some early Christians believed Melchizedek to be an early incarnation of Jesus. If the above message of the Dead Sea Scrolls can be believed, then the passage is very likely referring to Jesus himself and his Second Coming.

The Dead Sea Scrolls prove the Jewish mystical tradition of divine union went back to the first, perhaps even the third, century BCE. Jewish mysticism has its origins in Greek mysticism, a system of belief that included reincarnation. Among the Dead Sea Scrolls, some of the hymns found are similar to the Hekhalot hymns of the Jewish mystics. One text of hymns gives us clear evidence of Jewish mysticism. The text is called "Songs of the Sabbath Sacrifice." [87] Fragments of 1 Enoch, considered to be the oldest text of Jewish mysticism, were also found with the Scrolls.[88] Since evidence shows Jewish mysticism existed in the third century BCE, as Enoch indicates, then it would certainly have existed in first-century Israel. As stated earlier, the ideas of divine union and reincarnation can both be found in early Christianity. One may easily conclude it was the key to the very heart of Jesus' message.

Reincarnation has been a belief for thousands of years for certain Jews and Christians. The Zohar is a book of great authority among Kabalistic Jews. It states the following: "All souls are subject to revolutions." and "Men do not know the way they have been judged in all time." (Zohar II, 199b) That is, in their "revolutions" they lose all memory of the actions leading to their being judged.

Another Kabalistic book, the Kether Malkuth states: "If she, the soul, be pure, then she shall obtain favor... but if she has been defiled, then she shall wander for a time in pain and despair... until the days of her purification." (Kether Malkuth) [89] How can the soul be defiled before birth? Where does the soul wander if not on this or some other world until the days of her purification? The Rabbis explained this verse to mean that the defiled soul wanders down from paradise through many births until the soul regained its purity.

In the Talmud, Din Gilgol Neshomes (reincarnation) is constantly mentioned. The term literally means "the judgment of the revolutions of the souls." Rabbi Manassa, one of the most revered Rabbis in Israel, states: "The belief or the doctrine of the transmigration of souls is a firm and infallible dogma accepted by the whole assemblage of our church with one accord, so that there is none to be found who would dare to deny it... Indeed, there is a great number of sages in Israel who hold firm to this doctrine so that they made it a dogma, a fundamental point of our religion. We are therefore in duty bound to obey and to accept this dogma with acclamation... as the truth of it has been incontestably demonstrated by the Zohar, and all books of the Kabalists." (Nishmath Hayem) [90]

In conclusion, from all that has been said concerning reincarnation, one can safely draw the conclusion that reincarnation was well understood by the people of Israel in Christ's day. Jesus Himself taught reincarnation to his followers. The Holy Bible teaches reincarnation. Reincarnation appears in many NDEs. Reincarnation should be a doctrine accepted by every follower of Christ. The NDE should be accepted as truth by every follower of Christ as a revelation from God.

APPENDIX

NOTES

[1] From the ABC News documentary program, Turning Point, on NDEs. Produced by Joseph Angier and Ann Reynolds.

[2] International Association for Near-Death Studies publication Vital Signs, Volume XIX, No. 3, 2000, May Eulitt's experience is also described in more detail in her book entitled Fireweaver, published by Xlibris.

[3] https://www.near-death.com/experiences/group.html

[4] https://www.near-death.com/oakford.html

[5] https://www.near-death.com/experiences/exceptional/david-oakford.html

[6] https://www.near-death.com/experiences/exceptional/karen-schaeffer.html

[7] https://www.near-death.com/experiences/exceptional/linda-stewart.html

[8] https://www.near-death.com/experiences/exceptional/ricky-randolph.html

[9] https://www.near-death.com/experiences/gay-and-lesbian.html

[10] Raymond E. Fowler, The Andreasson Affair: Phase Two, p. 111-115.

[11] https://www.near-death.com/experiences/exceptional/brian-krebs.html

[12] https://www.near-death.com/psychology/experiences/extreme-meditation.html

[13] https://www.near-death.com/experiences/exceptional/josiane-antonette.html

[14] https://www.near-death.com/experiences/exceptional/mellen-thomas-benedict.html

[15] https://www.near-death.com/archives/false/john-bunyan.html

[16] https://www.near-death.com/science/evidence/some-people-receive-verified-visions-of-the-future.html

[17] https://www.near-death.com/religion/judaism/beverly-brodsky.html

[18] https://www.near-death.com/religion/christianity/don-brubaker.html

[19] https://www.near-death.com/experiences/exceptional/grace-bubulka.html

[20] https://www.near-death.com/experiences/exceptional/edgar-cayce.html

[21] https://www.near-death.com/experiences/children.html

[22] https://www.near-death.com/religion/buddhism/lingza-chokyi.html

[23] https://www.near-death.com/experiences/children.html

[24] https://www.near-death.com/experiences/exceptional/lynnclaire-dennis.html

[25] https://www.near-death.com/religion/judaism/jeanie-dicus.html

[26] https://www.near-death.com/experiences/exceptional/ned-dougherty.html

[27] https://www.near-death.com/experiences/exceptional/betty-eadie.html

[28] https://www.near-death.com/experiences/exceptional/richard-eby.html

[29] https://www.near-death.com/religion/native-american.html

[30] https://www.near-death.com/experiences/suicide/angie-fenimore.html

[31] https://www.near-death.com/experiences/children.html

[32] https://www.near-death.com/religion/christianity/kenneth-hagin.html

[33] https://www.near-death.com/experiences/gay-and-lesbian.html

[34] https://www.near-death.com/experiences/group.html

[35] https://www.near-death.com/religion/christianity/valvita-jones.html

[36] https://www.near-death.com/experiences/exceptional/carl-jung.html

[37] https://www.near-death.com/religion/christianity/gerard-landry.html

[38] https://www.near-death.com/experiences/children.html

[39] https://www.near-death.com/experiences/children.html

[40] https://www.near-death.com/experiences/exceptional/laurelynn-martin.html

[41] https://www.near-death.com/religion/islam.html

[42] https://www.near-death.com/experiences/exceptional/dianne-morrissey.html

[43] https://www.near-death.com/science/experts/melvin-morse.html

[44] https://www.near-death.com/religion/hinduism.html

[45] James M. Robinson, Apocalypse of Paul, Nag Hammadi Library, 1988.

[46] One experiencer, Mary Pollack, was asked for a password by two beings in the light in order to progress during her NDE. When she asked the beings, "You mean this is this all I had to say?" They replied, "You had to learn it for yourself. We couldn't have told you. We couldn't have taught you. This is something that had to come from you." Her entire NDE is profiled in the NDE video entitled Round Trip, by Timothy O'Reilly, Wellspring Media.

[47] James M. Robinson, Apocalypse of Paul, Nag Hammadi Library, 1988.

[48] https://www.near-death.com/experiences/exceptional/howard-pittman.html

[49] https://www.near-death.com/science/evidence/ndes-have-been-known-throughout-history.html

[50] https://www.near-death.com/experiences/with-pets/jan-price.html

[51] https://www.near-death.com/science/evidence/people-have-ndes-while-brain-dead.html

[52] https://www.near-death.com/experiences/exceptional/george-ritchie.html

[53] https://www.near-death.com/religion/judaism/virginia-rivers.htmll

[54] https://www.near-death.com/science/evidence/some-people-were-dead-for-several-days.html

[55] https://www.near-death.com/experiences/suicide/sandra-rogers.html

[56] https://www.near-death.com/experiences/exceptional/daniel-rosenblit.html

[57] https://www.near-death.com/experiences/exceptional/thomas-sawyer.html

[58] https://www.near-death.com/experiences/rich-and-famous.html

[59] https://www.near-death.com/experiences/exceptional/kimberly-clark-sharp.html

[60] https://www.near-death.com/experiences/exceptional/jayne-smith.html

[61] https://www.near-death.com/science/research/time.html#a05

[62] https://www.near-death.com/experiences/exceptional/howard-storm.html

[63] https://www.near-death.com/religion/christianity/lorraine-tutmarc.html

[64] https://www.near-death.com/religion/christianity/emanuel-tuwagirairmana.html

[65] https://www.near-death.com/science/evidence/people-born-blind-can-see-during-nde.html

[66] https://www.near-death.com/experiences/exceptional/ranelle-wallace.html

[67] https://www.near-death.com/experiences/exceptional/arthur-yensen.html

[68] From the NDE video, Life After Death, Episode 1, hosted by Tom Harpur, Sleeping Giant Productions, Wellspring Media, 1998.

[69] From the Discovery Channel's NDE documentary "Into the Unknown: Strange but true?"

[70] https://www.near-death.com/afterlife-evidence.html

[71] https://www.near-death.com/experiences/children.html

[72] https://www.near-death.com/science/research/future.html

[73] From the NDE video, Life After Death, Episode 8, Sleeping Giant Productions, Wellspring Media, 1998.

[74] https://www.near-death.com/science/experts/michael-sabom.html

[75] From the ABC News documentary program, Turning Point, on NDEs. Produced by Joseph Angier and Ann Reynolds.

[76] P.M.H. Atwater with David H. Morgan, The Complete Idiots Guide to Near-Death Experiences, p. 92.

[77] https://www.near-death.com/psychology.html

[78] https://www.near-death.com/experiences/out-of-body/charles-tart.html and https://s3.amazonaws.com/cttart/articles/april2013articles/Six+Studies+of+Out-of-Body+Experiences.pdf

[79] http://www.holotropic.com/

[80] From the NDE video, Life After Death, Episode 8, Sleeping Giant Productions, Wellspring Media, 1998.

[81] From the movie, Jacob's Ladder (1990), starring Tim Robbins, Elizabeth Pena; Director: Adrian Lyne.

[82] Fred Alan Wolfe, Taking the Quantum Leap: The New Physics for Non-Scientists, HarperCollins, 1988.

[83] Richard H. Drummond, Ph.D., Unto The Churches, p. 50.

[84] From the NDE video, Shadows: Perceptions of Near-Death Experiencers, by Norman Van Rooy, 1994.

[85] ScienceNet, http://www.sciencenet.org.uk/database/Physics/Original/p00350d.html

[86] From the NDE video, Shadows: Perceptions of Near-Death Experiencers, by Norman Van Rooy, 1994.

[87] Margot Grey, Return from Death: An Exploration of the Near-Death Experience, p. 12

[88] From the NBC documentary, Ancient Prophecies, hosted by David McCallum

[89] http://www.lunarpages.com/stargazers/millen/ndeproph.htm

[90] Kenneth Ring, Ph.D., Return from Death: An Exploration of the Near-Death Experience, p 55-56

[91] Raymond A. Moody Jr., Ph.D., M.D., The Last Laugh, p. 188.

[92] Raymond A. Moody Jr., Ph.D., M.D., The Last Laugh, p. 187.

[93] Howard Storm, My Descent Into Death, p. 129-130.

[94] Arthur Yensen, "I Saw Heaven", p. 33, 1979, C/O Eric Yensen, 3407 Fair Oaks Circle, Caldwell, Idaho 83605, email: Yensen@earthlink.net

[95] For more info, visit De Civ. Dei, XXI, xxiv

[96] For more info, visit Dial., IV, xxxix

[97] Commentary on this text

[98] For more info, visit Sermo lxvi in Cantic., n.11

[99] For more info, visit P. G., XIII, col. 445, 448, quoted from http://www.newadvent.org/cathen/12575a.htm

[100] Don Brubaker, Absent from the Body, p. 87.

[101] JewFaq, http://www.jewfaq.org/death.htm

[102] William Whiston, trans., Josephus: Complete Works, Wars of the Jews, Book II, Ch. 8, p. 478.

[103] Richard H. Drummond Ph.D., Unto The Churches, p. 86.

[104] For more info, visit Zohar I, 57b, quoted from http://web.wt.net/~cbenton/kabbalah/life.htm

[105] Letter attributed to Clement of Alexandria, found by Morton Smith in the Mar Saba monastery, southeast of Jerusalem, in 1958, translation by Morton Smith, http://www.webcom.com/gnosis/library/secm.htm

[106] Besant, Annie, Esoteric Christianity, quoting Clement, Miscellanies, Bk VI, ch. vii.

[107] G.R.S. Mead, trans., Pistis Sophia, p.323.

[108] Elizabeth Clare Prophet, Reincarnation: The Missing Link In Christianity, p. 57.

[109] The Dead Sea Scriptures, by Theodor H. Gaster, p.433-436.

[110] Neil S. Fujita, A Crack in the Jar: What Ancient Jewish Documents Tell Us about the New Testament, p. 170.

[111] Elizabeth Clare Prophet, Reincarnation: The Missing Link in Christianity, p. 61.

[112] http://www.blavatsky.net/index.php/reincarnation-in-the-bible

[113] http://www.blavatsky.net/index.php/reincarnation-in-judaism-and-the-bible

BIBLIOGRAPHY

Antonette, Josiane, Whispers of the Soul, J. Antonette, 1998.

Atwater, P.M.H., Beyond the Light, Morrow, William & Co., 1995.

Atwater, P.M.H., Children of the New Millennium, Crown Publishing Group, 1999.

Atwater, P.M.H., with David H. Morgan, The Complete Idiot's Guide to Near-Death Experiences, Macmillan USA, Inc. 2000.

Bailey, Lee Worth, The Near-Death Experience: A Reader, Routledge, 1996.

Bennett, Rita, To Heaven and Back, Zondervan Publishing House, 1997.

Berman, Philip L., The Journey Home, Simon & Schuster Trade, 1996.

Besant, Annie, Esoteric Christianity, Theosophical Publishing House, 1975.

Brinkley, Dannion, with Paul Perry, Saved by the Light, HarperCollins Publishers, Inc, 1995.

Brubaker, Don, Absent from the Body, Peninsula Publishing, 1995.

Bubulka, Grace, Beyond this Reality, Word Dancer Press, 1994.

Cornford, Francis, The Republic of Plato, Oxford, 1945.

Dennis, Lynnclaire, The Pattern, Integral Publishing, 1997.

Dougherty, Ned, Fast Lane to Heaven, Hampton Roads Publishing Co., Inc, 2001.

Drummond, Richard H., Unto The Churches, A.R.E. Press, 1989.

Eadie, Betty, Embraced by the Light, Bantam Books, Inc., 1994.

Eby, Richard, Caught up into Paradise, Baker Books, 1984.

Farr, Sidney Saylor, What Tom Sawyer Learned from Dying, Hampton Roads Publishing Co., Inc., 1993.

Fenimore, Angie, Beyond the Darkness, Bantam Books, Inc., 1996.

Fowler, Raymond E., The Andreasson Affair: Phase Two, Wild Flower Press, 1994.

Fujita, Neil S., A Crack in the Jar: What Ancient Jewish Documents Tell Us about the New Testament, Paulist Press, 1986.

Gaster, Theodor H., The Dead Sea Scriptures, Peter Smith Publishing, 1976.

Gibson, Arvin S., Fingerprints of God, Horizon Publishers & Distributors, Inc., 1999.

Gibson, Arvin S., Journeys Beyond Life, Horizon Publishers, 1994.

Hagin, Kenneth E., I Believe in Visions, Faith Library Publications, Inc., 1984.

Harpur, Tom, Life After Death (video), Sleeping Giant Productions, Wellspring Media, 1998.

Holy Bible, New International Version, Zondervan Publishing House, 1995.

Jung, Carl Gustav, Memories, Dreams, Reflections, Vintage Books, 1989.

Layton, Bentley, The Gnostic Scriptures, Doubleday, 1987

MacDermot, Violet, Nag Hammadi Studies 9, E.J. Brill, 1978.

MacLaine, Shirley, Out on a Limb, Bantam Doubleday Dell Publishing Group, 1984.

Martin, Laurelynn G., Searching for Home, 1996.

Mead, G.R.S., Pistis Sophia, Garber Communications, Spiritual Science Library, 1984.

Meyer, Marvin W., The Secret Teachings of Jesus: Four Gnostic Gospels, Random House, Vintage Books, 1986

Meyer, Marvin W., The Gospel of Thomas: The Hidden Sayings of Jesus, HarperSanFrancisco, 1992.

Moody. Jr, Raymond A., The Last Laugh, Hampton Roads Publishing Co, Inc. 1999.

Morrissey, Dianne, You Can See the Light, Stillpoint Publishing, 1997.

Morse, Donald R., Searching for Eternity, Eagle Wing Books, Inc., 2000.

Neihardt, John G., Black Elk Speaks, University of Nebraska Press, 1989.

O'Reilly, Timothy, Round Trip (video), Wellspring Media, 1996

Pittman, Howard, Placebo.

Plato, The Republic, Penguin USA, 1976.

Price, Jan, The Other Side of Death, Ballantine Books, Inc., 1996.

Prophet, Elizabeth Clare, Reincarnation: The Missing Link In Christianity, Summit University Press, 1997.

Ring, Kenneth, with Evelyn E. Valarino, Lessons from the Light, Perseus Publishing, 1998.

Ritchie, George G., with Elizabeth Sherrill, Return from Tomorrow, Revell, Fleming H. Company, 1983.

Ritchie, Jean, Deaths Door, Dell Publishing Company, Inc., 1996.

Robinson, James M., The Nag Hammadi Library In English, San Francisco: HarperCollins, 1988.

Rogers, Sandra H., Lessons from the Light, Warner Books, Inc., 1995.

Rosenblit, Daniel, Transformed by the Light, 1998.

Sabom, Michael B., Light and Death, Zondervan Publishing House, 1998.

Sharp, Kimberly Clark, After the Light, Morrow, William & Co., 1996.

Storm, Howard, My Descent into Death, Clairview Books, 2000.

Sugrue, Thomas, There is a River: The Story of Edgar Cayce, A. R. E. Press, 1990.

Van Rooy, Norman, Shadows: Perceptions of Near-Death Experiencers, Part 1, 1994.

Wallace, RaNelle, with Curtis Taylor, The Burning Within, Gold Leaf Press, 1994.

Whiston, William, Josephus: Complete Works, Kregel Publications, 1960.

Wolfe, Fred Alan, Taking the Quantum Leap: The New Physics for Nonscientists, HarperCollins, 1988.

Yensen, Arthur E., "I Saw Heaven", 1979, C/O Eric Yensen, 3407 Fair Oaks Circle, Caldwell, Idaho 83605, email: Yensen@earthlink.net

ABOUT THE AUTHOR

Kevin R. Williams is a computer programmer with a Bachelor of Science degree in Computer Science. He is the webmaster of the website "Near-Death Experiences and the Afterlife" at www.near-death.com. The website is one the most comprehensive website on the internet about near-death experiences. He is an active member of IANDS, the International Association for Near-Death Studies. His interests also include metaphysics, early Christian history, and comparative religions.

Williams believes his mission in life is to bring information about the NDE to the internet. He states, "My mission is to magnify the truth and to shine a light in this world of darkness. I seek to end the ignorance and fear of death and to plant seeds of more spiritual love and light within my fellow human beings. I wish everyone could find the enormous love and the great light I have discovered in meditating on the profound truths revealed in the NDE. This is my mission in this life and my love."

Williams currently lives near Sacramento, California, where he continues to write and maintain his website.

Printed in Great Britain
by Amazon